Braving a New World

Recent Titles in
Contemporary Urban Studies

The Cultural Meaning of Urban Space
Edited by Robert Rotenberg and Gary McDonogh

Creating Community in the City: Cooperatives and Community
Gardens in Washington, D.C.
Ruth H. Landman

Homesteading in New York City, 1978–1993: The Divided Heart of
Loisaida
Malve von Hassell

Two Towns in Germany: Commerce and the Urban Transformation
Norbert Dannhaeuser

Braving a New World

Cambodian (Khmer) Refugees in an American City

MaryCarol Hopkins

Contemporary Urban Studies
Robert V. Kemper, *series editor*

BERGIN & GARVEY
Westport, Connecticut • London

Library of Congress Cataloging-in-Publication Data

Hopkins, MaryCarol.
    Braving a new world : Cambodian (Khmer) refugees in an American
city / MaryCarol Hopkins.
       p.   cm.—(Contemporary urban studies, ISSN 1065-7002)
    Includes bibliographical references and index.
    ISBN 0-89789-392-1 (alk. paper)
    1. Cambodian American—Cultural assimilation—Case studies.
    2. Cambodian Americans—Social conditions—Case studies.
    3. Refugees—United States—Social conditions—Case studies.
    4. Urban anthropology—United States—Case studies.   I. Title.
    II. Series.
    E184.K45H66   1996
    305.895'93073—dc20   96-15353

British Library Cataloguing in Publication Data is available.

Library of Congress Catalog Card Number: 96-15353

ISBN: 0-89789-392-1
ISSN: 1065-7002

First published in 1996

Bergin & Garvey, 88 Post Road West, Westport, CT 06881
An imprint of Greenwood Publishing Group, Inc.

Printed in the United States of America

The paper used in this book complies with the
Permanent Paper Standard issued by the National
Information Standards Organization (Z39.48-1984).

10 9 8 7 6 5 4 3 2 1

IN MEMORIAM

Armand Hopkins (1901-1989)

This work is dedicated to my father, citizen of the world,

who instilled in me his fascination

with the Earth's people and their cultures.

Contents

Preface   *ix*

Orthographic Note   *xi*

Note on Place and Ethnic Names   *xiii*

1. Introduction   1

2. Material Culture: Meeting Basic Needs   17

3. Patterns of Kinship   47

4. Patterns of Social Organization   69

5. Ideology: Traditional Values in a New Setting   87

6. Agents of Culture Change: Individuals and Institutions   111

7. Formal Education: Cambodian Children in American Schools   125

8. Braving a New World: Maintaining Tradition, Transcending Barriers   147

References   157

Index   167

Preface

Braving a New World is a holistic ethnographic account of a small community of Cambodian (Khmer) refugees in a medium-size city in the Midwestern United States. It is particularly a study of cultural continuity and change. For anthropologists, it is axiomatic that culture is learned throughout the lifespan and in a great variety of informal settings. To this end, I have examined the changing patterns of technology, kinship, age, gender and class relations, community organization, religion, and aesthetics in the lives of these Cambodians within the various contexts of their families, their community, their rituals, and their institutions.

The research upon which this work is based was conducted during the years 1987 through 1995 using classic ethnographic methods, primarily participant observation and extended informal interviewing. Although all anthropologists intend to produce a "true" account of the cultures they study, inevitably our research comes to reflect the interests and experiences of those informants more interested in or more able to participate in our work, as well as our own skills in interacting with a broad range of personalities. Although my work necessarily is colored by my greater access to women, the young, and those who had more time to spend, I have attempted here to convey the broadest possible understanding of the vibrant, multifaceted, polyvocal, and rapidly evolving nature of this community of individuals whose adjustments to life in the United States vary widely according to origins, recent experience, age, gender, class, health, family, individual personality, and present situation. At best an ethnography can only be a still photo of an opera.

I've been most fortunate to have had the friendship and assistance of many Cambodians. In order to respect the wish of some to remain anonymous, I have identified neither the city nor individuals by name and thus cannot here give specific credit to those who so generously took me into their homes and lives, but my gratitude is heartfelt. Several Cambodians have read parts of this, but no one all of it; despite so much help, there may be inaccuracies or misunderstandings, and I of course claim all responsibility for such errors. I hope you will all find something of yourselves and something of truth in this book. I know it is not the book any of you would have written, but I hope you find it an acceptable account by an outsider looking in. Some Americans in the study, too, have been invaluable in sharing information and time with me. Most notable is "Ann," but many others in the schools, the church, and the Agency have helped me throughout the years. To each of you, my everlasting thanks!

Many others have been indispensable to the research and writing of this work. For initial inspiration and continuing support in the course of my life as an anthropologist, I am indebted particularly to Beth Dillingham, James Vaughan, Margaret LeCompte, Mary Anne Pitman, and James Hopgood. Many anthropologists and colleagues have done research foundational to the present work; most notable, of course, is May M. Ebihara, whose study of Village Svay remains the only holistic ethnography of village Cambodia. I am especially grateful to my colleagues in refugee studies whose research has informed the present study and who were always willing to share their insights; foremost among these are Pam DeVoe, Nancy Donnelly, Bea Hackett, Ruth Krulfeld, Judith Kulig, Judy Ledgerwood, Jeffery MacDonald, Susan Needham, Lance Rasbridge, Ann Rynearson, and Amy Zaharlick. I also thank Northern Kentucky University, the University of Cincinnati, and the University of California at Long Beach for financial and other support. Special thanks, too, to Robert Kemper, the series editor, who waded through the first draft with judicious scissors and gentle advice; Michael Burch and Justin Bowen who provided the lovely illustrations; Judy Ketteler who carefully proofread every page; and Lynn Flint, Nina Pearlstein, Marcia Goldstein, and Norine Mudrick from Greenwood, who oversaw the production of this book.

Finally, but not at all least, I thank my own sons, Joshua and Gabriel. Josh, with great patience, taught me to use the computer and cajoled a difficult program to do things its developer said were impossible. Both of them accompanied me in the field, but Gabe, particularly, was a constant companion and became, perhaps more than I, a part of the community. Thank you, sons, for your endurance!

Orthographic Note

I have chosen not to use the International Phonetic Alphabet but rather to follow the conventions of Khmer transcriptions into the Latin alphabet with English spellings where they exist (particularly Ebihara 1971 and Sam-Ang Sam 1995), French spellings when they have become conventionalized into English usage (such as with "Khmer," pronounced "Khmaer" with a silent "r"), and my own approximations into English spelling when precedents vary or are not in wide usage. Although this decision may render transcription less precise, my intent is to make the text more accessible to nonlinguistically trained anthropologists and others. The following linguistic conventions may aid in pronunciation, though of course sounds in one language can never be conveyed precisely using the orthography of another:

th   is an aspirated "t"

ph   is an aspirated "p" not an "f" sound

r   lightly trilled, as in Spanish

Many final consonants, such as "t" and "k," may only be aspirated if followed by an "h"; this leads to a general dropping of final consonant sounds in English. "V," "w," and "b" are more similar to one another than they are in English. Several consonant combinations do not regularly appear in English, such as "km" and "ph"; nevertheless, both consonants are pronounced with no vowel sound before or between.

Note on Place and Ethnic Names

There is some confusion regarding the place names Cambodia and Kampuchea and the adjectives Khmer, Cambodian, and American. In this work I use those terms as closely to the emic use as possible, recognizing of course that emic use varies among individuals and across time. For centuries, until April 1975, the name of the country was Kampuchea in their language and Cambodia in English (Huffman 1981). Other writers spell the original name of the people "Kambuja," meaning children of Kambu. From Kambuja it is easy to see the derivation of the French "Cambodge" and the English derivative of that. The Khmer Rouge, or the Pol Pot regime, changed the name of the nation to Democratic Kampuchea; in 1979 the Vietnamese changed it to People's Republic of Kampuchea; in 1989 the official name again became Cambodia. All but one of my informants refer to their country as Cambodia (pronounced closer to "Comboja," actually), and so I do here.

The vast majority of people from Cambodia are ethnic Khmer, and their language is Khmer, thus that term is used by many Cambodians and Americans to refer to all nationals of Cambodia. There are also, however, many ethnic Vietnamese, Chinese, Cham, and several smaller ethnic minorities collectively referred to as "Phnong," or "savages" (Ebihara 1971:55), as well as many ethnic mixtures. All of the adult refugees in Middle City speak Khmer as their main language; when speaking English they refer to their language as either Cambodian or Khmer and to themselves as Cambodians. The other ethnic groups within Cambodia, such as Cham-Malay or Khmer-Chinese, consider themselves and are considered by others to be Cambodians and would very rarely be called "Cham" or "Chinese" and then only to make a specific point. They refer to Vietnamese-Americans, who have been here longer and are more acculturated, as "Vietnamese." I have never heard the term "Cambodian-American" used by the members of this community, and so I do not use it, though that perhaps best describes the culture that is developing among them and well reflects the self-identity of many of the children.

Cambodians, like many people, use the term "American" to mean people of the United States. Again I follow emic usage here, despite the unfortunate imperialistic connotation.   The term "Black" or sometimes "Black American" is used by Cambodians, and thus here, for people of African or African-American ancestry. As the refugees in Middle City have little or no contact with actual Africans or other North Americans, these emic terms are clear in this context.

Braving a New World

Chapter 1

Introduction

The 1990s may be the decade of refugees. The United States opened its doors briefly in 1975 upon the fall of Vietnam and again in 1980–1981 to Cambodian refugees, but world crises in the 1990s are precipitating the flight and displacement of more people than ever before. In the past few years we have sought, in different ways, to aid Kurds, Somalis, Bosnians, Haitians, Russians, Cubans, and others. A million or more Rwandans spilled over their borders in 1994, fleeing a most brutal and massive slaughter between Tutsis and Hutus. Never before in history has there been such massive flight of people, on such a global scale. The United Nations' High Commissioner for Refugees estimates there are more than 20 million refugees and displaced persons worldwide (UNHCR 1994).

Anthropology, as a holistic science of humankind, is uniquely suited to study the complex situation of refugees, who face chaos both during their period of flight and in their process of adaptation in resettlement countries. In the latter half of this century, anthropologists have increasingly applied their skills and knowledge to fields of service such as education, health care, and international development. Now refugees may be the neediest people of all, having lost everything and in danger of losing their very culture itself. Anthropologists can contribute both to the refugees and to the people who work with them by studying the traditional cultures of the refugees and their current problems, and by serving as culture brokers and translators between the refugees and their new cultural environments.

At the same time, it is also incumbent upon anthropologists to address the urban problems of our own nation. The United States is experiencing an urban crisis, our own situation of chaos, with deterioration of schools and an increase of youth gangs, violence, and homelessness. Refugees, despite their generally rural origins, are typically resettled in urban areas, often in the worst of urban decay. In their particularly vulnerable state, refugees may become either victims of or participants in those urban problems: they may struggle in inadequate schools, or they may drop out; they may become gang members or gang prey. By intensive ethnographic research, anthropologists can comprehend the refugees' situation from the emic perspective and thus help legislators and assistance agencies develop policies and programs that can aid refugees both in maintaining their own cultures and in adjusting to life in the United States.

The study of refugees, for its part, has much to offer anthropology. For a variety of reasons, anthropology has, in recent decades, turned toward research at home. The proximity of a research population can enable us to stretch scarce research dollars to cover more research and longer periods of time. Third World countries are slower to welcome foreign anthropologists, preferring to employ their own. Proximate research is particularly advantageous in training the next generation, permitting regular supervision of graduate students in the field and providing senior researchers with their own carefully trained research assistants. Finally, and perhaps most importantly, studies of refugees lend themselves perfectly to the sort of long-term research necessary to an understanding of culture change. In refugee studies, anthropologists witness rapid and forced culture change and can also observe closely the consequences of policy decisions in resettlement, education, health care, and urban planning.

WHY CAMBODIANS?

Over one million Southeast Asian refugees have entered the United States since 1975 (USDHHS 1993:5); of these, approximately 150,000 have been Cambodians (Ebihara, Mortland, and Ledgerwood 1994:18). Until that time, the United States had very few Cambodians, some having entered as immigrants or students and some as Vietnamese in previous years. The largest numbers arrived in the years 1980–1982. By 1987, when I began my study, ethnographic research on Cambodian refugees was just beginning, and even the field of refugee research was new in anthropology.[1] Academic journals on migration focused on economic issues and immigration law, and refugee research in the United States tended to focus on larger groups, such as the Vietnamese. Cambodians, for reasons that will unfold in this ethnography, remained relatively ignored, in both the popular and the academic presses. Particularly because of the ethnographic dearth, I have chosen to develop the broadest possible portrayal of the life and culture of a specific refugee community. I intend this work to contribute to the development of a body of ethnography on refugee communities, an essential foundation for the development and testing of refugee theory.

There were other reasons for my choice of Cambodians. As recent arrivals, they were at the beginning of the process of culture change. I hoped to see, at that early date, which elements of their traditional culture were being maintained and which were already undergoing change, and what influences fostered or hindered their initial adjustment. Now the Cambodians have been in the United States nearly fifteen years, and it is possible to begin to examine the course of that change. This book focuses on the original ethnographic data collected between 1987 and 1991, but also includes material on more recent acculturation and some comparative material from other U.S. cities.

Attention has been called in recent years to the dangers of treating all Southeast Asian refugees as members of a cultural whole and to the necessity of understanding the many cultural and experiential differences among them. Cambodians, in particular, have a unique constellation of characteristics, including their ancient history, their traditional culture, unfamiliarity with Western urban culture, and the traumatic circumstances of their flight, which may render their adjustment patterns different from those of other more well-studied groups such as the Vietnamese. In fact, even when I began my research in 1987, preliminary studies were suggesting that Cambodians might not be adapting as rapidly nor as "successfully" as other Asians, even other Southeast Asian refugees. Then, as now, Cambodians in the United States were beginning to appear slow to learn English, to have high rates of unemployment, and to be having trouble in school. I wanted to see to what extent Cambodians were being empowered to establish lives that they themselves considered fulfilling. A holistic study of home and community seemed a promising basis for understanding their aspirations as well as for discovering areas of conflict between Cambodian and American social patterns and values that might be contributing to difficult adjustment.

Finally, I discovered early in the course of this research that many of those who work with and establish policy for Cambodian refugees had little knowledge regarding their traditional culture, their recent history, or their present situation. I hope the ethnographic information in this work will increase the understanding on the part of educators, health care professionals, and social workers, as well as those who develop and legislate policy regarding refugees, so that they may provide more culturally appropriate services to Cambodians and other refugees.

The specific community described here is a small Cambodian refugee community in a midsized Midwestern city, which I call Middle City.[2] It should be emphasized at the outset that this is not meant to represent a "typical" refugee community. Not only are Cambodians not Vietnamese, but Middle City is not on the East or the West Coast, regions which have long experience with in-migration and multiethnicity; Middle City itself, then, was undergoing a new experience. Finally, this specific group is distinguished from many other Cambodian refugee communities in the United States by its small population, which is under five hundred, as compared to, for example, the communities in Long Beach or Minneapolis with their many thousands. It is my hope that the community portrait offered here will contribute to the growing literature on and understanding of urban Cambodians in the United States, and perhaps more broadly to refugee issues as a whole.

THE ANTHROPOLOGICAL PERSPECTIVE

Theoretically and methodologically, this work follows in the tradition in American and British anthropology of holistic community ethnography and is a product of that view of the world, of culture, of human nature, and of social science which we may call the anthropological paradigm, including an interest in the emic, a holistic perspective, and a focus on culture as rich, complex, and dynamic.

Such a theoretical orientation and the qualitative methods it demands lend themselves to an understanding of complexity particularly important for researach on refugees. If all cultures are complex, refugee cultures are complex to the point of chaos: the chaos in the homelands that initially propels flight, chaos during flight, chaos in refugee camps, and chaos in new lands of seemingly incomprehensible language and culture (Donnelly and Hopkins 1993). Long-term participant observation not only allows for but seeks multiple views from within the culture, even when that creates a portrait that other sciences might regard as ambiguous. Anthropologists observe culture as it is enacted by or expressed by individuals, members who not only have different beliefs but also different ways of expressing those beliefs in words and action, and who may change those beliefs over time. We have a responsibility to capture those multiple views as well as variations across gender, age, and class. Pat Caplan sums up the mandate for contemporary anthropologists: "Ethnography should not be homological, plagiaristic, positivist. . . . The name of the game now is aesthetics, pastiche, collage, juxtaposition, framing, heteroglossia, polyphony/polyvocality" (1988:9).

METHODS OF STUDY

We had finally gotten to bed after hours of dancing and loud music and a long trip home. Six year old Theary leaned back against the headboard, crossed her ankles, and folded her hands behind her head. "Well, Mary, how does it feel to be sleeping in our new house for the first time?"

Although I never specifically found children with notebook in hand playing "anthropologist," my identification as anthropologist did not escape the attention of even the youngest members of the culture. My questions to everyone and intrusions into their lives were reciprocated: "What do you teach?" "Why aren't you married?" "You're not Catholic are you?" and so on.

I began my research through three American institutions: an elementary school, a social agency, referred to here as the Agency, and a church, which I call Hillside Church. Soon people introduced me to their families or friends and much of my fieldwork came to be by invitation. For many months Cambodians and Americans kept refering to Ann, an American who they said would tell me everything I needed to know. Ann was connected with Hillside Church, which had sponsored the first Cambodian family in Middle City, and she seemed to have won the trust and friendship of the community. Indeed, Ann welcomed my research project and became a key informant, a mode of entrée, a mentor, and a friend to me. Eventually my research sites came to include other American institutions, such as social agencies, clinics and other medical facilities, and other schools, and also many Cambodian settings, such as family homes during ceremonies and on ordinary days, the temple, and a variety of community gatherings such as weddings, funerals, and New Year celebrations. I also visited Cambodian communities in California, Minnesota, Ohio, Maryland, and Virginia, where I visited neighborhoods, businesses, temples, public schools, Mutual Assistance Associations (MAAs), and Khmer language classes in public, temple, and Christian church schools.

Allowing informants to guide the research process through invitations or requests for help, while in keeping with postmodern efforts to empower one's subjects, has certain drawbacks. Since people knew I was "studying" them, they at first chose events and activities they wanted me to see and excluded me from events and discussions they didn't want reported. Eventually, though, I became witness to situations that people would not necessarily like me to write about; in those cases, although the events have of course informed my own understanding, they are not included here.

Methods used in this study included observation, participant observation, formal and informal open-ended interviews, maintenance of a daily calendar for one woman for two months, collection of artifacts and documents, and viewing of family videotapes. By far my most usual method was participant observation, including such things as cooking and eating in one another's homes, wearing one another's clothes, sleeping with their babies in my bed and leaving my children with them, dancing at weddings, praying in the temple, and eating fetal chicks. Simple observation is useful early in research because it clarifies from the outset one's role as researcher and may prevent a few early blunders. I often used open-ended interviews to supplement and clarify experiences, but they usually were also somewhat participatory, involving simultaneous cooking, eating, baby tending, or language study.

It is important to emphasize that ethnography is never cinema verité. The ethnographer's very presence affects the culture, and in notetaking the ethnographer becomes an active filter through which the culture comes to be represented. Ethnography demands "experiencing strong relationships . . . not involvement with a site at arm's length" (Erickson 1973:15); in studying refugees, whose stories are so tragic and whose needs are so great, it is inevitable that the ethnographer will become involved to some extent in people's daily problems and in helping them with the adjustments they are striving to make.

Language was an issue from the beginning. To learn Khmer beforehand would necessitate postponing the research, but early research was critical to document culture change and adaptation on the part of both the Cambodian and the American cultures. The decision hinged on whether I could learn Khmer faster than they were learning English, and since they had had a six-year start, I felt chances of that were slim. Since I was not doing life history interviews and was not focusing on highly personal or sensitive material, interviews proved adequate with informants who had little English. Informants' freedom to choose whichever language they wished and to translate at their own discretion afforded them a measure of control and privacy that I do not regret.

SPECIAL CONSTRAINTS ON REFUGEE RESEARCH

Some of the dilemmas of this project are faced by all ethnographers. Classic of course is the degree of involvement, which is rightly controlled by the community as a whole and by the specific individuals with whom one becomes most involved (not always the ethnographer's choice either). Other constraints arise from the cultural situation itself; in this case the refugee condition, the poverty, and the lack of transportation may have led people to seek me out on occasions in which, given more options, they might not have. Ethnographers do not often enough address this issue of the ways in which the mutual dependence of ethnographer and informant influences our work. We have become more conscious (and apologetic) of our tendency to study Third World, minority, or marginal people because they are vulnerable to us, having no means to avoid being studied, but we often do not consider the precise ways in which specific vulnerabilities affect our data.

For example, I spent much time with widows and with the poor, simply because my help or friendship could be more useful to them than to some others. Teenagers, too, made themselves more accessible to me, probably because they hoped for a sympathetic ear when they complained about their parents and because they were interested in my sons and curious about my parenting style. For my part, I was most accessible to the young because they were most able to speak to me and understand me. I was more likely to help adults if asked, but I was asked for help more often by teenagers. These were not personal, but cultural, constraints upon selection of informants and subjects for study.

The balance between insider and outsider that all ethnographers struggle to maintain is especially difficult in refugee research. For me, there were actually two subject communities, the refugees themselves and the Americans who were professionally or otherwise involved with them. Although I was obviously not a true member of the first group, at one time or another we all thought I was a legitimate and true member of the second—an American "involved with them." The role of outsider is also complicated by the fact that refugees are, in some ways, some of the time, trying to become Americans. When asked, "What should I do?" I couldn't simply answer back, "I don't know, I'm just watching." So although one of the anthropologist's responsibilities is to *not* change the culture, this is particularly difficult when studying refugees since refugees are trying, very hard sometimes, *to* change their culture. Naturally, at times they saw me as a means to that end. Thus I may at times have been less effusive about my own culture, shared it less than an anthropologist studying a more distant society might have. Laura Bohannan (1966) could tell Shakespeare stories as an entertainment, as a bauble, but when teenagers grilled me about birth control or dating, it was not just myself being examined—my own and their own cultural practices were being held up for scrutiny and for decision making. The other group I was studying, the Americans, were in fact change agents, so when I was being a member of their culture, I was of course changing the other. Again, this was not a matter of choice for me. I could not avoid the role of cultural model.

Other difficulties arose from the ongoing nature of the project: people move, grow up, change their minds. Although a study of culture change clearly demands long-term research, the very length of time results in continually changing data and continually fluctuating ideas and conclusions.

Many directions of research that I attempted were either never possible or were unproductive. After the end of the school term the first spring, I hoped to gain entrée into family life by offering to tutor children. The teacher was enthusiastic and loaded me with books and materials, but her efforts to find even a single child were futile. Parents said the children didn't want to do schoolwork over the summer or needed to rest; the parents may also have needed the children themselves for farm labor or sibling care.

Michael Agar says ethnography "requires . . . an improvisational style to meet situations not of the researcher's making, and an ability to learn from a long series of mistakes" (1986:12). In keeping with a concern not to exploit informants, I often allowed my informants to control the research situations, thus occasionally becoming an unwitting fieldworker. Once I consented to drive a teenager to her friend's house. Before I could blink, she had all five younger siblings out of the house, bottles and diapers in hand, and had locked the door without a key. No adult was home at the friend's house, and so I had the children for the night, with no way to contact their mother. On another occasion I ended up keeping an infant after having said, "Oh no, I can't! I'm having a whole class of students for dinner!" The mother responded, "Oh, that's okay, he loves people! He'll sleep with your son; your son will take care of him." These are simply two examples of serendipitous events which developed into rich field experiences. So, as Agar suggests, my research was often in "situations not of the researcher's making."

As for the "long series of mistakes," that is practically definitional to the course of my fieldwork. Often I didn't stay long enough, didn't greet properly, wasn't deferential enough to an elder, sat improperly, took the wrong photographs, dressed wrong, spoke wrong, wore my hair wrong, ate wrong. But none of these blunders seem to have hindered the work at hand—I was often corrected and often teased, but I did, slowly, in this way, learn many of the correct behaviors. I also learned, like the children, to take the sharp, direct, but cheerful criticism.

LEARNING CULTURE

A study of refugee adaptation or adjustment is a study of learning in the broadest sense: refugees are faced with learning an entire new culture, a whole new way of life. They will need to make, and most of them will make, profound changes in their material, social, and ideological lives. The sociocultural setting in which those changes take place is a primary factor in the success of the eventual adjustment; members of the receiving culture can either facilitate adjustment by making some broadening compromises and adjustments of their own or can impede adjustment by erecting or maintaining barriers.

Refugee studies must focus in on a more specific kind of learning as well, that of formal education. As refugees continue to flow into the United States, their children continue to flow into our schools. While Asian children have in general gained a reputation for school achievement, Cambodian children do not appear to be fitting that pattern (Mitrosomwang 1992; Rumbaut and Ima 1988; Rumbaut 1989). The teachers in Middle City recognized that their own Cambodian students were having difficulty with school. Thus, although this work is intended as a holistic ethnography, it is worth keeping in mind how each facet of culture and each experience of cross-cultural encounter may influence the school experience. It is in the interest of educators and of this nation as a whole to see that all children, including refugee children, are situated to receive the best education possible. Scholars of the educational process and schools themselves must seek an understanding of how best to provide that education.

These two forms of learning are intimately related. Solon Kimball and Jaquetta Hill Burnett point out that the process of learning itself may be culturally prescribed and urge anthropologists to recognize the importance of "simple routines of life" in shaping world view and "the overarching conceptualizations which give meaning to behavior" (1973:xiv). They warn that conflicts may develop when the school experience does not build upon those home-based simple patterns for some children and instead may conflict with them. This book presents just these "simple routines" of Cambodian refugee lives in Middle City. I believe an understanding of some of these simple routines and "overarching conceptualizations" may explain some of the conflicts facing Cambodian children in American schools.

In a similar vein, Frederick Gearing points out that there are many educational systems present in a person's life, and "one cannot adequately comprehend the operations of any one education system in a community unless one comprehends as well the operations of the variety of educational systems which coexist and may compete" (1975:2). Thus, only by studying refugees within their own community and in the various new cultural institutions with which they come into contact can we begin to see the inherent conflicts among those systems and appropriately address the needs of refugees and their children.

BACKGROUND TO THE COMMUNITY

Cultures exist in geographic and historic contexts. In the case of refugees, there is a triple set of contexts: the context of their own history and traditional culture,[3] the context of the culture in which they now find themselves (in this case, Middle City), and the special context of refugeeism. The first and last of these are well documented elsewhere, and I give but the briefest overview here; as for Middle City, the name is, of course, a pseudonym, so I'll try to convey a sense of the city without precise identification.

Cambodian History

While most of this book describes Cambodian refugees in their present U.S. context, to understand the magnitude of the changes they face requires an understanding of the environment which they have left and the historical processes in which their traditions developed and which, most recently, have propelled them to our shores.

Cambodia is a small but fertile nation bordered by Thailand on the west and by Vietnam on the east and southeast, two neighbors with which it has had uneasy relationships for much of its history. The three seasons are dry and warm, dry and hot, and rainy and hot, so much of daily and ceremonial life is carried on outdoors. Most of the Cambodians in Middle City come from agrarian backgrounds, growing rice and other vegetables on small but very productive plots of land. Population density was low for Asia, so there was not a press for land.

Americans have some knowledge of the recent history of Cambodia from the news media and the popular film *The Killing Fields* and some have a vague mental image of Angkor Wat. Few, though, have much sense of the history of Cambodia, ancient or recent. This section offers a very brief review of the history of Cambodia in order to provide the essentials necessary to understand the Cambodian culture in Middle City.[4]

The Austronesian ancestors of the present Khmer and other Southeast Asians migrated from Southwestern China from about 2500 to 1500 B.C., establishing the Funan Empire in what is now south central Cambodia. During the Funan Period, Indian influence began to penetrate Southeast Asia, and Indian scripts and classic Hindu literature and Sanskrit poetry were adopted. With the worship of Shiva and other Hindu deities came other practices: marriages were celebrated on auspicious days (as they are in Middle City today, on dates set by monks), triple prostration was required before the king (in Middle City this practice continues in respect to the monks), and mourning required the shaving of the head (still reported to be required, but actually rarely practiced in Middle City). The Naga legend of Indian royalty became an important theme in Khmer art and literature and is still manifest in Khmer religious architecture in the United States. After the death of Jayavarman I in 681 A.D., the kingdom split, fell into confusion, and by the eighth century fell out of Khmer control.

The Angkor Period, from 802–1432 A.D., is the classic period of Cambodian history to which contemporary Cambodians refer with pride, and the monuments of which appear in posters, calendars, and paintings in Middle City homes. This Angkor Period dates from the reign of Jayavarman II, who gradually recaptured and reunited Cambodia. Indian influence became even stronger, especially in government and religion. The royal family, political and religious officials, and the intellectual class were Brahmans, although they apparently intermarried freely with the Khmer and became racially blended. Royal and priestly inheritance was matrilineal. Complex irrigation and road systems were built, and canals were used for transport. The divine king "owned" the people as well as the land; trial by ordeal was practiced occasionally, with loss of fingers, toes, or limbs, or live burial as punishment (practices later adopted by the Khmer Rouge).

The palace was ornate, with gold furniture and mirrored halls. The king and the ladies of the court wore crowns, necklaces, belts, rings, and anklets of gold, as well as pearls and flowers, all items worn today in Middle City by brides and by the short-lived dance troupe. Royal processions included horses and elephants and hundreds of women carrying lighted candles, banners, umbrellas, and gold and silver palace utensils (Cady 1964). Many elements of this former glory can be seen in the the costumes, ritual paraphernalia, and processions of Cambodian ceremonies in Middle City today. The architecture at Angkor Wat was a major achievements of beauty and technology; technical advances in stonework permitted much larger, taller, and more daring buildings and the elaboration of bas-relief carving.

The Khmer Empire reached its peak in the early twelfth century, during the reign of Suryavarman II, who expanded the kingdom to include much of what is now Laos, Vietnam, Thailand, and Malaya. An increasing interest in Buddhism during the late twelfth century led to the building of 20,000 Buddhist shrines, richly inscribed with Sanskrit poetry, and the resultant "several hundred thousand nonproductive monks and temple servants" (Cady 1966:52). Some scholars attribute the decline of the empire partly to this development of Buddhism and to Buddhism's democratic and egalitarian doctrine, which freed people from the complicated intervening hierarchy of priests and deities (Briggs 1951:259). Furthermore, the monks embraced and honored poverty and devoted themselves to good works for the common people (such as teaching) rather than to the service of the nobility. The hydraulic systems eventually fell into decay, resulting in decreased agricultural production. Vassal states rebelled, sea trade declined, and in 1431 Thai armies sacked and captured Angkor, specifically killing off the elite and intellectuals (Briggs 1951), much as the Khmer Rouge did five and a half centuries later.

Although it was the Thai who captured Angkor Wat, it was the Vietnamese who invaded in large numbers, took over trades, tried to impose their language and other cultural systems, and eventually closed Phnom Penh to outside trade. May Ebihara points out, though, that the general populace was little affected and that major elements of the culture remained unchanged: the strict hereditary class system, the divine right of the monarchy, the use of corvée and slave labor, the hierarchical system of government officials, the general disenfranchisement of the peasantry, and the system of patron/client relationships all seemed to remain into the nineteenth century from the earlier periods (1971:36–42).

By the time French observers were visiting Vietnam in the early nineteenth century, Vietnam had established itself as the dominant power in Southeast Asia. In an 1863 pact with Vietnam, the French acquired legal power over part of Cambodia, while Thailand acquired the rich provinces of Battambang and Siem Reap, the western homelands of many Middle City Cambodians. Although French political authority was absolute, the king retained "an illusion of royal authority and national independence" (Cady 1964:550), important to ordinary villagers, who continued to consider the palace the magical center of the world and the king a divinely authorized god-king (Cady 1966:112). French influence was minimal except in Phnom Penh, and even there the French imported Vietnamese to administer the government and control the trade. In villages, Buddhist schools run by the monks remained, continued to teach only boys, and refused to teach the Romanized alphabet introduced by the French. Village headmen remained in charge of corvée labor, taxes, and local police. Since the French developed no systems of roads, schools, hospitals, mining, or industry, as they did in other Southeast Asian countries, the ordinary populace, used to political and economic dominance by outsiders, scarcely felt French presence.

There is a surprising dearth of anthropological research on traditional Khmer culture. The outstanding work is May Ebihara's unpublished dissertation on a Khmer village in 1959–1960, *Svay, a Khmer Village in Cambodia* (1971), and her articles based on that research (1960, 1964, 1966, 1974, 1990). Until recently, Ebihara has been the only American anthropologist to have done ethnographic fieldwork in village Cambodia; as she explains, most of her predecessors' work was in French and was primarily historical rather than anthropological. Happily, her own fieldwork was done at a critical time in Cambodian history, after the changes brought about by World War II and French colonial occupation but before the traumatic dismantling of the culture beginning in April 1975. Thus from her work we can see ordinary or "traditional" village life as it was when Middle City adults were in their youth and early adulthood. By documenting in rich detail the traditional culture from which the Middle City Cambodians have come, her work provides a basis for comparison and, as such, has been continuously informing of my own research and foundational to this book. Subsequent to Ebihara's original study, there was little ethnographic work in village Cambodia because of the wars and subsequent upheavals.

Following World War II, King Norodom Sihanouk won Cambodia's independence from France and attempted neutrality in the relations between Communist and non-Communist nations but was unable to prevent Communist Vietnamese troops from establishing bases along the eastern border. The United States began to bomb these in 1969, forcing the Communist troops deeper into Cambodia; all of Cambodia became a stage of war, with Cambodia's own Chinese-trained Communists, the *Khmer Krahom* (Khmer Rouge or Red Khmer), fighting the non-Communist government. People fled to the capital, Phnom Penh, for protection.

In the early morning of April 17, 1975, Khmer Rouge soldiers walked into Phnom Penh, declaring the war's end. At first people were joyful to have peace at last; the ordinary citizen didn't much care who was running the government. But some of the more educated and those involved in the government were wary and did not join the rejoicing in the streets. Within a few hours their anxieties were affirmed.

The soldiers, many of them teenagers, began a rout, storming into homes, looting, and chasing the people out. It is important to understand the nature of the Khmer Rouge soldiers. They were not foreigners; they were Khmer, but generally from remote areas. There had always been distrust between the rural people and the westernized, French-educated city people. Many of these Khmer Rouge had never seen running water or electric lights; they shattered mirrors and burned books, bathed themselves in toilets, and slaughtered pets and hung them in doorways.

The people were told this rout was merely a temporary move of a few days to "clean the city up" (presumably of squatters, but some residents were also told that the United States was planning to bomb the city [Yathay 1987]), but when the soldiers began clearing out hospitals and orphanages as well, and killing or arresting government officials, lawyers, teachers, and monks, the city dwellers realized they must shed their urban identity. Merely getting out of the city took days, because people were herded in all directions and not allowed to use their cars or motorcycles. People tried to bring rice and a few cooking items, but they were primarily concerned with locating family members, especially grandparents or married children not living in the household. That theme of trying to locate and reunite family dominates the entire period from that first morning, through the exodus from the city into the slave camps, and during the flights into Thailand four years later. It is a dominant theme still, in the daily life and dream life of Cambodian refugees in Middle City.

It is impossible to even begin to understand Cambodian refugees in the United States without considering their experience under the Khmer Rouge. Most

Americans know that refugees have suffered, but not everyone comprehends the full extent of the atrocities of life and death suffered at the hands of the Khmer Rouge and the consequences of those horrors which are ever-present in the daily, and nightly, lives of Cambodians in the United States.

The world was told that "2000 years of Cambodian history have ended" (Chandler 1990). The city people became the "new people" in the villages. They would not have been particularly welcome anyway, but in this case they poured into already war-torn villages under the criticism of the Khmer Rouge, who labeled them parasites. To have been a teacher, monk, or artist, or even to be able to speak or read French, made one suspect, liable for imprisonment, torture, or death.[5] Many forms of torture are described in various autobiographies as well as by my informants: chopsticks in the ears, hanging by the feet, children swung by the feet and smashed against trees, children witnessing the beatings or killing of their parents, and the infamous Chinese water torture. Children from the age of six were separated from their families and sent off to other labor camps according to age. The forced labor itself was a torture, because many did not know how to do the work, and all were sick, underfed, and very frightened. The infirm, the aged, and those who became too sick to work simply died. Medicines were forbidden because *Angkar* ("The Organization"—meaning the central organization of the Khmer Rouge) was supposedly able to care for all the people. Although the daily rations were a meager cup of rice, people were forbidden to grow their own foods, and many starved to death. Some were forced by the Khmer Rouge and by starvation to commit horrendous acts for which they now suffer deeply (such as killing others, walking over or sleeping with dead bodies, and abandoning their own children and parents).

Few people escaped during these years, but when the Vietnamese overthrew the Khmer Rouge in January of 1979, those who were able took this moment of confusion to escape westward on foot, sometimes literally crawling, to Thailand. The trip was long and arduous. Jungles were loaded with dangerous snakes, the rivers leech-filled, the trails mined. Many Cambodians were robbed, raped, and killed along the way by soldiers or by those hired to guide them; others died of exposure and starvation. Some reached Thailand only to be hauled off in trucks and chased at gunpoint back over the border into the mined jungles of Cambodia.[6]

The years in refugee camps were another ordeal. Many refugees died shortly upon reaching the camps because their health was so severely damaged; others were raped, robbed, beaten, or otherwise mistreated by the guards. Once settled in, a few people were able to contribute to their support by gardening, giving lessons, or sewing, but for the most part people were idle and dependent upon strangers for their sustenance and for decisions about their future. Schooling was minimal, "just a-b-c," as my informants said, despite the United Nations High Commissioner for Refugees (UNHCR) mandate for fourteen weeks of "intensive" language training. This lengthy stage of idleness and helplessness has had lasting consequences for their adjustment in the United States.[7]

When the first Cambodians arrived in Middle City, they suffered from parasites, disease, malnutrition, severe depression, nightmares, rotten and missing teeth, and other permanent injuries. These problems were the result of physical and mental torture, forced labor, starvation, loss and murder of family members, general religious and cultural upheaval, and family disintegration due to death and loss. Post-traumatic stress syndrome and survival guilt are endemic; many people, including children, had helplessly witnessed the torture or murder of family members.

For those who were left behind in refugee camps, matters have not improved. In 1990 there were over 300,000 Cambodians in camps along the Thai-Cambodian border (USDS 1990), mostly classified by the Thai government as "displaced persons" and therefore ineligible for third-country asylum. Since 1993 the United Nations has been encouraging repatriation, although the Khmer Rouge still control large areas and much of the countryside is covered with land mines. Many who return to Cambodia flee back to Thailand; others lose limbs to the mines. Cambodians in Middle City are acutely aware of the terrible conditions of their kin in Thailand and Cambodia. The *New York Times*, May 4, 1994, reported,

The guerrillas have stepped up attacks . . . thousands of people have taken refuge . . . along roads, in temples . . . sleep in fields at night. . . . Virtually the entire population of Battambang's Rattanak Mondol district—27,000 people—fled . . . last week.

For a broader view of the post-war situation in Cambodia, the reader should consult *Cultural Survival Quarterly*'s special volume on Cambodia (Volkman 1990) or May Ebihara, Carol Mortland, and Judy Ledgerwood's more recent *Cambodian Culture Since 1975: Homeland and Exile* (1994).

Middle City

In contrast to the land from which the refugees have come, Middle City is distinctly urban. Located in the midwestern United States, it can be bitterly cold in the winter. As an old city, its downtown area is fairly dirty and many buildings, though architecturally beautiful, are in grave disrepair. There are several large parks beyond the city, but few truly urban parks and little greenery along city streets. The inner-city neighborhoods where the Cambodians were originally placed are particularly densely populated and devoid of trees, though a few Cambodian families set pots of flowers on their cement yards. Trash litters the streets and sidewalks, and the city is noted for its air, soil, and water pollution.

Middle City is also noted for its sociopolitical conservatism. Although it is not a particularly "poor" city, as it has several strong industries and well-subscribed arts organizations, the schools and social agencies are in almost constant financial trouble. The central city houses the very poor, who are mostly American-born minorities and now the Cambodians; the outer edges have working class and middle class neighborhoods; the wealthy live well outside the city and their children go to separate schools. Few Cambodians except those who work as maids ever see those distant neighborhoods. In past decades, Middle City was proud of its multicultured history, referring to the European immigrants of the last century, who have left their signature in the city's arts, cuisine, and architecture. But the city has been relatively impervious to recent immigration, and most citizens and services are unused to dealing with people of other cultures. One can spend weeks without meeting anyone of foreign birth; many residents live in the same neighborhoods in which they grew up, send their children to the same schools they attended, and cannot imagine living elsewhere. Most are deeply loyal to their city and their nation; it seems natural to them that foreigners would want to come, and it seems obvious that foreigners would want to become as American as possible as quickly as possible. For the Cambodians, the most significant feature of Middle City may be that it has no Buddhist temple or other Buddhist organization. In a survey of Cambodian communities in the United States, most communities rated as "good places" had Cambodian temples or other nearby Buddhist temples; the authors conclude "the existence of either a strong MAA (Mutual Assistance Association), or a temple, usually indicated a strong community" (North and Sok 1989). Although there was discussion of both forms of institution, Middle City had neither throughout my research.

Cambodians as Refugees

The body of general work on refugees is growing exponentially, so the reader is referred for bibliography to such publications as *Selected Papers in Refugee Issues,*[8] the *Southeast Asian Refugee Studies Newsletter* from the University of Minnesota, and Linda Camino and Ruth Krulfeld's recent work, *Reconstructing Lives, Recapturing Meaning* (1994).[9]

Material specifically on Cambodians as refugees is less abundant. John Marston's *Annotated Bibliography of Cambodia and Cambodian Refugees* (1987) contains over five hundred entries, many of which are guides for refugees or their American teachers, social workers, and sponsors. Testimonials and autobiographies by refugees, noted earlier, also provide insight into the flight process and the early days in the United States. Most of these were written by the earliest-arriving refugees, who often had better English and urban skills and who came into a somewhat more welcoming environment than those rural Cambodians who arrived in Middle City. The most recent work is the previously noted collection by Ebihara, Mortland, and Ledgerwood (1994).

Finally, because we are dealing with a topic so current, much fine research is as yet unpublished. I refer particularly to several recent doctoral dissertations by anthropologists: John Marcucci's *Khmer Refugees in Dallas: Medical Decisions in the Context of Pluralism* (1986), Beatrice Hackett's *Family, Ethnicity, and Power: Chinese Cambodian Refugees in the Washington Metropolitan Area (District of Columbia)*, (1988), Judy Ledgerwood's *Changing Khmer Conceptions of Gender: Women, Stories, and the Social Order* (1990), Judith Kulig's *Role, Status Changes and Family Planning Use Among Cambodian Refugee Women* (1991), Lance Rasbridge's *Infant/Child Feeding Among Resettled Cambodians in Dallas: Intracultural Variation in Refugee Iron Nutrition* (1991), and Bo Sin's *Socio-Cultural, Psychological and Linguistic Effects on Cambodian Students' Progress Through Formal Schooling in the United States (*1991). The reader is encouraged to seek out these works for more thorough coverage of those topics. The present study is intended as a broader, more holistic ethnography of a particular community of Cambodian refugees as they are in the processes of maintaining their culture and adapting it to life in the United States, while at the same time learning American culture and adapting it to their needs.

NOTES

1. The Committee on Refugee Issues (CORI), a committee of the General Anthropology Division (GAD) was founded at the Annual Meeting of the American Anthropological Association in New Orleans in 1990.

2. In keeping with anthropological concerns to protect anonymity, this and all names of people, places, and organizations in this book are pseudonyms.

3. The word "traditional" is of course subject to interpretation. In this work, I generally mean the culture of rural Cambodians just before the wars beginning about 1970. I don't mean to imply that the culture was at that or any time static or monolithic—there had always been much cultural exchange with neighbors and much inter-village variation. Nevertheless, the intent in this work is to distinguish the culture and life typical of peacetime Cambodians, particularly those who became refugees, with the life of Cambodian refugees in Middle City.

4. For more on early Cambodian history, see Briggs 1951, Cady 1964 and 1966, Chandler 1992, and Kalman and Cohen 1975; for recent history, see Barron and Paul 1977, Becker 1986, Chandler 1983, 1990, and 1991, Jackson 1989, Kiernan 1985 and 1993, Martin and McLeod 1994, Ponchaud 1977 and 1989, Shawcross 1979 and 1984, and Vickery 1984 and 1990.

5. Sam-Ang Sam reports 80 percent of performers, 90 percent of classical dancers, and 90 percent of teachers or professors died during this time; he cites Cheng Phon, "There were 380,000 artists and intellectuals. During Pol Pot, just 300 people survive" (Pack 1989, cited in Sam-Ang Sam 1994).

6. For excellent biographies and autobiographies of this period, see Criddle and Mam 1987, May 1986, Ngor 1987, Noup 1988, Sheehy 1987, Welaratna 1993, and Yathay 1987.

7. See Mortland 1987 and Tollefson 1989 for more on Cambodian refugees in the camps.

8. This series, *Selected Papers in Refugee Issues*, is published by the Committee of Refugee Issues. To date there are four volumes: 1992, edited by Pamela A. DeVoe; 1993, edited by MaryCarol Hopkins and Nancy D. Donnelly; 1994, edited by Jeffery MacDonald and Amy Zaharlick; and 1995, edited by Ann M. Rynearson and James Phillips.

9. Very recent studies of specific refugee groups are too numerous to name, but particularly notable ones, in addition to those already cited, include Burns 1993, Donnelly 1994, Gold 1992, Hagan 1994, Haines 1989, and Kibria 1993.

Chapter 2

Material Culture: Meeting Basic Needs

Material culture is not only the most visible and most readily understood component of culture but also the most receptive to change, and it therefore provides an appropriate point from which to begin a study of the process of culture change. By "material culture" I refer here to those objects and processes by which culture satisfies the most basic physical needs of a population—what anthropologists generally term "technology"; but I mean in this case to distinguish these from what is sometimes called "high tech"—electronic and other devices of recent invention and new in American culture as well (video cameras, VCRs, computers, pagers, etc.).

FOOD

A paper plateful of clear noodles is brought to our table; they're thicker than spaghetti, raggedy textured. I can only think of Gummiworms. I ask, and dutifully write down "ski'paw." A heap is put on my plate; they're a little rubbery, but taste deliciously of vinegar, garlic, chopped peanuts, and coconut. Later, when a teenager joins our table I ask her to tell me the name in English.

"Ski'paw."

"Yeah, I got that," showing her my notes, "but do you know a name for it in English?"

"That *is* English!" and she spells for me, "s-k-i-n p-o-r-k."

Rice is the staple and most important food of Cambodians, and a group of small teenagers said to me once, "Rice, we need rice to grow. Rice make you big." Rice is bought in Asian stores in large plastic sacks, and American rice is scorned as tasteless (and comparatively, it is—the rice imported from Thailand fills the house with a rich, sweet, baking smell). There are many brands and several varieties, preferred for different purposes and by different families. *Bobo*, or "soup rice" (a sort of rice porridge), is the first nonmilk food of infants, a common breakfast, and is also eaten at other times. As in Ebihara's village Cambodia of the early 1960s, almost every major meal includes boiled white rice. However, noodles made of rice wheat or rice flour, served either hot or cold, are also used abundantly, as are a great variety of meats, fruits, and fresh vegetables.

Meats such as pork, chicken, ham, sausage, beef, shrimp, crab, clams, mussels, sardines, shark, and various fish are ordinarily used in small amounts, but they are plentiful for parties and for guests; sometimes a trip is made out of the city to buy a whole pig or to buy parts that are less often used by Americans—stomachs of cows and pigs, for example, tongues, and the above-mentioned pig skin, which is boiled, seasoned, and served up like noodles. Eggs are used hard boiled or as ingredients for various dishes. "Baby eggs," eggs at various stages of incubation, are hard boiled and served with a sauce of lemon juice, salt, and pepper. These and the developing eggs from inside chickens are saved and eaten as special delicacies. Dried fish and cryopacked cooked fish are purchased in Asian stores.

Many raw and cooked vegetables are eaten, such as bamboo shoots, bean sprouts, beans, peas and peapods, bok choy, spinach, water chestnuts, cabbage, lettuce, tomatoes, carrots, green beans, long beans, spaghetti squash, potatoes, onions, garlic, taro, corn on the cob (fresh and tiny canned ones), cucumbers, cilantro, lemon grass, coriander, and many varieties of small leafy plants which we call "basil" and Cambodians translate, accurately, as various kinds of "mint" (*chi krahom, chi angkam, chi t'pol traiy, chi sang houm,* etc.). I include these last as vegetables rather than as herbs because they are eaten fresh and in larger quantities than Americans would, more as salads than as seasonings, so they are a more significant source of vitamins than they would be in an American diet. Some are hard to obtain fresh in Middle City but can sometimes be found in the few Asian stores. A few families have small backyard gardens in which they grow vegetables and flowers, which are shared with friends. Fresh fruits such as pineapple, apples, strawberries, bananas, oranges, coconut, Asian pear, mangoes, and grapes, and some imported canned fruits, such as lychees and jackfruit, are used for ceremonies, snacks, desserts, and sometimes in main dishes such as sweet and sour pork. Other items common in the diet are peanuts, whole as snacks or finely chopped in sauces or salad dressings; seasonings such as garlic, tamarind, coriander, ginger, Thai fish sauce, soy sauce, vinegar, salt, and pepper; beans; popcorn and chips; and a great deal of soda pop, particularly Mountain Dew (the English name is used, sometimes as a generic term for soft drink; the Khmer word for orange, *toeukroat,* is also used to mean soft drink). Many adults drink beer, at least at parties, and cognac (usually referred to as "Hennessey") is usually served at wedding parties.

Most foods are not eaten plain, but in combination. Common dishes are fried rice with egg, peas, ham, and intricately slivered green onion; spicy sauces of shrimp, bamboo shoots, and tomato; stews of fish, shrimp, or meat with vegetables; tiny eggrolls filled with potato and onions or mixtures of pork, onions, cabbage, carrots, vinegar, sugar, and soy sauce; cold noodles with beef and peanuts; cold transparent rice-flour crepes filled with lettuce or cabbage, shrimp or pork or both, chi krahom, cold rice noodles, perhaps bean sprouts, and cucumber; grilled skewers of slivered beef or pork marinated in onion, fish sauce, garlic, and ground peanuts; chunks of sauced beef or chicken on a bed of lettuce; layered salads of shredded cabbage, cucumber, coriander, and basil, or red bell peppers, onions, and sprouts, with a variety of dressings; very thin noodles with peanut sauce and slivered cucumbers; dressings and dipping sauces made of vinegar, sugar, salt, garlic, and peanuts, or fish sauce and sugar; and many delicious varieties of soup, eaten plain or spooned over rice. To Americans, the cuisine as a whole resembles both Thai and Vietnamese cooking but is often less spicy.

Although sweets do not have a high position in the cuisine, several kinds of slightly sweet dishes are made, such as a white coconut jell served in squares or diamonds about an inch deep; dumplings made of a sweet dough with bean filling, in sweet coconut-based sauce; a sort of custard or sweet coconut milk sauce that may contain various noodles, rice cake chunks, beans, or rice dumplings; a wine-based sauce with shredded coconut; a firm black jell made from canelike syrup and served in coconut juice; and a variety of rice cakes with bananas, sweetened beans, or other fillings, wrapped in banana leaves and steamed. Children love ice cream and popsicles, but most adults do not care for American desserts.

Meals and Mealtimes

Cultures vary in their ideas about the timing of meals and the appropriateness of certain foods for certain times. Cambodians are more likely to eat traditional foods during leisure times such as weekends and summer vacations and at celebrations, whereas they eat American foods when their time is more strictly scheduled. So, for example, on a schoolday children may have a hasty 6:30 A.M. breakfast of dry cereal (sometimes with milk), candy, a popsicle, or "nothing." But on weekends, the meal may be late in the morning and consist of rice, noodles, fish, chicken, vegetables, fried eggs, and other rather substantial foods. The popsicle breakfasts may cause teachers concern, but in more traditional homes, or when the mother is able, breakfast just as likely consists of rice cooked the night before, with a little sugar or salt, or occasionally bobo, the rice porridge. Family meals later in the day vary greatly, again according to social class and degree of Americanization, but also according to hours the adults may work, which is often during the evening or night.

Most of the children do not partake of the school-provided breakfast because it means being at school before dawn, but for those who do it usually consists of a doughnut or sweet roll. If there is milk, they seldom drink it. They say "it for babies," or "it make me throw up," or they just wrinkle up their noses. Despite the milk intolerance of many Asians, the teachers continue to urge them to drink it. The children also eat selectively from the free school lunch—they may eat the canned peach and the chips but leave the tuna sandwich and the milk. The high school kids may bring sandwiches or noodles for lunch, but most of them, like their American peers, neither buy nor bring lunch, but typically spend the lunch hour with soda pop and friends.

Different foods are appropriate to different occasions. For the large public New Year party, a group of women will make fried rice, skewers of grilled beef, sweet and sour grated cabbage, and tiny eggrolls, because these things transport and sell easily. At family celebrations and weddings there are more elaborate dishes, and far more variety, perhaps eight or ten different "main dishes" and perhaps soup and dessert as well. Everyday family meals show more western influence: fried chicken, airy white bread, sandwiches, chips, reconstituted orange juice, granola bars, and canned peas, beans, and spaghetti.

Shopping for Food

Shopping is generally done in nearby grocery stores because transportation is difficult, but those who are able prefer to shop in the bigger suburban supermarkets for lower prices and in Asian groceries for better prices on rice and also for their traditional foods. Only people with cars can easily get to the Asian stores that have the kinds of fish, vegetables, spices, and other ingredients they need for their customary diet; they must travel over 100 miles for the nearest "Cambodian" stores. These stores sell the appropriate cookware, the elaborate silver ceremonial dishes, incense, fresh vegetables and fruits, dried roots, beans, large bags of rice, cooked, dried, and frozen fish, and a great variety of canned foods, as well as jewelry, cloth, floormats, music tapes, and videotapes. However, all these foods and other goods are imported from Thailand, not Cambodia; the stores are "Cambodian" because they are run by Cambodians and cater to Cambodian customers.

People are alert to price differences from store to store. I have had price comparisons quoted to me—according to pound for beef at various supermarkets, and for the bags of rice at the different Asian stores. Almost all of the families received food stamps when they first arrived, and many still do. Teenagers and often younger children are helpful in the shopping because they can read the labels and ask questions.

Preparation

Generally women and teenage girls do the cooking, but sometimes the elderly are alone to cook for themselves during the day and have learned to use microwave ovens to reheat food cooked by a younger adult the day before. Boys and men often know at least the rudiments of cooking. I've seen boys small enough to need a chair to see into the pot, set up with a chair at the stove to reheat a large kettle of fried rice, and eight- and ten-year-olds are fully capable of making a batch of noodles, perhaps adding egg or vegetables to round out the meal.

For communal events, women gather the day before, kneeling or squatting on a blue plastic tarp in a kitchen or an adjacent room or on a porch or patio in the yard, to cook in large quantities. They chop, peel, season, stuff, wrap, mix, fry in huge woks, and grill outdoors. One group may make hundreds of eggrolls, another make and grill hundreds of skewers of marinated meat. Many are cooking in the kitchen or yard while more ceremonial events are taking place in another room. There may be fifteen or more women at any one time, and others may come and go over the course of the day; they work late into the night, sometimes all night. Teenage girls help with this, and small children, boys, and men come in and out to join in conversations. It's a major social event in itself, filled with gossip, teasing, stories,

Michael M. Burch

Women cooking for a celebration

and laughter as the women share food, cooking tips, and criticism. For the children, always close by, it's an important arena for enculturation.

In addition to American-style pots and pans, many use electric woks, which has caused some landlords to refuse to rent to them because they find the grease splatter on the floor impossible to remove. Large and small stone mortars and pestles are also used in traditional cooking, as well as huge aluminum pots purchased in the Asian shops. Women work deftly with large knives, cutting away from the body, creating precisely uniform matchsticks or tiny cubes; they scorn the use of graters and peelers.

Serving and Eating

Serving and eating styles also vary according to occasion. When they first arrived, the Cambodians tended to eat on mats on the floor, but most families now have tables and chairs, and some families gather at these for ordinary meals.

Communal meals are of two sorts: more religious, such as wedding ceremonies and funerals, and more festive, such as wedding receptions and the New Year. At the more religious events, in homes or in the temple, mats cover the floor or carpet, and people kneel in small, informal clusters. Foods are brought out, usually by bowing women and young men, in serving bowls—rice in very large (2–3 gallon) bowls or kettles or dishpans—and placed in the midst of a cluster of four to eight people. There is also a stack of shallow bowls for individuals, a pile of serving-size spoons (larger than what Americans call soup spoons) for individual use, and a stack of paper napkins or a roll of paper towels. There may also be chopsticks if noodles are served, and occasionally some forks. Very small amounts are put into the individual dish at a time—a serving spoon of rice and only a tablespoon or two from one of the other dishes. The individual spoon is poised above the personal dish; from there it dips into the communal dish, gestures above the personal dish, but actually goes straight into the mouth. Dishes are not passed once they are on the mats; the diner reaches forward into the center of the cluster of people, not usually moving the communal dish. Such meals usually finish with cigarettes for older adults.

At these meals adult men and women may sit together in one room, or, if there is a large crowd or two rooms, they may segregate by sex, but this seems to be a casual practice, not a rule. Infants, toddlers, and girls of all ages may be present, but most children over five and especially boys usually do not attend or may be found outdoors playing or in a nearby home watching television. The elderly are given quite a bit of attention, and children up to four or five may be spoon-fed.

At less religious occasions such as wedding parties, which are generally held at large recreation centers or rented halls, tables are set with paper cloths, napkins, and plates, and food is brought out on serving plates by young men and women. Again, small bits at a time are put onto individual plates, but people are less likely to eat directly from the serving plate. Food never seems to run out; if one dish is finished, another soon appears in the hands of a youth.

At the large communal New Year party, also held in a community recreation hall, bare tables with chairs are set up, and individuals go to the kitchen to buy single items. People may bring back a plate for themselves or a large plateful of items to share with the tableful of friends and kin. A few bring coolers and baskets with salads, sandwiches, chips, and other foods to share with friends; other people frown on this practice, however, because the profit from the food selling helps to pay for the hall and the band.

At the more traditional events and at home, people eat with chopsticks, spoons, forks, or with forks and spoons used together, depending on family preference and the kind of food (spoons for rice, chopsticks for noodles). It is good form to raise a dish up to about eight inches from the face and lift trailing noodles with chopsticks, but it is not acceptable to bring the bowl quite up to the face "like Chinese do," as one little girl told me with a grimace. At wedding receptions, though, in the large rented halls, places are usually set with plastic forks and spoons.

Drinks may be brought out on a tray with filled glasses, or glasses, ice buckets, and two-liter bottles of soda pop may be set out on tables or on the mats. Alcohol is not served at the temple or at more traditional, more serious meals.

Cleaning Up

Women and girls do most of the cleaning up, whether from family or communal meals. Food may be returned from an individual plate into a serving bowl, and plates may be wiped with paper towels before being stacked and sent to the kitchen. Few people have dishwashers, so dishes are washed by hand, usually by teenage girls. For large events, washing may be done in the backyard or basement of a house; a special short hose is used, with an on-off valve and spray trigger at the end. In other cities, temples have a special outdoor area with spigot for this purpose.

Ideas about refrigeration sometimes differ from American views. Food may be left out all night, or all day and night, and reheated and eaten the next day, and food carried on picnics or to other events is not kept on ice. In Cambodia few people had refrigerators except in Phnom Penh, and even there people preferred to shop daily, as refrigerated food was not considered fresh.

Feeding Babies

In infant feeding, the newly developing refugee culture is at variance both with its own traditional practices and with American customs. Breastfeeding was the custom in rural Cambodia because other milk was not available and among educated urban Cambodians because they believed it was healthier, as do many Americans. However, in Middle City (as in other American cities; see Rasbridge 1991 and Rasbridge and Kulig 1995), young Cambodian mothers prefer to bottle feed with formula, often provided free through the Special Supplemental Food Program for Women, Infants, and Children (WIC). The young women tell me it's healthier, or that you can't breastfeed in the United States because Americans would stare at you; the older women say the young mothers are just lazy. Rasbridge points out that the consequence is a high rate of iron deficiency anemia among infants.

Babies are fed bobo as a first food and eventually almost anything others eat, including many sweets. Often at Agency classes mothers would take punch or cookies for their babies, but none for themselves. A baby over a year old is as likely to have cola or Kool-aid in a bottle as milk, and children up to four carry these bottles around. They are not impressed by American ideas of nutrition—some mothers see American babies with bottles of water and believe that the reason Americans give babies water is that they can't afford milk.

Babies and young children are fed on demand when food is being prepared, so often they've already eaten by the time adults gather for a meal. Slightly older children are quite capable of getting their own food, so one might encounter a five-year-old eating a bowl of rice as the children gather around the television or a nine-year-old cooking noodles for himself and a small sibling.

Cross-Cultural Differences

Food is fertile ground upon which to explore ethnic identity, cultural differences, stereotypes, misunderstandings, and sometimes conflict (Francis 1988; Germer 1986; Katona-Apte and Apte 1980). Several times I heard Americans comment that the refugees' diet is much healthier than Americans' because Cambodians eat brown rice; it took a Cambodian some effort once to convince a woman who works with Asians that no, indeed, they eat polished white rice just as Americans do. A church school teacher, planning a picnic, said to me, "We'll pack peanut butter sandwiches. All kids like that." Once when a group of kids came hungry into my kitchen at noon, I offered turkey sandwiches, peanut butter, hamburgers, eggs, cereal, and noodles. They all looked quite blank, then made noodles. Teachers and other Americans constantly urge children to drink their milk, which they clearly are not pressed to do at home. One little boy returned from a week at summer camp "so skinny—he not eat at all, not once." As many of the younger kids do, he said simply, "I don't know how to eat American food." Family and friends bring food to someone in the hospital, because, similarly, they "don't know how to eat hospital food."

Of course, food can also be a positive meeting ground for cultures: Cambodians are proud of their foods, which indeed Americans seem to find delicious and not entirely unfamiliar. But they are often willing to try American food, too. When I offered one small boy breakfast, I ran through what I had come to think were the obvious things: noodles, rice, chicken; he said, "You know how to make pancakes?" Another time, I asked a mother what I should serve her family for dinner. She said "You know hot dog?" Feeling a need to be a more impressive hostess than that, I also made chicken, spaghetti, fried rice, and several other dishes. They ate the hot dogs.

The Cambodians' main sources of American-style foods are institutions—school, camp, church, and the Agency. At church the children are offered chunks of ham, tomato soup, pizza, fruit, cheese, and fruit-flavored punch—but mostly cookies, which is what they take. The children about eight to twelve years old seem to be the most amenable to trying American foods. The younger ones eye it suspiciously and stick to cookies and punch. Teenagers, too, often say they prefer Cambodian food. For a school picnic, children were given bags with baloney sandwiches, apples, raisins, and chocolate milk; though told emphatically to "drink the milk first," few ate anything except the baloney out of the sandwich. The women seldom take the cookies and soft drinks offered at the Agency. Perhaps because of the type of snack they normally offer, more conscious efforts at the Agency to teach American ideals of nutrition are of doubtful value. At one such nutrition class, as the teacher pointed to the "Four Food Groups" on a chart and discussed daily nutritional needs, a mother broke candy and fed the bits to her infant and toddler, while other tots drank coke from baby bottles. One day the lesson was on calcium, and the women were told they must eat cheese, milk, tofu, and broccoli each day, because calcium is not stored in the body. This, they were told, was why they must sign up for the WIC program—to get such important foods as milk, cheese, cereal, and cream of wheat. Since these foods are either unfamiliar or disliked, the lesson was lost.

Although food may seem a simple arena for culture change, American foods, food vocabulary, and preparation are not so readily adopted as one might expect. Even with this most basic and primary element of culture, learning a new culture is neither swift nor easy, perhaps not predictable, and certainly not necessarily advantageous. We can hardly view the popsicle/doughnut breakfasts an improvement over the traditional rice or bobo, the soft drinks more nutritious than breastmilk. On the other hand, maintaining the traditional foods and eating patterns is increasingly difficult for economic and other practical reasons.

HOUSING

I enter the sideyard, walk down the concrete past the broken bike, the rain-soaked couch and rusting refrigerator, up the step. The door is unlocked. Pitching into the darkness of the long hallway, I grope for the stairs, the rotted wood soft underfoot. "Sary," I call out, "it's me."

The three women are kneeling, filling eggrolls; they make room, and I join them on the blue plastic tarp. There are no counters and, besides the ancient stove and sink, only a short, wobbly wooden bench for work space. The floor slopes away from the entrance, and at the stove it angles down steeply, so that pots slip to the back of the stove. Two woks sputter, and swarms of flies buzz merrily in the sweltering heat.

Most Cambodians in Middle City were originally placed in one-, two-, and three-room apartments in two inner-city neighborhoods that happened to have available housing. The buildings are two or three stories, with one or two apartments on each floor, and are in acute disrepair. Roofs leak and water seeps in onto the floor when it rains. Yards, usually concrete or bare packed earth, often have standing water left from rains or coming from within the house. Yards and sidewalks are littered with broken beds, couches, appliances, and general trash such as broken bottles and assorted rusty parts of ancient things. Stairs are broken and tilt crazily; windows are cracked and screenless; faucets run steadily; ovens don't work. Some have single heaters, and simple hooks for locks. Widows with children live in basement apartments because it's cheaper, but often they have no phones and are afraid. Most of the neighbors are poor, unemployed, and resentful. The refugees have their tires slashed, their car windows broken, and eggs, chairs, threats, and epithets thrown at them.

Decoration

Inside, the feeling is different. Most homes are clean and very neat. Despite the dark, peeling walls, cracked plaster, and sloping floors, there is an air of gaiety. Doorways have ruffled or lace curtains, beds and couches may be draped in brightly colored Asian fabrics. Calendars and posters of Cambodia (especially of Buddha and Angkor Wat), photos of kin and friends in Thailand or long ago at home, and rows of school awards cover the walls. Tables and dressers hold small shrines to Buddha or to ancestors, with photos, figures, incense, and flowers. Profusions of flowers in red, pink, fuschia, turquoise, yellow, and gold, real or made of silk or plastic, are on dressers, in vases on the floor, on tables, at shrines, in little girls' hair, looped in curtains. Tinsel and metallic fringes and blinking multicolored lights may garland the shrines or doorways. Despite somewhat crowded conditions—families of eight or ten may have a kitchen and one or two other rooms—most of the homes are very tidy, with shoes lined up at the doorway, beds made, and utensils out of sight. Sounds of taped Cambodian music and smells of sweet cooking spices, incense, and tiger balm fill the air.

Furniture has been donated by sponsoring families or churches or is purchased at yard sales. There may be enough chairs, small tables, and beds, but seldom enough chests of drawers and often no kitchen counter space. Kitchen tables are too small for whole families to sit together. Much of the furniture is in very poor condition—stained, wobbly, leaking stuffing, or missing parts; sometimes there are only a cot and a few lawn chairs. But every home has a television, and most have VCRs, sometimes two, and often a stereo system with large speakers; many have Nintendos, cable television, and cordless phones, although some also have no phones. Very, very few have dishwashers or washing machines. Most have no books or magazines about, although a few have Bibles, partial sets of encyclopedias, and 30-year-old *Reader's Digest Condensed Books*—donations from sponsors.

Use of Space

For ceremonial occasions, furniture is removed and imported handwoven mats in flowered or geometric patterns (Thai made, purchased from the "Cambodian" stores) are laid over the carpeting. Satin cushions are set out for monks. Participants sit on the floor in small clusters for eating or in a large circle for other events. In this way a small room can accommodate thirty or forty people.

Though teenagers sometimes express an interest in more privacy, six or eight children sharing a bedroom or a bedroom with their parents is not as uncomfortable as it might be to Westerners. Young children find security in bed with adults or older siblings. One night, three little girls just would not go to sleep until their older sister joined them in bed. When I checked on them later, all four were on one half of the bed, snuggled together in the July heat. Children are also quite comfortable on a blanket on the floor; again, with that larger space, they tend to cluster together. Once, when keeping a toddler, I couldn't get him to go to sleep in bed with my son or with me, but as soon as my son feigned sleep on the floor, Vanna plopped on top of him and was immediately asleep. One of the children's major concerns about summer camp is that they may have to sleep in a bed alone.

Location and Availability

Some families have moved out of the neighborhood in which they were originally placed, some to purchase homes in middle-class suburbs, some to working-class neighborhoods where they rent apartments and houses that are bigger and in better condition, and others simply to other inner-city apartments. The original neighborhood remains, though, what one little boy calls "you know, the Cambodia place." There is some sense of community—most people have lived there at one time or another, some have married children living there, women feel comfortable in their sarongs on those streets, the children play together from house to house, and important events such as family and religious ceremonies draw former residents back.

Rental of adequate, safe, clean housing is difficult. The type of housing needed is in very limited supply, partly as a result of the American inclination toward small families and partly because the conversion of many larger apartments to condominiums has resulted in a dearth of large, inexpensive apartments. Thus not only do the Cambodians have trouble locating housing, but when they do they find themselves competing with low-income Americans in the same situation. This contributes to hostile relationships with American neighbors, sometimes leading to violence. The general shortage of housing was exacerbated by the refugees' sudden arrival in large groups.

Even when appropriate housing is available or people are willing to accept inappropriate housing, many landlords refuse to rent to families with so many children or say there is "no way" you could have brothers and sisters share a bedroom. Indeed, three generations in one room may have worked better in an environment where much of daily life was spent outdoors. Landlords also dislike the custom of wok cooking and say neighbors complain of the cooking smells and the noise of the children. There are exceptions, though; one landlord has become a special friend to some of the Cambodians, finding them apartments, fixing cars, attending New Year parties, and offering advice on medical or legal difficulties. But even he won't rent to a family with eight children.

Variation

I don't mean to paint an overall picture here. Some people have moved out of the original neighborhood, and their homes shine with middle-class suburban newness: spotless carpets and walls, bright fashionable furniture, built-in matching kitchen appliances, crisply mown lawns—nothing distinguishes these homes from their American neighbors except the neat row of shoes at the door. But others remain in very grim conditions—cold, wet basement apartments, rooms without windows, minimal furniture, dim bare bulbs lighting only a spot of ceiling, showers that leak through to the neighbors below, exposed pipes and wires, hallways heaped with trash, flies everywhere. And some of the homes are in between.

CLOTHING

> The interview was for a job at McDonald's. I called Thea ahead of time to suggest that she not wear shorts—"just school clothes, a plain skirt and blouse." When I picked her up, she had on a long-sleeved ruffled blouse of turquoise, fuschia, and pink plaid silk, and a long taffeta skirt in a bold red, green, black, and white plaid. Spiky high heels, black lace stockings, pearl barrettes, and many gold necklaces and bracelets completed her outfit.

Clothing is an aspect of material culture that does not appear to present problems for the refugees once they have been settled a while. Beyond the initial confusions, most of them dress quite adequately, and teens seem to dress much like their American peers most of the time. Because of rapidly changing styles, and perhaps for other reasons, Americans shed used clothing frequently enough that free stores and churches are full of last season's fashions.

Initially the Cambodians came without warm clothing (literally nothing but the clothes they wore and a plastic bag of documents). Inexperienced with cold weather, they wore rubber sandals and cotton clothes out in the snowy midwestern winter. When first presented with gloves, they thought it was a joke. But today, ten or fifteen years later, they're used to warm coats, boots, scarves, and even gloves. Still, though, many children arrive at school on cold days without jackets. I've seen children playing in the snow with bare feet and bare hands. This is more a result of parenting styles than lack of adequate clothing: in the case of the kids in the snow, they were finally admonished to put on shoes and gloves, but they put on shoes without socks, and no gloves.

Cambodians in Middle City wear a variety of clothes, depending upon their age and income, factors which also of course relate to their level of acculturation. In general they are more likely to wear traditional clothes at home and at community events, particularly the more serious religious ones, and Western-style clothes in public.

When they first arrived, there was some confusion about clothing, such as about gender appropriateness and rules of modesty. Women felt comfortable going about publicly in fancy lace bras (and still sit in their homes by open doors and windows without blouses) and raised considerable antagonism in neighborhoods and attention from the newspapers for doing so. On the other hand, it took some of the teenage girls six or eight years to succumb to shorts, and then only the longer styles. Gym shorts were a source of acute embarrassment; the girls tried to wear huge T-shirts to cover their upper legs. Some women bathe in their sarongs, and children in swimsuits.

In some cases clothing is not really adequate. During the first years children arrived at summer camp without swimsuits, shoes, or raincoats. For a while the church tried to make sure each child had at least that, but I've seen kids leave for camp with 10" x 14" packs containing all their clothing, bedding, and gear for a week. One cannot generalize: some children, perhaps with more acculturated mothers, bring new suitcases filled with new and stylish clothes.

Men and Boys

Adult men typically wear slacks and Western-style shirts outside the house, sometimes suits for more formal wear, and sometimes a simple sarong at home. Teenage boys and young men wear Western-style clothes exclusively and are very style conscious at community events such as weddings and New Year, wearing the currently fashionable baggy pants, wide-sleeved shirts, and spiked hair. Except for one infant, boys wear only Western clothing. Little boys' clothes seem to be the least carefully chosen: they are likely to be too small or too big, mismatched, girls', torn, or dirty. This fits Ebihara's observation that in Village Svay baby girls were clothed in pants or a sarong after about one year, whereas boys were permitted to go unclothed until about seven or eight.

Women and Girls

Adult women show the most variation in clothing styles. When I first met them, the most common dress was black slacks and a polyester or knitted top, with or without sleeves. Older women wore black slacks or ankle-length skirts. Over the years more women have come to wear slacks of various colors, Western-style dresses and skirts, and suits or jackets, though many still wear long skirts and sarongs of imported cloth at home. Teenage girls and young women of even the poorest families wear the latest fashions; for school they wear jeans and baggy shirts and jackets like American girls. At first they wore elaborate clothes for the New Year and wedding receptions—sequined and gold lamé gowns or elegant sarongs with gold thread. After ten years in the United States, teenagers are just as likely to wear miniskirts with black lace stockings and spiky-heeled shoes or metal-studded designer jeans. For very special occasions, some women wear a long skirt of handwoven silk or very fine cotton, usually dark reddish brown ikat-woven with tie-dyed threads of rich yellow. This is worn with a closely fitted lace or eyelet blouse lined with plain cotton.

Little girls wear almost exclusively Western clothes, but they may wear them in ways which distinguish them from middle-class American kids, such as in unconventional combinations of patterns (plaids with flowered prints) and colors (fuschia dress with green, navy, red, and gold flounces added). Like the little boys, they occasionally wear clothes that are too small or simply worn out, but usually a great deal of care has been taken to dress girls up in lace and ruffles and jewelry, at least for special occasions. Even little girls of four and five may wear rouge and lipstick, and even infant girls have gold earrings and nail polish. Around the house, girls of all ages wear long skirts of traditional cloth, gathered onto elastic at the waist, but they don't wear them beyond their own front yards, feeling that Americans would tease or criticize them.

Jewelry, Hairstyles, and Shoes

Women, girls, infants, and young men wear 18-carat or 24-carat gold jewelry, sometimes quite a bit of it. Many married women wear gold wedding bands. Jewelry is given, especially by family members, on important occasions such as engagements and weddings. Many boys and men wear simple gold chains at their neck, usually under their clothes.

For many women, hairstyle customs still follow the patterns Ebihara described for village Cambodia in 1960, where most young and adult women wore their hair long, in a ponytail or braid, or pulled back with barrettes. Other Cambodian women in Middle City wear their hair shorter, more in keeping with American styles. Also as Ebihara describes for village Cambodia, "perms" are considered special, and many girls and women have them done for special occasions beginning at about the age of ten or twelve. I was offered a perm several times in order to be really appropriately decked out for New Year (I was also occasionally admonished to grow my nails longer and to wear nail polish, more makeup, etc.).

Reciprocal grooming is fairly common, particularly among women and girls. Women and teenagers give each other haircuts and permanents and do makeup and nail polishing for one another; a teenager might paint her mother's nails or a mother might shave her daughters' eyebrows with a straight razor. Several women make a little income by giving haircuts and permanents and by arranging hair for special occasions such as weddings. Men and boys wear their hair as Americans do and as they did at home; they too may cut one another's hair or the hair of their wives and children, but they also use barbershops.

Hair, and particularly the length of it, is an important social symbol. Traditionally and in the United States, women begin to cut their hair shorter during middle age and very short in old age. Widowhood seems to be a factor in this. Traditionally, women shaved their heads upon the death of a husband, though this is rarely still practiced in Middle City. Certainly, though, some women cut their hair after the death of a husband, and very old women, with living husbands or not, wear their hair as short as one inch. A shaved head represents innocence, purity, and honesty, and a vow to shave one's head is an assurance of one's truthfulness. This custom is not actually carried out in Middle City and perhaps was not in Cambodia in recent years either. As part of the wedding ceremony, the bride and groom go through a ritual hair-cutting ceremony, with perfumed scissors and much joking, but the hair is not actually even touched.

Everyone removes shoes as a sign of respect at temples, in the presence of monks, and whenever there are mats on the floor. Most people also remove them upon entering private homes, and so most homes have neat rows of shoes by the door and immaculate carpets. Children are less careful about this and tend to run in and out of houses either shod or unshod, perhaps because the American-style laced shoes are difficult to manage. This may result in a culture change over the generation. Generally, shoes are kept on in public places, but there was often a pile of shoes under the table at the Agency classes.

Special Clothing

Especially elaborate clothing is worn by the bride and groom at the traditional wedding ceremony. Typically the bride's dress is one-shouldered and has an attached scarf of the same fabric. The fabric may be silk or synthetic brocade, patterned or plain, and may be heavily sewn with metallic and pearl beads and sequins. The skirt is long and straight, of the same or a contrasting color, and perhaps similarly bejeweled. The groom wears a jacket and pants of similarly elaborate fabric, and both of them change clothes several times during the three-day ceremony. Another kind of wedding outfit, for both the bride and groom, consists of a long brocade skirt, gathered at the waist and pulled through the legs, and then fastened at the waist with a broad belt. These wedding clothes are of bright or light colors such as red, pink, fuschia, turquoise, gold, and yellow, which symbolize life and happiness. In addition to much real gold, the bride wears a large bangle on her upper arm, a gold or silver belt, and other costume jewelry. The outfits are generally rented from another city. If there is a Christian wedding as well as a Buddhist ceremony, the bride will have a white American-style dress and veil in addition to the traditional garments.

Mourning clothes worn by the immediate family are white or sometimes black, and a family may make and wear all white clothing for a week or 100 days after the death. More usually, they may simply pin a square of black fabric to their regular clothes after the first days of mourning. Friends and others, however, just wear ordinary nice clothes to a funeral.

Sewing

Many women and teenagers are skilled at sewing and make their own clothes. A few women were professional seamstresses at home, or even owned sewing shops, and have relied on that as a job skill here. Unfortunately, few know how to sew from patterns, and lack of English hampers those who are old enough to have been truly experienced seamstresses back home. A few girls had sewing lessons in the refugee camps, but apparently these lessons were fairly rudimentary and did not teach them the use of patterns. Many families, but not all, have sewing machines.

Clothing and Culture Conflict

Because they are so replete with symbolism, clothing and customs of dressing can easily be misinterpreted, subjecting people to cross-cultural misunderstanding and hostility. Americans often disapprove of what they see as precocious dressing on the part of very little Cambodian girls—lipstick, rouge, earrings and other expensive jewelry, stockings, heels. The older girls sometimes dress in a way that Americans misread as provocative or risqué—slit skirts, very high heels, heavy makeup, sequins, gold lamé, tight or thin or low-cut blouses. This can lead to cultural conflict. Americans unfamiliar with Cambodian culture criticize what they see as the ostentatious display of jewelry. Teachers complain that little girls are "inappropriately" dressed and sometimes take them to the sink to wash off the makeup. The camp director worries about the dangly earrings, but the little girls don't know how to take them off. The Americans also worry about loss and theft. One three-year-old did lose her gold earrings in a swimming pool and told me about it repeatedly for the rest of the summer. In recent years, young people have said that their clothing, particularly the fancy dressing, was one of their major embarrassments in school during their first years in the United States; they wanted to wear jeans and T-shirts like their American peers, but their parents made them wear ruffles and flounces to show respect to the schools.

TRANSPORTATION

Ann comes into the Sunday school classroom. "Where is everybody?"
   "Not here!" a couple of children reply.
   "Where's Mony?"
   "Didn't come!"
Phea is assigned to phone Mony, to find out why he has not picked up the children. She reports back that he is asleep, not coming today; it seems that everyone went to Riverside last night for a wedding, and he didn't get back until 5:00 AM. And so the elaborate Easter festivities the teachers have spent weeks planning for today—the egg hunt, the movies, the party and games and prizes—will be unattended.

Traditional transportation for most Cambodians was by foot, oxcart, bicycle, cyclo, or motorcycle. Villages were small enough that everyone was within easy walking distance, and occasional trips to neighboring villages or Phnom Penh could be made by bus or cyclo. Ebihara reported that people commonly walked distances of several miles, even occasionally up to forty miles into the city (1971:556). She also reported few bicycles in Village Svay, but one Middle City woman told me she had a bicycle at age thirteen and her own motorcycle shortly after that, so those vehicles may have become more common in the late 1960s. Since cars were common only in Phnom Penh and completely disappeared after 1975, few Middle City refugees arrived with driving skills.

Even though many households in Middle City now have cars, transportation is a constant problem. The main drivers are adult men and a few adult women; the elderly don't drive and few teenagers drive. Since many of the women are widows, many households lack drivers. Like most poor, many refugees either can't afford to buy cars or buy used cars which are in a frequent state of disrepair, so that even those who have cars often need alternate transportation. A few Cambodians (men and women) give driving lessons for a fee, and at one of the driving test locations they can now request a tape of the driving rules in Khmer, listen to it, and then take the written test in Khmer.

Buses can be problematic too. In Middle City they are infrequent and seldom go out to the suburbs where some women work as maids. Most of the services available to refugees, such as the clinic, the city hospital, and the Agency, are in areas of the city generally considered unsafe after dark, and women recognize the dangers of waiting for buses there. Others fear they will get lost or not know when to get off. Some are more willing to ride buses when traveling together or when tokens are provided, as the Agency sometimes does for people who come to its classes.

Buses can also be expensive. After a long effort to find jobs for a group of women, an Agency worker found they were spending $2.10 for bus fare each day. Since they were only making $3.50 an hour and working short days, this was unreasonable. She offered to get them passes, which for $34 would allow them to ride anywhere in the city as much as they wanted for a month. Their first paychecks were going to be $40, and the women just laughed, "No way!" She could not convince them that their next checks would be larger, that they wouldn't have to buy passes every week, and that owning a car actually cost her more than that. The women quit the jobs.

Inadequate transportation causes other job-related problems. Since most Cambodians in Middle City are from rural backgrounds, they readily accept seasonal farm work and feel the pay is good, but they have no way to get out to the farms. If a group relies on one member to get them all to a job and that person or car can't go one day, the whole group misses work, which understandably annoys the employer.

For many reasons, people often must rely on others to get them places. In the early years, the Agency and Hillside Church sent out vans for Sunday school, and the schoolteacher occasionally rounded up children for a Saturday field trip. Some relied on individual Americans—church members, sponsors, neighbors, me—to get them places. This was complicated by a reluctance to use the phone with Americans and by weak English skills in general; even when a child was used to translate, confusions resulted in missed appointments and annoyed clinics. On rare occasions, the translator at the Agency or one of the Cambodian school aides drove people to doctor appointments or job interviews. Unfortunately, they were paid only if these trips were during business hours, though they often did the driving voluntarily at other times. The school aides could be paid only to help with school-related trips, and the Agency would not send a driver if anyone in the family owned a car, even if the car were off at a job every day. Also, people said that the Agency personnel merely dropped them off, stranding them with no way home.

Reliance on Americans has hazards for the Americans too. When I first began my research, driving people was an easy mode of entrée because it was always needed, but I found myself taking carloads of women who spoke no English to places I didn't know and to which they could not direct me. Worse, I was soon picking up children I didn't know from parents who didn't know me and with whom I could not speak. I would simply leave church with a carload of children, hoping some of them would know where they lived.

Interested in serving the children even if parents couldn't come, for a few years the church sent a van with a Cambodian youth to collect children for Sunday school. Even this was difficult; few teenagers drove, and those who could were reluctant to make commitments because family obligations must come first, even if announced later. Because of this, agreements to help out often collapsed, even if the youth really wanted the job. Changing residence patterns led to the final demise of that program. Eventually the van traveled so widely that it had to begin very early, meaning earlier pickups, longer rides, and extra time waiting at church while a second run was made; fewer and fewer children came. The American congregation was exasperated. "Why don't their parents drive them?" The parents didn't drive them because they hadn't cars, or the cars didn't work, or the only driver in the family worked on Sundays or had worked all night the night before. In Cambodia, children had taken care of their own amusements, and the culture of carpooling children has not taken hold in the refugee community. The congregation didn't question the benefit of the Sunday school for the children, but they ended the project because they felt the parents' lack of participation demonstrated a lack of appreciation. This theme—Americans not perceiving enough gratefulness on the part of the refugees—was a constant throughout my fieldwork.

Most commonly, Cambodians rely on one another for transportation. This too is problematic, because a person with difficulties is relying on someone else with similar difficulties: a car in poor condition, a houseful of children to leave, a job with irregular hours, no telephone, unfamiliarity with the city layout or institutions, and so on. Again, when people lived close together, shared transportation was easier; moves to the suburbs are dismantling the transportation networks.

There are other transportation difficulties. American cars are not big enough and haven't enough seatbelts for families with six or eight children and perhaps grandparents, in-laws, or other relatives as well. Insurance is another problem. Some companies will not insure young people except on their parents' policies, a problem if the parents don't drive or have no insurance, yet driving may be essential for these youth who often make substantial contributions to their family's income. Other companies won't insure a new driver, regardless of age, unless that person is added to a policy the company already holds. When I tried to arrange a policy for a young woman, several companies insisted on meeting her before they would quote a price. The Cambodians attribute this to prejudice: "They don't like Cambodians." Some people seem unclear whether they have insurance or not, others drive knowingly without it because they can't afford it, and some pay very high premiums.

Inadequate transportation limits families' abilities to keep in contact, keeps the elderly housebound, and hinders community interaction. It also hinders cultural maintenance by preventing many people from going to Riverside, several hours away, where there a few Cambodian stores and restaurants, a larger and more organized Cambodian community, and a temple. Many important ceremonial events take place in Riverside, often lasting into the night. Participation in these demands frequent long-distance travel by Middle City Cambodians, whose cars are often not in adequate condition for such journeys.

Difficult transportation can also become a health issue, because people try to ignore a problem if they cannot get to a doctor, or they must carry very ill children on long bus rides with long waits. One woman carried a child with pneumonia to the clinic through a January snowstorm, transferring buses several times, only to find that she had to go to a different location, on a different series of buses, to get the prescription.

HEALTH AND HEALTH CARE

All of them arrived in very poor physical condition; at first, the very early ones were literally just skin and bones. The ones who come now are just very sick: venereal diseases, hepatitis A and B, leprosy, consequences of starvation.

All of them, every single one, is or has been depressed. Clinical depression. Without exception.

—social workers, 1988

When I began this study in 1987, one of the first things I noticed about the children was their poor physical condition. Only one had glasses; another had a short leg, another had contracted polio in the refugee camp and was in a full-body brace, many were missing secondary teeth; they all seemed small for their age.

Many other major and minor physical ills are found in the population as a whole—blindness, clubbed feet, scars, herniated disks, cysts, diabetes, malaria, venereal diseases, tuberculosis, hepatitis, pneumonia, scoliosis, every variety of cancer, high blood pressure, high cholesterol, lice and intestinal parasites, decayed teeth, anemia, and ulcers. Some of these illnesses are consequences of the appalling health conditions under Pol Pot and in the refugee camps, but some health problems have developed here. For example, those who work at meat cutting find their hands "locking up"; they waken with their fingers tightly curled and can't open their hands; some get their tendons cut. One young man's hands became so raw and infected from scrubbing floors with harsh chemicals that he had to have them surgically drained. Worry and fear often cause physical ills. Women become so frightened or worried that they can't sleep or eat, leading to exhaustion and then vulnerability to other problems such as headaches, colds, infections, flu, general dizziness, weakness, aches and pains. Nightmares and sleeplessness are common, and several men may have died of Sudden Unexplained Death Syndrome (SUDS—also found in other Southeast Asian refugee populations).

Cross-Cultural Perceptions of Health and Illness

Cambodian and American ideas about health and illness are sometimes quite different. Many Cambodians believe, and almost all at least half-believe, that illness and death may result from social causes such as jealousy, anger, or vindictiveness on the part of one's enemies, a phenomenon anthropologists have referred to as witchcraft. Thus Western medicine may relieve the symptoms of an illness, but doesn't remove the causes, which can therefore recur. When a person dies despite proper Western treatment, beliefs in supernatural causes are strengthened.

Even physical principles regarding health and medicine, such as the concept of contagion, can differ. Despite explanations from several Americans, many people felt that an entire family was likely to carry the cancer from which the father died, and some felt that visitors could get it if they chanced to use his spoon. This idea was supported by the fact that the public health clinic took blood samples from the entire family (checking for hepatitis). There was a wariness around me when my father died of cancer, and several people urged me to get tests. If one parent has one disease and the other another, they will mix together in the children, who may then carry a more potent illness.

Many people mention ailments I cannot identify, for example, eye pain when reading or in sunlight. In other instances, their words for diseases or reactions are uncommon to Americans; for example, I have heard of children dying of chicken pox and of people having it for a year and being blinded by it. "Do you mean smallpox?" I asked. "No, no, kitchen paw."

Traditional Medical Care

Cambodians have several sources of traditional health care. Many favor Chinese medicine, but this is not easily available locally. Some feel they must travel to a large city, a distance of five hours, to find good Chinese medicine. Some problems, particularly those Americans would call psychological, could be treated by a monk were one available. Monks can, for example, expurgate curses or general bad luck or can convince a person to give up alcohol or other unhealthy habits. Some people visit the monk in Riverside, a city several hours away, or in critical situations he can come to Middle City, moving in with a family in the case of immanent death in order to prolong life, protect the family from further harm, and ease the death with prayers and incense. But this is difficult and expensive, and of course he cannot always come. Mental health care absolutely requires a monk, who may be called from other cities or visited by the patients and their families. A family may send a senile grandparent to stay with the monk in Riverside for a while; the elderly enjoy this but miss their grandchildren. People have different attitudes about specific monks, and those who don't like the one in Riverside must travel at least five hours to find another, a major strain on families as well as on the ill.

The third form of traditional medicine derives from *proeman*, or folk religion. Sometimes this is provided by a *kru khmer*, sometimes translated (by Cambodians and Americans) as shaman and sometimes as teacher. The kru can make herbal medicines or give a patient a "shower" (sprinkling water over the person from a small bowl). A few men have protective tattoos, particularly to protect them in war; these tattoos are in Pali and cannot be read by most people. Similarly, women sometimes wear a protective red string around their waists. Other forms of folk medicine are not considered religious. A few elderly are well versed in herbal cures and make medicine from roots and herbs purchased locally and in Riverside. Many people use this medicine for minor ills, rather as Americans use over-the-counter and "home" remedies. Coining, briskly rubbing the surface of the skin with a coin and an ointment such as Tiger Balm or Vick's Vaporub, can be done by anyone and is practiced widely for various ills such as flu, colds, asthma, and general aches and pains. As with Ben-Gay or Vick's, the mild skin irritation creates a soothing warmth.

Thus, people can choose from a wide variety of traditional medicines, although these are not always available in Middle City. Many people feel traditional medicines are more appropriate to their culture, their body size, or the specific illness than are American medicines, which are perceived as too harsh or strong.[1]

American Health Care in Middle City

American-style health care seems to be either of very poor quality or inaccessible. Children do not have the legally required shots for school, medical records are not retained by the parents, doctors refuse to prescribe critical medication because they feel that this population takes it too fast or shares it among friends (they do). It took me five hours one day to get blood tests on four children, and four weeks later the clinic said they had done the wrong tests. The only doctor in one clinic would frighten anyone: he drools, he shuffles as he walks, and his speech is barely comprehensible to an American; he has had a stroke, but that does not explain the filthy gray of his coat, the frayed cuffs, the torn dangling pockets, and the blotches of blood on the sleeves. A woman was not allowed to breastfeed her newborn because she needed medicine for parasites, but she was never given the medicine, or if she was she didn't know it. Patients are released from hospitals at midday, when no one is available to drive them home or interpret instructions. Ann, the American woman who has been such a friend to them but who also speaks no Khmer, said once, "There have been six hospitalizations [in the last three months], and I have been the only interpreter." She is called by the hospitals and by Cambodians at any hour of the night and is relied upon absolutely, although she has no formal training in nursing, medicine, counseling, Southeast Asian cultures, or the language.

The most usual interpreters/liaisons are schoolchildren, often brought out of class to convey complicated medical information to parents; if a child is unavailable, there is likely to be no translator at all. The use of children in this role is awkward and embarrassing, and it puts a strain on family and age relationships. For example, a thirteen-year-old girl was asked to translate birth control information to a woman of forty, and a teenage boy was brought in to translate a discussion of postpartum difficulties and intestinal parasites with a new mother. It can also have serious consequences for both the parents and the child, not the least of which may be the undermining of parental authority. Children may receive information the parents don't want the child to have or personal information the parent would rather tell the child under more private circumstances. The child is placed in the uncomfortable position of having to relay instructions to the parent, thus seeming to give orders to the parent—a completely impossible situation in Cambodian culture. The child may also have to relay frightening or bad news, such as that the parent is dying. Parents may avoid important medical care because they are hesitant to upset their families in this way. Finally, there is medical danger in this, because children may not have a grasp of either English or Khmer sufficient to translate complicated medical explanations or instructions. Thus a doctor's order, "Tell her it's very important that she take three of these every day for two weeks, and then call me," may become in translation, "He says you can take this." Americans feel such translation is an opportunity for the teenagers to gain important knowledge (such as information about reproduction and birth control) and like to see the children taking helpful, important roles. For the families, it contributes to adults' feelings of inadequacy and helplessness, and it also hastens the disintegration of traditional generational roles and parental authority.

This is a population generally unfamiliar with and somewhat fearful of hospitals, and hospitals do little to ease that situation. In one case, the hospital assumed a man was crazy because his English was so poor and they wouldn't believe his story (which was true) that a car had driven through his window. It was only when Ann brought his baby into the Emergency Room that he was able to relax. Rules may be posted but are not explained in a way the Cambodians understand. One young woman (who had been through American high school) did not know she could see her newborn any time and did not know what time she was going to be released, although the nurse assured me she had explained both these matters, and the rules were posted in the hallway. Another woman gave her daughter bubble gum immediately after the dentist explained she should have only "soft foods" following a tooth capping; in the mother's view, the chewing gum was "soft." Still another resisted surgery because she was afraid of dying and leaving her small children. Many Cambodians leave hospitals as soon as possible because they believe the care is inappropriate: they are served unfamiliar foods which they can't eat; they are urged to drink cold fluids, considered inappropriate for many illnesses; and their traditional medicines are taken away.[2]

Most women are afraid of doctors in general and are particularly uncomfortable with male doctors. Women go home after waiting hours because they are embarrassed to undress in front of male doctors. Obstetricians have found their patients, feet in stirrups, ready for a pelvic or baby on its way, with their underpants on or holding their skirts down. "In Cambodia, boy doctor boy, girl doctor girl." Actually, in rural Cambodia women go to women midwives and seldom go to doctors at all.

Mental Health

Mental health is always an issue with victims of torture. Despite the existence of organizations and professionals specially trained for this, I know of no professionals with such training in Middle City. At least one man has been repeatedly violent, attacking his children and grandchildren with knives and making wild threats and accusations. Words of violence are common: "I'm gonna kill you," "I'm gonna shoot her," "I'm gonna tear his eyes out," "I'm gonna beat her with a stick until she's dead"—not said casually or carelessly, but spat out with fury and venom. Many people experience nightmares and sleeplessness, hear voices, and have feelings of generalized hopelessness and depression. Physical fights, particularly among women and within the nuclear family, are not uncommon, though they are denied and are a source of shame. And yet counselors and psychiatrists treat Cambodians as if they are Americans, as though their problems and their culture are the same as ours. As a test of his wits, an elderly man was asked to name his grandchildren; many adults would be unwilling or incapable of doing that—names are just not used in that way. A mother and daughter were dismissed by the counselor because he felt they were so well adjusted, the mother doing such an excellent job; but the girl continued to receive beatings and to run away from home.

Traditionally the head is sacred and the brain the most important part of a person, the location of the soul; psychological problems therefore indicate spiritual and moral problems and are thus shameful. This idea contrasts sharply with the American idea of the brain as simply an organ which can be opened and fixed like any other, so brain surgery is far more frightening to Cambodians than to Americans. In fact, the American concept of "mental illness" does not exist traditionally in Cambodia and is not widely accepted by refugees. People may be troubled by manifestations such as irrational or dangerous behavior, but they don't connect these symptoms to illness or particularly look for cures. They tend to be much more tolerant of unusual personalities, particularly in the elderly, than are Americans. When Americans introduce the idea that these may be signs of "illness," people are led to expect quick relief such as they get for other pains.

Americans sometimes view low usage rates for mental health facilities as an indication of high adjustment rates for an immigrant group, but in the case of Cambodians in Middle City low usage is more likely due to fear, shame, embarrassment, lack of language skills on the part of the doctors and clients, misinterpretation of silent language cues, and cultural differences such as misunderstanding of why doctors would ask personal questions, distrust of the sincerity of a sixty-minute appointment, expectation of an immediate cure, and failure to include family members in the process. Some researchers (Cohon 1981) feel that any mental health treatment by Westerners is too interfering—that Buddhism teaches much more accepting attitudes toward psychological differences and that people may do better if left to deal with these problems in traditional ways.

The recent "increase" in mental and psychological difficulties is probably a consequence of several factors. First of all, people were so desperately ill and needy in so many critical ways when they arrived that Americans focused attention on these obvious problems. Also, as people's immediate lives have become safer and as food, clothing, and shelter have become less serious problems, and as people begin to have time to think about their terrible past, worries, fears, guilt, and remorse begin to play. Finally, as people become more familiar with American ways and ideas and get to know caring Americans more closely, a few have begun to try, or at least to consider, American-style treatment. I have not seen any cases for which this has been particularly helpful, probably because of lack of commitment on the part of both Cambodians and Americans—the Cambodians begin with skepticism and are further discouraged when they see no results after a session or two; American providers have not made efforts to learn about Cambodian culture in order to offer culturally appropriate help.

Pregnancy, Childbirth, and Postpartum Care

Teenage girls and even adult women are purported (by their parents, by Americans, and by researchers) to have been completely lacking in knowledge regarding the biology of conception when they first arrived. Many of them reached the menarche with no preparation from their mothers, and initially the male translator for the schools had to sit them down and explain to them what it meant and what to do. "This was very embarrassing for them, and for me too!" Now there is a woman aide who takes care of this, but Ann also tries to instruct the girls that she knows, at least before they go off to summer camp.

Sometimes her lessons fall on informed ears. One summer, just before camp began, an eleven-year-old giggled, "Ann asked me did I know what 'period' meant!" Sharing Ann's concern, I probed: "Well, do you?" "Of course!" and she proceeded to give a simple but reasonably accurate explanation, after which she and her two sisters, age five and six, launched into a general discussion of sex and intercourse. So the fund of knowledge varies from family to family.

It seems the schools teach little about birth control, or not enough that the teens really understand, so Ann sometimes arranges to have teenage girls act as interpreters for women having doctor appointments, so some of them are learning in roundabout ways. But the knowledge is uneven. Several girls have asked me if you can get pregnant by kissing or French kissing. Their confusion about American mores also leads them to worry about pregnancy. "If a boy take you out and you really love him, should you do whatever he want? You know what I mean!"—this is an eighteen-year-old referring to a first date with a boy she has not yet met. Although they also say "Cambodian girls don't do that!" in fact they do, and they get pregnant rather frequently. In general, Cambodians neither approve of nor practice birth control. Young women usually want to limit births, and I was told more than once, after a first birth, "She's going to be an only child," or after a second, "That's it. In America, two is enough!" But third and fourth pregnancies ensue. They feel that birth control pills make them gain too much weight, make them sick, or give them headaches, in keeping with a more general feeling that American medicine is too strong or comes in doses too large for their small bodies. One young woman had another child after believing her tubes had been tied. Another was discouraged by stories from friends who had been very sick after the surgery. When I asked about condoms, I was told, "Cambodians don't like it," or "My husband wouldn't like that." Young women are sometimes willing to have abortions, though unmarried girls are frightened of the procedure, and both married and unmarried women are likely to be talked out of it by their mothers or other older women. Nevertheless, it is the method of choice, or last resort, for quite a few.

Although Ebihara (1971) reported no particular pregnancy taboos, several young women cited a few: the rice on the bottom of the pot (ordinarily considered something of a treat) will make the water too thick, and drinking water will make the mother gain too much weight, make her too fat. Sex of the child can be determined by the size and shape of the mother's abdomen or by the mother's complexion. I asked if they were taking vitamins: "No! Too big—look like for a horse!" You could crush them up? "No, still look like medicine; not good to take medicine when pregnant." Again, rice is considered to be the most important food for the growth of the fetus, and milk is spurned.

Traditionally in Cambodia, as in most of Southeast Asia, women are kept on raised platforms with small fires going underneath for a week after birth. This "roasting" is to "help the veins and blood and stuff come together better." In Middle City, at least when they have their mothers to look after them, young mothers are kept warm, though by other means than fire, such as by wearing layers of sweatsuits and sweaters, keeping jugs of hot water on their abdomens, and eating and drinking hot foods, particularly hot water with roots and herbs. The hospital gives them ice and cold drinks rather than hot water, so they drink nothing. Alcohol also gives a warm feeling, so a dried herbal mixture called "Loving Tiger" is put in a bottle of vodka and drunk as medicine; they are afraid to bring this into the hospital, however, so this means of recovery must wait until they get home. Some young women told me they could not take showers or comb or wash their hair, but others knew of no such restrictions.

Newborns are kept at home, close to the mother or grandmother, and are carefully protected from physical, emotional, or spiritual harm. Some food taboos after the birth are for the baby's benefit. For example, a mother avoids spicy foods for several months after the birth, because such things can cause mental disorders or lack of discipline in the child (regardless of whether or not the child is breast-fed). Care is taken that babies sleep straight lest the head be injured, that they not be frightened by the bathwater lest the umbilicus "bloom up," and that they they are not left to cry lest they take air into the stomach and become sick. Their heads and bodies are washed often and rubbed with ointments. An elderly woman explained a newborn's need for frequent bathing: "A leaf, which when taken out from the tree, has some water put on it and an hour later it would be dying; this may be compared to a baby's skin—we have to care about it carefully, as the leaves."

The infant's health may be looked after by the maternal grandmother if she is available. She may put a paste of herbs on the newborn's head, a red thread around the wrist, mitts on the hands to prevent thumbsucking, or lipstick on a rash. Young parents don't seem to question the grandmother in these affairs, but they may take a baby to the hospital if a situation appears to become serious.[3]

Dental Care

The condition of people's teeth was sometimes extremely poor when the refugees arrived, and some people were in such pain that they had most of their teeth pulled. Others have waited, but because of the severe and early malnutrition, pulling is necessary even for many young people and children. Some dentists blame the parents and give the mothers lengthy lectures about their neglect; the dental and medical practitioners seem to have little awareness of Cambodian culture or history and little patience with these patients' special needs. Again finances are a constant problem: the understanding in Middle City is that Medicaid will cover the pulling of teeth but will not replace them. Consequently, some people wait until they are in excruciating pain with serious abscesses before they seek dental care.

Health Insurance

Most people have Medicaid if they are unemployed but lose it if they get jobs, which usually do not begin health insurance until six months after employment, if at all. This presents a great risk for families with many children and serious health problems. Most employers do not provide dental coverage, and this too is very serious in a population where even children require major dental work. There is confusion among the Cambodians and the Americans who help them just what Medicaid will cover.

Adaptation and Conflict

The refugees clearly have some access to both American and traditional health care and medicine, but that access is often quite limited, so that it would not be quite accurate to say people always have a "choice." Those with ties to friendly Americans may use American doctors and hospitals because there is someone to encourage them to do so and to help them make appointments, get them there, deal with the staff, and ask questions; they may do this out of loyalty to the American rather than out of any conviction that such care will be effective. People who might prefer traditional medicine may resort to American medicine when traditional medicine is not available or doesn't work; similarly, those who might prefer American medicine cannot always afford it or find it too confusing or difficult to obtain.

Perhaps because of lack of faith in the efficacy of Western medicine and perhaps because of fears of overdosage, many Cambodians do not follow the recommendations of their physicians. They may find their family disagrees with the diagnosis or recommendations, or they may find that a prescription medicine has no immediate effect or has side effects that may have been explained but not understood. They may make appointments but have a change of heart and not go, or they may fail to appear at follow-up appointments. Doctors hesitate or refuse to prescribe certain drugs because they know they may be taken incorrectly or shared around the community.

Although I've met physicians, psychiatrists, and social workers in Middle City who are interested in the Cambodians and profess a willingness to try to develop culturally appropriate practices for Asian patients, I know of no instances there in which American doctors have collaborated, or even attempted to collaborate, with traditional Khmer curers in cases of physical or mental illness, although I know this has been successful elsewhere.

ELECTRONICS AND OTHER TECHNOLOGY

Three-year-old SoVy leaps into my arms and plants a kiss on my cheek. She grins mischievously, "I give you a kiss!"

"She learn from TV! American!" her mother explains, laughing but embarrassed.

"Cambodians wouldn't kiss?"

"No, no! Not Cambodian, only husband-wife, in bedroom! No!" She is shocked, but also a little proud that her daughter is so precociously picking up American mannerisms.

The refugees have rather readily adopted certain elements of Western technology, particularly televisions, VCRs, cameras, and videocameras. Homes have televisions on most of the time, and most also have VCRs on which they play rented movies from India or Thailand, sometimes dubbed into Khmer and sometimes not. Films in Thai or Indian languages are stylized romances, and even though the language cannot be understood, most people know the plots by heart anyway. Parents feel television is a good way for the children to learn English, and most adults attribute their own knowledge of English to watching television. Children learn other things from television and radio as well. Preteens know advertising jingles and sing along with popular American songs. One little girl recited the entire story of *The Little Mermaid* to me in bed one night. "How many times have you seen that?" "Oh, hundreds!" she replied. Some families have two VCRs and copy tapes they rent or borrow. Cable television is also quite common.

Many families have videocameras and regularly film funerals, weddings, New Year parties, and other events. These tapes are often played in the background when there are guests. Ceremonial tapes would seem an ideal way to teach artistic and ritual traditions to children, who are not always present at the more religious ceremonies, but neither children nor adults seem particularly attentive when tapes of classical dance or theater are played at small gatherings. I tried to elicit commentary from a little girl one day when a court dance was on a neighbor's player, but her only response was that it was "boring" (see Sam-Ang Sam 1994 for similar commentary from other Khmer children in the United States).

Tapes of important events are sent to relatives in other states who may not be able to otherwise attend. They are also sent to relatives in Cambodia and in camps, and tapes come back of tearful kin describing their poverty, pointing out the ruined farms and homes, declaring how much they miss their family, and pleading to be sent for.

Cameras are also very common. Most families and individuals have albums of pictures of relatives at home or in Thailand and recent pictures of themselves. The pictures sent from Cambodia and Thailand look, to an American, formal and grim. One elderly woman shows me pictures of her sisters lined up, expressionless, and points to them, one by one: "She: five kid, all dead. She: eight kid, two live. She: all dead. Husband dead, husband dead, husband dead. Khmer Krahom [Rouge]." Pictures from Florida or California or Minnesota are more cheerful—large gatherings, wedding pictures with glittering gowns, abundant flowers, and grins. Cars and televisions are important backdrops for formally-posed photographs in the United States.

Other modern communication technology in general use includes microphones and sound systems, telephones, and videogames. The microphones and speaker systems are used with other Western band equipment (drums, electric guitars, keyboards) at large parties and weddings, but also by the monks for prayers and rituals at the temple and even in small rooms. Almost every household has a telephone, although that was not the case as recently as 1987, and many have cordless phones. There is still some reluctance to use telephones with Americans, though this has dissipated greatly over the last few years. Many adults have a child make the call and the initial contact, then take the phone themselves; one woman had her daughter call me to ask me to telephone the minister to tell him they miss him. Making appointments by phone is especially difficult because times and dates may be misunderstood, and because Cambodians are unlikely to reject an assigned time, even if it is impossible to meet it; they will accept the appointment but then just not go. Several young couples and children, particularly boys, have Nintendos, the currently fashionable home videogame; some families have two. One child's room was furnished, for a while, only with mats and his Nintendo. Children also go to corner minimarkets to play videogames.

The adoption of these devices presents a different pattern than the adoption of other "American" technology; here we see a true blending, a true adaptation, not of their own culture to American ways, but of American culture into their own lives. For the most part, objects and systems of American electronic technology are drawn upon to enhance and preserve the traditional culture, particularly by facilitating communication within the community, with Cambodians in other cities, and with friends and family in Cambodia.

MATERIAL CULTURE AND CULTURE CHANGE

Even in material culture, this most elemental component of culture, processes of cultural maintenance, cultural adaptation, and cultural acquisition are varied and complex. In each area we see elements of traditional culture, elements of mainstream American culture, and a great variety of blends.

The Cambodians arrived in the United States uniquely lacking in material goods, most bringing literally only the clothes on their backs and a plastic bag of documents, and yet they have in just a few years amazingly reconstructed many forms of the material culture of their homeland, material culture that was brought not physically but in the memories of recipes, in skills, and in the mental constructs of what material life should be like. At the same time, many elements of every refugee's daily life are not traditional and are either direct adoptions of American culture or adaptations of American ways to suit their own needs. For example, American paper plates and plastic utensils are used at weddings and large parties because they are easily available and disposable—an efficiency for a gathering of five hundred—while for smaller events held in the home, traditional-style dishes and utensils can be borrowed if the household does not own enough. In other situations, American customs are followed mainly to avoid friction with Americans in public; for example, American clothes are worn by schoolchildren and increasingly more adults, who find themselves out in the workplace with Americans on a daily basis, while at home most people prefer to wear their traditional clothes. Transportation, entirely outside the home, is entirely Western, bullock carts being neither available nor practical in Middle City.

Closer examination reveals several patterns which influence use or nonuse of American technology. One pattern is that American material culture such as clothing may be adopted for outside the home, while within the home the preference is for the traditional when possible. Another pattern is to retain techniques when they are satisfactory, such as cooking and serving customs or sewing without patterns, but when a completely new technology is available here for which there was no traditional tool, such as televisions and telephones, the new customs are adopted widely. Another variable is age: schoolchildren, daily exposed to Americans, pick up American technology such as clothing styles and videogames more readily than do adults and the elderly, who, though they watch a great deal of television, are less comfortable with other elements of American material culture such as Western clothing, telephones, and transportation. Time in the United States is surely another factor: those who have been here longer use more American technology, although that pattern may also be influenced by differences between the early arrivals, who were more familiar with Western technology, and those who came later, who tended to be of more rural background, and also by different reception patterns in the receiving culture, such as varying types of sponsorship, housing, and jobs. Cost is yet another factor; those who can afford to buy houses or rent larger apartments do, and those who can afford cars have them. Gender, age, and income combine to influence who gets what: teenage boys seem to have no trouble acquiring pagers, electronic games, and cordless phones, while their mothers often work without blenders, graters, or vegetable peelers, not to mention more significant appliances such as dishwashers and vacuum cleaners. Finally, availability may be most important; either Cambodian or American goods and methods may be prohibitively expensive or otherwise entirely inaccessible.

Anthropologists note that cultures are most likely to change in ways that prevent further or more drastic change; in this community, it seems that material culture which fosters better communication within the community and with those left behind, such as driving cars and videotaping events, is adopted or adapted more readily than that which is more individual, such as expensive housing or furnishings. Many changes take place merely to avoid embarrassment in public or friction with Americans. Female-headed households may be more retentive of traditional material culture, although I haven't enough data on husband-wife households to be certain of this. Some culture changes occur because they are offered or withheld by the American community: for example, much Cambodian food is simply not available because of import laws and because of American preferences. Finally, some choices about material culture are affected by the traditional social standing of a family in their home culture. One family, which often speaks of buying a house but says it cannot afford to do so, gives generously to temples in other cities and spends more on traditional clothes and ceremonies than most. This family views these expenses as an obligation demanded by its leadership role in the community, although this ritual spending may be the major dimension of that leadership.

Some seemingly innocent culture changes, manifestly adopted merely for convenience or even to make carrying out traditional customs easier, may in the long run subvert or at least interfere with significant aspects of traditional culture. For example, VCRs purchased by parents in order to play tapes from friends and relatives may be used primarily by children watching American movies their parents may not approve. Microwave ovens intended to reheat lunch for grandma when the family is off at work can also be used by children to fix American-style frozen dinners, thus changing the nature of family meals and diminishing the importance of the mother's role as provider of traditional sustenance.

Thus simple observation of material culture reveals a complex and constantly shifting network of patterns of cultural retention, adoption, and adaptation. The following chapters will show some of the same factors functioning similarly to affect patterns of maintenance, adoption, and adaptation in social and ideological culture as well.

NOTES

1. For more complete information on traditional and Western-style health care, see Aronson 1987; Brown, Corbett, and Freeman 1987; and Marcucci 1986; for more information on refugee mental health and mental health care, see Cohon 1981 and 1986; Heigel 1982 and 1984; Holtzman and Bornemann 1990; Keo 1987; Mollica 1990; Stein 1986; Sue 1973 and 1981; and Williams and Westermeyer 1986.

2. Hospital staff actually gave me different answers about this. Some said no, they didn't take anything away, they just discouraged its use. When I was more specific, citing, for example, alcohol-based medicine, I was told, "Oh, well! No, we couldn't allow that!"

3. For more complete information on women's health, beliefs about conception and childbirth, etc., childbirth, etc., see Fishman, Evans, and Jenks 1988; Kulig 1988, 1990a, 1990b, 1991, and 1994; Sargent and Marcucci 1988; and Sargent, Marcucci, and Elliston 1983

Chapter 3

Patterns of Kinship

My brother and I were so close. He's two years older than me, but we were so close, like one. Sleep together under one net, share rice, share water. If one have food, both eat; one have water, both can drink. Hungry together, hurt together, cry together. When it rained, we hid under one tree. We took care of each other, you know?

When they took my brother's age group off to work, I held on to him and cried and cried. I wouldn't let them take him and not me. They said I was too young, I would die with that kind of work, but I hung on and cried, and they had to take me. I did almost die. I was so skinny, lifting those big rocks, but they couldn't separate us, they had to take me too.

—young man, recalling life under the Khmer Rouge

Among the Cambodians in Middle City, as in many non-Western cultures, kinship is the primary form of social organization. This is manifested in daily behavior and in expressed values. In school activities, children choose to sit with or be grouped with siblings when possible; sisters dress alike for parties and festivals; when conflicts arise, people answer the demands of their families before the responsibilities of job or school; adults long to return home not so much to see Cambodia or their friends, but to see their siblings or honor their dead parents. This primacy of kinship can be both a source of strength for the refugees and also a source of some anguish. It also brings them into occasional conflict with American society. Throughout this chapter, references are made to and comparisons made with Village Svay studied by Ebihara in 1959 and 1960 (Ebihara 1971).[1] The reader will see that the basic structures of kinship and also the patterns of the kin relationships as they are manifested in everyday life are substantially the same as Ebihara described them of Village Svay thirty-five years ago.

The typical Cambodian family is a nuclear family, much as in the United States. Other kin may be important, but the nuclear family is the core of the household, the unit of production and consumption, and the source of love and respect. Most families have or wish to have more children than prescribed by the American ideal, so the family of which an individual sees her/himself an integral part is a much larger unit than that meant by an American. A dominant theme in life histories of refugees is the death or loss of family members, and by this an adult means not only spouse and children, but equally and perhaps more importantly, family of origin. Thus a Cambodian living in a household of ten or twelve individuals may still feel deeply and constantly distressed at the loss of so many other family members who have died or become separated during the war, during the Khmer Rouge era, or during flight.

KINSHIP, ECONOMICS, AND RELIGION

The importance of kinship for the Cambodian refugee community derives in part from its centrality to traditional Cambodian life. Although without corporate kin groups such as clans, so instrumental in the Hmong's economic adjustment in the United States, the Cambodian kinship structure figures importantly in Cambodian economic system. The household is the primary economic unit, but gifts and financial support are expected among other kin as well. Wealth is maintained in the form of jewelry worn by the women in a family (and by some men as well), and gifts of money and jewelry to kin are large by American standards. As François Ponchaud says, "nothing can be refused a brother, sister, or even distant cousin. Financial or other aid is compulsory within the family" (1977:10).

In Middle City, this economic function remains important; the household, which may be larger than the nuclear family, pools money, tasks, and investments. Money brought in by all workers buys the family food, which is stored, prepared, and eaten by the family as a unit. Some teenagers in the family may work and some go to school, but their income is pooled. When children (sometimes as young as eleven) do summer farm labor or other work, they spend most of the money on younger siblings or give it to their mothers for family use. I never heard children being advised to save their earnings (although the boys do save "bride money"), but they willingly and proudly spend it on the family. As one mother said to me of her thirteen-year-old's summer plans, "'Mommy,' she says, 'I going to get a job, help you out. You don't need to buy me things; I get a job, then I buy for myself,' and she did." Other teens bought Easter dresses for little sisters or paid the family phone bill with the money I paid them for interpreting. An older teenager may be the primary support of a family, particularly if the father is dead.

Even absent kin may make substantial contributions to the economic life of their families. Young adult or teenage sons may find employment in other cities and send the money home. One young man paid the down payment on the house for his mother (this is a two-parent family) although he doesn't work or live in Middle City. Many families send money to Cambodia or to the refugee camps in Thailand, though the risk of theft is high, to help support relatives, usually siblings or parents, left behind. Even more of an economic strain, but more reliable, is actually carrying thousands of dollars in cash, clothing, and other goods to Cambodia to distribute to huge gatherings of family.

Family celebrations can be important economic events as well. Gifts at rites of passage such as first birthday, weddings, and One Hundred Days ceremonies are generally in the form of cash. A family may expend $6,000 to $9,000 on a daughter's wedding, much of which goes to feed the hundreds of guests and much of which comes back as bridewealth from the groom and his family and also as large cash gifts from the wedding guests.

Kinship is also intimately tied to religion. Reverent display of respect to parents and ancestors is a fundamental element of religious worship at ceremonies such as New Year, *Phchum ben* (Soul's Day), *Kathen*, weddings, funerals, and *Boun muy roy ngay* (One Hundred Days). In fact these ceremonies are excellent examples of the triple relationship of kinship, religion, and economics, as much money is given to or in the name of the ancestors at some of these ceremonies. This relationship will become more apparent in chapter 6.

SYSTEMS OF CONSANGUINITY AND AFFINITY

Marriage

Traditionally, monogamy was by far the most common form of marriage; polygyny is legal but rare (Ebihara 1971:96) and is generally considered appropriate only for the most wealthy. Cambodians in Middle City can cite cases of polygyny in the past among their acquaintances or kin, but it is not overtly practiced in the United States. Among refugees, difficulties arise because U.S. law permits a polygynous family to enter the country, but not to remain married. Occasionally a man has entered the United States with a "camp wife," having lost contact with his real wife for many years during Pol Pot and the camps in Thailand. The relationship with the camp wife may have begun out of necessity (in the border camps men were not issued food, and thus association with a woman was a man's only way of avoiding starvation), but these relationships often grew strong and loving and resulted in children. In this country, they may or may not be legally recognized common law marriages (depending upon the particular state). When a long-lost wife, and perhaps children, are finally located in Thailand or Cambodia and are sent for, one marriage ceases to be a legal relationship in the United States, though the husband may support both women and all the children equally.

In traditional Cambodia, a fiancé gave his bride's family a monetary gift representing the worth of a house, even though the actual building of a house would probably be partly supported by the bride's family as well (Ebihara 1971:125). Similarly, in Middle City the groom gives a large sum—perhaps $5,000 to $8,000— to the bride's family, specifically to the bride's mother as a sign of the groom's appreciation for her careful raising of the daughter. Much of this may be spent on the wedding celebration itself. Although this custom of bridewealth is common in much of the world, American friends of Cambodians in Middle City worry that the parents may get in trouble for "selling" their daughters, or may even be accused of child prostitution, since some of the girls are young and most of the marriages do not involve American-style weddings with American legal documents. In addition to this amount of cash, there may be major expenses for the prewedding ceremony as well. These expenses—for new clothing, engagement rings, food, and ritual gifts such as perfume and cognac—may be considered part of the bridewealth also, since they too are paid for by the groom.

The incest taboo extends to the nuclear family, grandparents, aunts and uncles, and nieces and nephews (Ebihara 1971:97-99), and I know of no deviance from that rule in Middle City. Among the most grievous of incestuous relations, comparable to nuclear family incest, was "polygyny with two women related to one another" (Ebihara 1971:97), surprising given the very close relationship between sisters and their disinclination to be separated in adulthood. The taboo does not extend to cross or parallel cousins of any degree, and Ebihara found cousin marriage common in Svay. Cousin marriage is rarely practiced in Middle City since few people have cousins nearby, but occasionally a young man will travel to a distant city, or even back to Cambodia, to wed a cousin chosen by his parents.

Residence

Ebihara reports a tendency toward village and hamlet exogamy for Svay, and this seems to be characteristic in Middle City as well. Though young men and women may be in daily association in the high school, in the neighborhoods, and at church, they quite often develop romantic relationships in other cities. They cite this as a reason for wanting to go to weddings, the temple, and New Year parties in those cities—"to see my boyfriend"—and it is a reason parents are sometimes reluctant to take them. Though many young people are choosing their own marriage partners, parentally arranged marriages are often negotiated between families in different and distant cities.

Traditionally, a Cambodian village was likely to be composed largely of kin, not through deliberate exclusion, but because fear and suspicion made people unlikely to travel to a village which did not contain kin (Ebihara 1971:561–563). Thus members of a community were either born there, married into it, or moved there to claim land inherited from a parent who had moved away the previous generation (Ebihara 1971:93–94). By contrast, the community in Middle City originally contained very few kin groupings beyond the nuclear or stem family. However, prior to and during the course of this study, several families moved to join kin in other U.S. cities or were joined by kin from other cities. Further, some families continue to live close to other families or individuals whom they knew in the camps in Thailand and to whom they refer as "cousins" in English, but who are not actually related. Thus although people may cite other reasons for moving out of Middle City, such as better public assistance or better jobs, many moves simultaneously reunite kin, and it would be difficult to assign priorities to their reasons. This propinquity toward kin extends within the city as well, perhaps as a variant of the stem family.

Ebihara reports a preference for (though not predominance of) neolocal residence with very common uxorilocal (matrilocal) residence and occasional virilocal (patrilocal) residence. In Middle City there is great variation, but permanent neolocal residence is not common in young marriages. Though there is great flexibility, a general pattern of ambilocal residence (residence with either the bride's parents or the groom's parents, with some mobility back and forth) is apparent. If a young couple does in fact set up a separate household, they often choose the same building, the same apartment complex, or at least the same neighborhood as one set of parents, usually the bride's. For example, one young couple first lived with the wife's family briefly so that she could finish in her own high school, then got an apartment near the husband's family where he could get a better job, then briefly lived with his parents while he was ill, then got their own apartment again, and then moved back to live with the bride's family. Occasionally, a young man may move into the bride's parents' household before the marriage, particularly if the bride's mother is a widow, because the young men often have more urban skills, more English, and more literacy than their older mothers-in-law, and thus can contribute significantly to those households. This appears to be an adaptive extension of the traditional (though uncommon in Svay) custom of brideservice.

Uxorilocal residence may be particularly common in Middle City because many of the girls are marrying younger than they did in Cambodia, sometimes pressured into marriage by parents who are scandalized by the girls' "dating" or a perception that they are dating (Ledgerwood 1990; Smith-Hefner 1993). Thus in Middle City, as in traditional Cambodia, an explanation often offered for uxorilocal residence is that the girl is too young to leave her parents, and because, as Ebihara says, "girls are thought to need more protection and surveillance . . . [and] girls are often apprehensive about the possibility of having to leave the comfortable warmth of home and community" (1971:128).

One further residence pattern reported by Ebihara, amitalocality (residence with bride's mother's sister),[2] is also found in Middle City. Although I know of only a few cases of this, it may be more common than is apparent; in one case, a young woman was adopted by her mother's sister in infancy and thus considers the older woman her mother and calls her *Mae* (mother). In other cases, kinship ties were rearranged during the Pol Pot times, in the camps in Thailand, and sometimes during the immigration process; this is an example of the social relations of kinship taking precedence over the biological ones, and these rebuilt families may be so well established that it may be inaccurate to call this amitalocal at all. Indeed, as Ebihara describes in Village Svay, "a maternal aunt frequently becomes a mother surrogate by collateral extension of filial sentiment along the female line. Warm affection between aunts and nieces is evident in daily interaction within the hamlet" (1971:132). This relationship between sister's-daughter and mother's-sister is less evident in Middle City because few pairs of adult sisters have managed to migrate together, but many adult women speak fondly and sadly of their dead or left-behind sisters, and the present pattern of closeness between sisters (see below) may presage the reestablishment of the si-da/mo-si relationship.

Descent

Eskimo kinship terms[3] and generally bilateral kin relationships continue the traditional patterns described by Ebihara. As elsewhere in much of Asia, kin terms reflect age relative to Ego as importantly as, or perhaps more importantly than, they do gender. For example, *b'ong srey* and *b'ong proh* refer to older sister and older brother, respectively, while *p'on srey* and *p'on proh* refer to younger sister and younger brother. However, in practice the terms *b'ong* and *p'on* are used, without the specification of gender.[4] Similarly, a parent is as likely to refer to her "older child" as she is to her "male child." In fact Ebihara does not even give gender terms for siblings, listing terms only for "younger sibling" and "older sibling." These customs continue in Middle City when people are speaking Khmer, but when speaking English, children use the terms "brother" and "sister" rather than "sibling." They also *very* frequently specify "my big sister" or "my little sister."

It should be emphasized here that kinship patterns in Middle City are distinctly *not* matrilineal, despite matrilocal residence and the frequency of mother-headed households. When describing their families, people mention kin on both their mother's and their father's side about equally and perceive of themselves as related to and descended from both parents equally. Family names (usually written first) are generally inherited from the father, but this was introduced by French colonial patterns. When there are two parents, about as many families seem headed by the wife as by the husband; Ebihara's term "a happy balance" (1974) is as appropriate to kinship and gender patterns in Middle City as it was in Village Svay. As these Eskimo and bilateral kinship systems are so similar to those practiced by Americans, and because they express important values of gender equality supported by American expressed values, these patterns seen unlikely to change.

There are two common forms of the household family, cited by Ebihara and found today in Middle City, the stem family[5] and the independent nuclear family. In Svay, the stem family accounted for about one-quarter of households (1971:123) and the nuclear family household about one-third of households (1971:129). In Middle City it is common for parents and their married children or adult siblings with their families to make some effort to live in the same neighborhood or in the same or adjacent apartment buildings, and often at least one married child lives directly in the household with an elderly parent. There are also nuclear family households. Most families necessarily entered the United States in this form, and although some of these have since acquired in-laws, many remain nuclear in form. Other nuclear families have formed when married children leave the parental household. There is much flexibility between these two forms (stem and nuclear families) as housing, jobs, and personalities vary; so, as described above, a young couple may make several moves between the two sets of parents before setting up, not necessarily permanently, a nuclear family household of their own, which may in time be joined by younger siblings or other kin. Thus the ambilocal nature of residence patterns creates a rather fluid family group.

PATTERNS OF KIN RELATIONSHIPS

Consanguine Kin

My parents took care of me, did everything for me; now they're old, I take care of them. They gave me life, now I give my life to them.

—two young men

How do these rules play out in the relationships between individuals in their daily lives? Again as in most non-Western cultures, consanguine relations are stronger than affinal relations; as one young man said to me, "Your wife die, your children die, you can get another; your parents die, you can't ever get another." Ebihara points out that even after splitting by marriage, the members of a nuclear family still "should (and usually do) offer one another daily support, loyalty, and consideration, as well as special assistance in time of trouble" (1971:111). She notes that all nuclear family relationships are strong and emotional, but that parent-child relationships are the strongest. My observations in Middle City indicate both strong parent-child relationships and very strong sibling ties as well, particularly between same-sex siblings. Specific relationships within a few sample families may serve to highlight some of the themes of kinship patterns within the culture.

Adult woman/father. Ebihara says that "the bond between parents and children is perhaps the strongest and most enduring relationship in village life" (1971:119). This still appears to be true in Middle City, although there are indications of impending change over the next generation. The following examples of two young women suggests that they have respectful and tolerant, though often disapproving, attitudes toward their fathers.

Sovanna, a young widowed mother, explained to me that she hadn't wanted to marry because she was too young, but her father said she must so that he could give her land—if she waited until he died, her share would be much smaller. It was her father who told the workers what crops to plant on her land. In the United States, and especially since the death of her husband, Sovanna seems to have become the leader of the family. She is the one who chose the United States over other countries, and she has urged her father to go to church and to be baptized, though he understands no English. "At first he didn't want to go, because he was Buddhist, but I told him, 'Come father, you'll have fun,' and I prayed God for him, and after around five months he believed."

Sovanna has worried a lot about her father. When I asked about him she would knit her brow and say, "Oh, he's not very good," but she didn't complain or ask for help. As time went on, there were incidents of his threatening violence to her, her children, and others. In addition, although the old man received his own welfare check, he didn't share it with the family for household expenses. There were hospitalizations, psychiatric care, sojourns at the temple and with relatives, but with little effect. All of this—revealing the problem to Americans, seeking psychiatric help, and finally sending the old man away—brought Sovanna much criticism from the community. One woman said, "She's just trying to get rid of him so she can have fun, just wants to run around with men," and another said, "She just dumped her old man. Not like us. Not a good Cambodian. Everybody's mad at her because she do that to him."

Sopheap is another young woman whose relationship with her father has caused her much anguish. She speaks of his accomplishments with pride. When first telling me of his abdication, she directed her anger not at him but at the woman who lured him away from the family, leaving her, a teenager, feeling the head of household and placing the responsibility of earning a living and getting married on her. When she showed me a tape of her wedding she said, "See, I'm crying. I'm crying because my father should be there. I needed him to be there . . . I felt all alone." When her baby was born she again expressed sadness, feeling that he should come back to recognize her achievements. At first her confidences seemed sad, but later there was a strength to her anger, fire in her eyes and words when she spoke of him. Once she yelled at me, "How dare you mention him to me! How can you speak of him when all he does is bring hurt! I don't want to ever think of him again!"

Both Sovanna and Sopheap seemed to be rather accepting, or at least passive, in their attitudes toward their fathers when I first met them. As Sovanna said, "He's my father, what can I do?" But subsequently they took action, either physically or verbally, to mitigate the anguish caused by the fathers. Sovanna's original plan, to rely on the monks for assistance with the father, would have worked in Cambodia, where each village has a *wat* (temple) where the elderly may live or visit. But that was impossible in Middle City, and her final solution, advocated by her American friends, caused a rift with her community. Sopheap could not so physically control her father, but her own verbal behavior is similarly inappropriate for a traditional Cambodian.

Adult woman/mother. The relationship between an adult woman and her mother is an important one. Refugee women often have their mothers living with them, as would have been the case in Cambodia; when brides come from another state (not the usual pattern), their mothers sometimes come too. One household in Middle City includes a woman and her children, her married son, his wife and children, and his wife's mother and wife's grandmother. Several women have gone to great lengths to get their mothers to the United States, and quite a few families arrived here with the wife's mother.

The birth of a child may enhance the relationship between a woman and her mother. Theary explained that she needed to marry at eighteen because her mother didn't "have anyone," and later she gave the same explanation for her pregnancy: "My mom not have anything to do—she need someone." The mother, Thea, gave her much advice about pregnancy and postpartum care and took over the complete care of the infant and new mother, placing Theary under fairly strict supervision about food, clothing, hair care, medicines, and general activity. My first visits after the birth were full of "My mom says I have to . . ." and "My mom says I mustn't. . . ." Theary said, "My mother brought me to the hospital," although it was her husband who drove the car. The mother was in the delivery room for the birth and in church the next day announcing the baby, though she seldom went otherwise. The baby slept with Thea, the grandmother, not Theary. During my early visits, it was Thea who was tending the baby, plopping her in my lap, handing me the bottle, and she has continued to care for the child as the young mother maintains jobs and school. Although Thea is not Theary's biological mother, but her aunt, Theary has often said to me, "She's my real mom. She raised me and took care of me all of my life, so she seems like my mom to me." When Thea went away for a month, Theary said, "I really miss my mom now that she's gone. I miss her a lot."

Occasionally mothers and daughters are in conflict. Theary often told me that she and her mother weren't speaking or were "having trouble"; sometimes she would threaten to move out. But more often young women in these circumstances stick by mothers whom Americans would consider difficult, unreasonable, overly dependent, or demanding, and obey the mothers' whims, arrange activities for them, and generally look out for their welfare. Several times Theary said to me, "Would you go visit my mom? I think she's lonely" or responded to invitations from me, "I can't go, but my mom would like to go with you."

Chantha provides a third example of mother-daughter relationships. She also lives with her mother (and father and young siblings), and she and her mother seem to have a particularly close and interdependent relationship. Chantha's two toddlers are close in age to her mother's two youngest, and the two mothers care for the four children together. Chantha takes her young siblings to dental and doctor appointments, sees to their school registration, bakes birthday cakes, and gives her sisters permanents; her mother owns the house, sews for the babies and tends them when Chantha is out, and mothered Chantha's older child when the second baby was born. The two women cook together, sew for each other, and attend parties together like good friends.

It's hard to explain the differences in the three patterns described above, but further knowledge of the individuals and their situations can add insight. Sovanna was an independent young woman early on: she drove her own motorcycle at thirteen, visited her soldier husband in Saigon despite everyone's protests about the danger, escaped the country alone with her small children, and elected to come to the United States despite her husband's preference for France. She also made conscious decisions and efforts to adapt to American culture: took English lessons and has learned English well, almost immediately moved away from other Cambodians, got her children into schools without English as a Second Language (ESL) programs, has American magazines around the house, takes great pride in her children's English abilities, and has American friends. Sovanna has always shown an interest in American culture and asks lots of questions. It is likely that, not finding solace or solutions to her father-problems in her own community, she willingly took the advice of American friends and doctors who assured her that the old man was cheating her, was physically and mentally ill, and was a danger to her and the children. Her compliance not only convinced Americans that she was trying hard and adjusting well; it also, very practically, freed her of the constant fear and trouble and expense of caring for him. One can't yet know whether the cost, in loss of Cambodian community support, will be too great or will be counterbalanced by the new friendships of Americans.

Theary, younger, might also be expected to have adopted much of American culture readily and easily, and in some ways she has. She completed high school, and her spoken English is excellent. As early arrivals, her family had more support, financial and otherwise, than most, and with more education, English, and urban skills than most, their potential for success in adjusting to American patterns seemed high. With no small siblings to support, and considering her good grades in high school and her high ambition, one might have expected Theary to fall easily into an American pattern of college and independence after high school. But other factors may have been at work. Her family's high status in the home culture, her own serious study of traditional court dance, and her mother's skills as a traditional herbalist may have developed in her more pride in the traditional culture, more concern to keep it alive, than some other young people have. It was Theary who tried to maintain the traditional dance for a few years and plays videotapes of it when there are guests. She recites to me without hesitation the necessary steps in a traditional wedding, the herbs to put on a baby's head, the salts a new mother must bathe in. She helped her mother when Thea was the leader of a major traditional multicity ceremony. So a family which had achieved high status in the traditional culture continues to derive status, community respect, and well-being through maintenance of traditional knowledge. In addition, Thea's traditional skills and competence have allowed Theary to rely on her to a far greater extent than Sovanna can on her very dependent father.

Finally, Chantha may have had more choices in the adjustment process because the intact nature of her family placed fewer immediate burdens on her. Perhaps her exuberant mother as a role model influenced her decision to leave school for marriage and motherhood, but she has the opportunity to finish school and attend college if she wishes. The family creates a comfortable environment for her to develop her own direction of adaptation, and she is not compelled to take on responsibilities before she is ready.

Sometimes, of course, the elderly mothers get responsibilities they may not seek. Chantha's and Theary's mothers have major roles in the raising of their grandchildren, which keep them housebound and less likely to seek jobs, ESL classes, or other association with Americans. One young woman was criticized for not helping more at the death of her father-in-law. When an American responded, "But she has two babies to take care of," she was told, "No! She has her own mother for that!"

Mother/teenage daughter. At first glance, women and their teenage daughters seem to have a relaxed, friendly, and mutually helpful relationship. Women express pride in their daughters and their accomplishments and often allow them more freedom than they actually think is best. For their part, the girls take major responsibilities in the home, caring for younger siblings, housekeeping, and earning money. In their American environment, it is often the teenage girls who go to the clinic or school to translate for the mothers. They often skip school and sometimes quit altogether in order to manage these tasks for widowed mothers. Women and their daughters seem to enjoy one another's companionship, and sometimes the mothers seem to rely on the daughters for what we might see as mothering. Kim almost always had her daughter Ra phone me and then would keep her nearby to help her with words she didn't know; once, although I had agreed to meet her at the clinic and her own English is quite good, she also brought thirteen-year-old Ra along. A daughter will remember to bring tissues to a funeral for her mother and will correct my pronunciation of her mother's name. There's often an air of camaraderie in the relationship between mothers and daughters; they may shop and sew for one another, sit together at community events giggling and talking, comb each other's hair, and paint each other's fingernails. When Sophy was banging away on my piano, her daughters teased her about the clamor, nudging her off the seat. In the adult ESL class at the Agency, the teenage translator went from woman to woman to help them, sitting down on the chair with each as she went.

There are also, however, strong tensions underlying many mother-daughter relationships. Girls who have been through several years of high school here have a different sense of independence than their mothers had at that age. The mothers did not associate with boys, and most did not choose their spouses. "If the parents tell them get married, then the girl has to get married." So now when their daughters want to go out with boys, there is a tension between wanting to help the daughters get along in this new environment and wanting to preserve the family's reputation in the community. One mother tells her daughter, "Go, have a good time, but be careful"; but if the girl does something disapproved, the incident is noticed, remembered, and recounted throughout the community.

Several girls have run off, sometimes briefly, sometimes for a long time. They say it is to escape the unreasonable burdens of housework and the impossible restrictions imposed by their mothers. One woman, whose daughter is a model of respectable behavior, said of another, whose daughter had just run away, "Of course, she lets those girls run wild! I saw that girl standing outside, right on the sidewalk, talking to a boy! The mother should stay home and watch her daughter, not let her be so wild!" When another girl appeared at a public event with a boyfriend, the mother was furious and the community scandalized. A young man explained to me, "She should never have brought him here, right in front of her mother. That was a terrible thing to do!" In fact the mother and daughter have reconciled, but the mother has been criticized because of it.

Mothers are not necessarily the family ogres, however. Fathers, when they are present, can be even more strict, with both sons and daughters; one father said to me, "If my daughter or son get a boyfriend or girlfriend, I would cut my blood out!" So teenagers keep their romantic affairs to themselves. One college student said, "Our mother knows we do it, because she knows we're in America now and she can't stop it. But we would never tell her. That would be disrespectful, hurt her feelings too much." This young woman has, at other times, claimed an especially close relationship with her mother: "My mother and me, we really communicate. I can tell her anything. That's the problem with most Cambodian parents—they have no communication with their kids."

Parents/children. Women seem to have very close and warm relationships with young children and are particularly solicitous of infants and toddlers. When I visited mothers, they usually had a baby, toddler, or grandchild hovering or in their lap. When I interviewed Maly, three-year-old Ry was usually cradled in her arms, either awake or sleeping. Maly would give Ry the bottle, but say "What nurse say about bottle? Nurse say you stop that, hunh?" Ry retained the bottle. In the church nursery, Sophy jumped up when a baby cried: "Oh, don't cry baby! Why you cry?" and promptly picked it up. When tending the church nursery, the Cambodian women never let the babies cry but carried them immediately to their mothers in the sanctuary.

Although I spent a great deal of time watching mothers and babies, it was not always clear to me which tot belonged to which mother. Mothers brought infants and toddlers to the ESL classes at the Agency, though they were implored not to. Toddlers climbed on and under the meeting table and seemed to be disciplined equally by anyone (or, more often, by no one). A three-year-old reached for a cup of juice; a woman nearby gestured as if to slap the child, saying "Ai!"; everyone laughed; the child's mother watched, smiling, but did not enter into the action. I saw this exact same scene on another occasion (where a baby also spent the evening sitting on the table where adults were eating dinner): again a woman not the baby's mother acted as if to slap the infant, again everyone laughed, again the mother observed passively.

The whims of toddlers are indulged. For example, a mother might take a full cup of juice for her toddler, a smaller serving for herself. Adults might sit through the ESL class without a workbook, but no one would suggest taking the one from the five-year-old. When the ESL teacher lifted a child from jumping around on the table, the mother did not respond, nor when the child immediately climbed back up. When a one-year-old bit a styrofoam cup into chunks, the mother casually removed the bits from the baby's mouth, then calmly watched as the child started in on another cup.

Many women also brought infants and toddlers into the Khmer language Christian services at the church (the older children were in Sunday school). The children seemed to arrive and leave, be tended, fed, scolded, or carried out by various "mothers." Once I came upon a small child about eighteen months old, standing outside the closed glass door of the chapel where the service was being held. I squatted down, and she came up to within two inches of my nose. She stared at me solemnly for a while. I asked her, "Where's Mae?" No response. I got up to go, and she reached her arms up to me, still silent and serious. I picked her up and played with her awhile. All this time, there seemed to be no notice from the chapel. When I tried to put her down, she simply kept her hands up, with that solemn look. I carried her into the chapel and stood with her a while longer, hoping someone would claim her. A few people smiled briefly at me, then ignored me. I finally handed her to the woman next to me. "Is she yours?" The woman smiled and took her, but was not the mother.

There seems to be a sort of ritualized spanking of children. I have seen many instances of pretend swatting of small children, and a few times when a child has actually been hit (that is, I was pretty sure there was contact), but I never heard a child cry from being hit. On the other hand, scoldings may sound (to American ears) extremely harsh, though they may be accompanied with grins and laughter. A four-year-old was loudly scolded by her grinning, laughing sister and others gathered around (she had accidentally gashed her brother with a knife); she spent most of an hour crying and shaking inconsolably, and huddled the rest of the long evening in a dark, scowling sulk. The intense humiliation had far greater impact than any physical punishment I ever witnessed.

On the other hand, some parents do "beat" (their word—I never witnessed the practice, so I am not sure whether they actually mean a "beating" or a "swat") older children. Even mothers may beat strapping eighteen-year-old sons, and the boys are expected to go down on their knees and beg forgiveness. American child-abuse laws are worrisome to parents, who aren't sure where the line is. Many fear that any punishment at all will get them in trouble; others feel their children are growing wild because of lack of discipline. The youngsters manipulate the situation by threatening to report their parents; some have actually done so. One father said, "Your rules are too tough [on parents]. If the police knew it, they would put me in jail. . . . I want my kids to be good people, not to be in jail. I have to conduct them to good behavior."

Of Village Svay Ebihara wrote, "Parents derive great pleasure and entertainment from children who are generally treated with considerable permissiveness and given much affection . . . parents generally receive obedience, deference, and devotion from their children" (p. 116). Though describing life in Cambodia thirty-five years ago, this quite accurately describes the relationship with preteens today in Middle City.

Sibling. The sibling tie, too, today in Middle City as in Ebihara's Village Svay, is strong and learned early. Child siblings share beds, clothes, toys, money, and tasks at home; at school they play together and help one another with their work when possible. When given the choice, they ask to sit together or be grouped together for outings. Four siblings may share one bus seat, while other seats remain empty. One mother was appalled that my sons, five years apart and very different in interests and personality, seldom played together. "Don't they love each other? Oh no, Cambodian children prefer their brothers and sisters over anybody. They love each other; why play with somebody else, strangers?" One young mother said to me, "I tell her [the four-year-old], 'You share with him, you play with him before others, because he's your little brother, he loves you'; and I say to him, 'You do what she says, because she's your big sister and she loves you.'" Three women began life stories with me by listing their siblings, "seven brothers and sisters, two boys and five girls," or by recounting how they lost them during the war.

Ebihara says, "the warmest sibling relations are between those who are of the same sex and close in age" (p. 121), and this is apparent in Middle City as well, perhaps particularly between girls, who dress alike for parties, sit or walk with arms around one another, fix one another's hair, share the household tasks and childcare, and generally confide in one another. One teenager felt abandoned when her sister left home; she hadn't minded the housework when they shared it because they talked and had fun together while doing it; school friends could not be confided in as a sister could. Sisters often dress alike. Boys close in age are also constant companions and look out for one another, sharing friends, play, homework, jobs, clothes. Young siblings share beds, either with one another or with an older sibling or in a group on the floor; small children seldom sleep alone. Siblings share toys in a way remarkable to Americans and are very generous with one another: three-year-old Sovann stretches out her hands for the popsicle four-year-old Sovy is eating and is given it without hesitation; nine-year-old Sophy opens her birthday gift and distributes the paperdolls among her brothers and sisters.

Siblings may be very close across ages, too, especially teenage girls and their younger siblings. Traditionally girls took care of younger siblings while both parents worked in the fields. One woman says, "When I was young, I didn't go to the field to watch the cows; I stayed home and took care of my little brothers and sisters."

Even urban girls had this responsibility; another woman, Chantou, said, when questioned about play, "I played with my brothers and sisters; I liked to help them and play with them . . . because I'm the oldest. You see, my parents were very busy, and sometimes they didn't have time to spend with my brothers and sisters, so I'm the only one that could help them get through life."

Many retain this closeness into adulthood, and one of the many sorrows of refugees is that siblings are widely scattered. Chantou later said she wishes she had not come to the United States—she wishes she were still in Cambodia "so I would be with my brothers and sisters." When she and others have gone back for a visit, they word it, specifically, "to see my sisters." Other women took over responsibility for their younger siblings during the Pol Pot time, as families became separated or parents died.

In Middle City, too, older siblings play an important role in taking care of their young siblings. They often stay home from school—if a parent is ill or working, for example—to care for the little ones and sometimes take care of the whole family if a parent goes out of town to the temple or for a wedding. The responsibility of sibling care seems natural to the older children. A twelve-year-old boy, contemplating his mother's getting a job, shrugs and says, "But she has to take care of my brothers when I'm in school," and when I mentioned summer camp to him later he responded, "But who would take care of my brothers?" Even in the context of American institutions, the older siblings are very responsive to the needs of the younger. In church and at Sunday school many teenagers have a younger sibling in tow. When two little girls hover at the Sunday school door, the teacher says, "Rim, come get your sisters"; the boy fetches them and settles them into chairs beside him, but they are soon sharing the chair with him. A whimper from the church nursery alerts the young teens: "Is that my sister?" murmurs Roeun, and she rushes out, returning a moment later with a little boy in tow, whom she turns over to his own sister.

Siblings take pride in one another's accomplishments and enjoy one another's company. In church, a teen motions me over, beaming, to point out the coloring her three-year-old brother is doing, staying in the lines. In another family the older kids announce proudly that the toddler has toilet-trained herself. When teenage Mohm enters the house, a joyful chorus of greeting rises from the younger siblings and their friends. Once in church, when I looked up and noticed that the toddler had gone from her lap, Mohm had a large teddy bear on her lap and was joggling it exactly as she had just been doing with her little brother.

Sometimes these responsibilities interfere with developing closer ties with American age-mates and hinder other activities that Americans consider important developmental tasks of adolescence. BunRoeun told a neighbor she couldn't spend the night because her little sister needed her; the mother explains that when the baby wakens during the night, BunRoeun is the one to "take her to the bathroom, always do things for her." Typically the teenagers have childcare responsibilities after school which infringe not only on social time but homework time as well. Sibling attachment can also prevent teens from seeking greater independence. One girl said to me, "I really want to run away, but I can't because who would take care of my brothers and sisters?" She contemplates an escape for even a few days, "But even then, I'm afraid for my brothers and sisters—who would take care of them?" When she finally does take off, she is miserable: "I miss my little sisters—they're so cute!" she grins through her tears. And the little ones worry about her and tell me, through tears, "I miss my big sister!"

Children may go to live with a mother's sibling in toddlerhood or later, or with their own adult sibling, especially an older sister who has moved away and is lonely for them. These moves may be permanent and similar to Western adoption, but more frequently there is instead a pattern of extended periodic visits. This flexibility serves wonderfully for a young bride or a young mother glad for a teenage helpmate and also for the teenager seeking respite from parental authority; it enables a widow to send an unruly adolescent son to an adult brother or brother-in-law for male discipline; it provides welcome temporary relief for a family who may have many children and an ill or widowed parent; it provides children with a variety of models of family relationships; and it provides children for adults who have not borne children. But it does not work well in American school systems.

Ancestors. It's difficult for Americans to appreciate the importance of ancestors in other cultures. We erringly refer to "ancestor worship" as if it were a particular religion. For Cambodians, as for many cultures, reverence for age extends to ancestors. One is bound, out of duty and love, to pay respect toward ancestors in various ways, and ancestors in turn bring blessings and a good life to their descendants. Conversely, mistreated ancestors can also bring misfortune to their descendants.

One of the most serious problems which Cambodian refugees face, and one which Americans seldom acknowledge, is the consequence of having left dead family members behind without carrying out the proper funeral rituals. It is not merely the sadness of the loss nor the guilt of the leaving, although these are very real and serious problems. But perhaps worse, and not understood by Americans, is the problem of ghosts, or *kmauit*, especially the spirits of dead who have been murdered and not properly buried. These spirits haunt their kin at night, giving people frightening nightmares and making them afraid to fall sleep. Since many refugees fled without knowing where their kin were or even whether they were dead or alive, many were unable to bury their kin or to perform the proper rituals for them. Here, they try to placate them by "doing good" by giving money, silk, and other gifts to the monks, particularly at Phchum, an autumn festival dedicated to the ancestors. In dire cases, people make an effort to go back to Cambodia, try to find the bones of their parents, dig them up, and give them a proper ritual burial. Considerable money and energy are spent on these pursuits, but they may bring spiritual peace.

Affinal Kin

Although consanguine kin are clearly the closest ties, today in Middle City as Ebihara found them in Village Svay, ties created by marriage become very important as well, and often emotionally close.

Wife/husband. Because most of my informants were women, most of the following observations are of women or focus on women's roles; in addition, most of the older women I knew were widows, and the young women had not been married long, so I have less information on marital relationships than on other kinship patterns. Nevertheless, a general picture presents itself of fairly accepting and egalitarian partnerships, much like those described by Ebihara. Though traditionally husbands in Cambodia were to some degree chosen by the parents (as Ebihara reported and my informants confirmed by their own experiences), women seem either accepting or praising of their husbands. A widow tells me, "I miss my husband. He was good to me"; another says (to a minister), "My husband was a good person. He love Jesus—love, love, love Jesus very much." Young brides say, "He's all right; I like him, he's really good to me," or, beaming, "Yeah, I'm lucky—really lucky!"

And indeed, many of the husbands do seem "good." Despite crowded living conditions, poor health, and lack of education, English, and job skills, many of them maintain two or three jobs, and some have saved enough money in a few years to buy houses. They help with children and are quite comfortable tending babies and toddlers. Although the literature reports wife beating in many refugee groups, no one raised this subject with me (though I heard complaints and fears of beatings by mothers and older brothers; and I don't mean to suggest that wife abuse does not occur, merely that it seems not to be widespread).

In Middle City as in Cambodia, husbands turn their paychecks over to their wives, who are in charge of the family money, making the purchases and paying the bills. When I tried to explain to one young woman that in some American families the wife has to ask the husband for household money, she was horrified: "What? That's like a whore or something! If you love me, you take care of me. I take care of your baby, but you take care of me." Since many families are uxorilocal, the financial responsibilities of the mother-in-law can be substantial.

On the other hand, there is much independence between husband and wife. One husband was debating whether to go to work the next day, and the wife said, "I can't tell him go or not; it's his energy, only he can tell if he can go or not." Another young man was going to get the tendons of his hands cut because of a work injury. The wife was afraid of the surgery and its consequences, but she felt she couldn't say that to him; "It's his hands, his decision; I can't tell him what I think." In another situation, a young man was musing about college: "I'd like to go, but right now my wife is going. Let her try. If she can do it, she'll finish. If she can't do it, then maybe I'll try."

In-laws. Perhaps partly because of the ambilocal nature of residence, perhaps partly because marriages are still so often arranged by the parents, perhaps partly because there is such a felt need for kin, still such an acute sense of loss, and surely partly because it is the customary pattern that the adults have learned, in-laws play an important role in the lives of the Cambodians in Middle City. A young couple may depend primarily on one set of parents, but the other set is available in times of need. This is practical in an unfamiliar environment where any connection for a job possibility and any coping skills are welcome. The two sets of adult parents usually have known one another before the courtship began, but even if they have not, they tend to cooperate in guiding the young couple's future decisions, and they may consult with one another if the young couple is in trouble of some sort.

Even when a young couple lives with the bride's parents, either of them may seek the groom's parents' aid in case of conflict within the household, if a job is available in the groom's hometown, or if the groom's family has more money or other means to help them. Or they may feel compelled to go live with the groom's family if that family needs the help. When a son-in-law moves into a widow-headed household, of which there are many, he makes a substantial contribution to the household budget, perhaps even assuming the rent.

Perhaps for some of the reasons already noted, such as close sibling ties, a desire for a wider circle of kin, and the loss of kin, siblings-in-law often develop close relationships as well. One young woman said, after an argument with her sister-in-law, "Cambodians are not supposed to fight, especially not us—we're like sisters; sisters-in-law, but almost the same." Since young children may live with their married siblings for short or long periods of time because of proximity to schools, because of parents' work schedules, because the children are unruly, because of illness or other difficulties in the home, or simply to continue the close bonds the siblings had before the marriage, the married-in spouse may adopt a parental role toward the young sibling-in-law: "I feel so bad for my little sister-in-law; they don't treat her right. I want her to come and live with us." Adult brothers-in-law, particularly, can assist with discipline and educational decisions for a young in-law that might be difficult for the child's widowed mother.

Thus, although the consanguine relationships, especially those between mother and child and those between same-sex siblings, seem to be paramount, affinal relationships may be strong, loving, and important on a daily basis. Few adults in Middle City are fortunate enough to have in-laws who have survived and moved with them, but as teenagers grow up and marry, the strong sibling bond, particularly, may act to reestablish the tradition of in-law cooperation.

Fictive Kin and Missing Kin

Adoption, both legal and informal, was common in traditional Cambodia and seems to be common in Middle City as well. This is a little difficult to track, since in most cases people just say they are siblings when they might actually be cousins, or cousins when there may be no biological relationship at all. Sometimes they use nuclear family kin terms in order to immigrate together but reveal more distant ties later to trusted Americans. The traditional patterns of easy family expansion to include in-laws, nieces and nephews, grandparents, and other kin, and the casual extension of kin terms to close friends clearly have adaptive advantages for refugees seeking to rebuild families along the same lines if not with the same individuals, and where a larger kin group means a larger pool of skills, economic support, and emotional support in frequent times of need.

This chapter has described relationships within families as I observed them in Middle City. Another kind of relationship can only be observed through the pain expressed in faces and in the efforts to which families go in order to locate or maintain communication with beloved members left behind—a wife and child, an elderly parent, a daughter or son—who may still be missing or were missing or believed dead at the time of flight.

Relatives left in Thai camps or in Cambodia live in terribly impoverished and dangerous conditions. Those in refugee camps are stuck, unlikely to be allowed to enter the United States, unwelcome in Thailand, and afraid to return to Cambodia. There, whole villages have been destroyed and the land laid waste; towns, schools, hospitals, libraries are in ruin; land mines are everywhere, and the Khmer Rouge still have control in some rural areas. Communication is practically impossible; people have to travel to Phnom Penh to receive a telephone call, letters seldom get through, money and packages sent are stolen, and so on, so the worry is constant.

Because mail doesn't get through, many families make an effort to hand-deliver gifts. After years of work, a family may save up enough for a plane ticket, and someone travels to Cambodia with money, clothes, and other gifts. A large group of kin in Cambodia or Thailand gathers, and the event is videotaped, with the family lined up, weeping, telling the relatives in America how much they miss them, how much they are suffering, who is sick, who has died. Like Phchum, these projects consume a great deal of family resources, but they provide some peace

It is unlikely that these families will ever be allowed to reunite. As each year passes, a child comes closer to becoming twenty-one, after which time s/he is no longer recognized as a "child" by U.S. immigration law (and therefore presumably no longer wanted by the parents?). Lives are put on hold, because if a son or daughter marries while in a refugee camp, the chances of joining the parents and family are further reduced. Nevertheless, families spend a great deal of time and money on lawyers and on acquiring citizenship because they still have hope. The desperate lengths and sacrifices to which Cambodian families go in order to reunite and the determination with which U.S. law seeks to prevent reunification dramatize the difference in the value placed on family between the two cultures.

FAMILY STRENGTH IN A CHANGING WORLD

As was evident in the discussion of technology, kinship patterns in this refugee community exhibit a wide range of variation. Nevertheless, one feature seems to stand out. Against a backdrop of violent family upheaval in which spouses were forcibly separated, children removed from their parents, strangers forced to mate, and young people taught that their own survival might depend upon torturing, killing, or abandoning their young siblings or old grandparents, and in a present setting of rapid and radical culture change, family ties appear, amazingly, to be strong, broad, and deep. In the preceding examples, certain relationships stand out: the respect toward the elderly parents (living and dead), the warm and intense relationship between mother and teenage daughter, the patient attitude of mothers toward young children, and the tender and responsible relationship of older toward younger siblings.

The relationship of adult woman to elder parent is one of respect and deference, though it may be mixed with a jocular friendliness and camaraderie. Some women complained to me a bit, but they did not in fact challenge the marriage decisions made for them by their parents, and they generally continued to obey parental directives and arrange their own lives for their parents' comfort. Many adults arrived here with old parents, although the difficulties of esaping with anyone not of sound body must have been enormous, and they continue to support these elderly despite the added financial burden on an already large and unemployable family. Others continue to support still-living, recently dead, or long dead ancestors or parents through money sent back to the camps or Cambodia and through elaborate and expensive ceremonies such as Kathen and One Hundred Days. On the other hand, it is possible that we may see a rift in this relationship as a few young adults are striking out on their own, leaving the parental households. At the time of my research, marriages and moves had not yet left parents living alone, but it is possible to imagine this in the future as young children raised entirely in the United States marry and establish neolocal households. One woman failed in her efforts to put her elderly parent out of her home through the traditional avenues of taking him to the monks and to other families, and when he finally had to be hospitalized, the community response was cold and critical. It would be interesting to know whether the community reaction would have been different had she been someone else—a community leader, for example. Because she is unusual and because of the community disapproval, this case is probably not precedent setting.

The convivial mother-daughter relationships that I witnessed at the beginning of this research were in striking contrast to those in our own society, which accepts or even expects animosity between mothers and teenage daughters. In the Cambodian community, there is a high level of mutual trust and support. As I've pointed out, teenagers, especially girls, take a major role in rearing their small siblings and also perform other tasks such as housekeeping, income earning, and writing and translating for the mother. Even though they are strikingly obedient and respectful toward their mothers, the relationship can seem at the same time breezy and almost sororal. Questions arise, then: is this relaxed and friendly mother-daughter relationship traditional (alongside the obedience), or is it a product of the fact that the older women have had a harder time adjusting to a new culture and are therefore dependent upon their daughters both for practical matters and for friendship? Or are the daughters taking a role traditionally played by a woman's mother, who would normally be in or near the home of her adult daughter? Since I have known primarily women without husbands, it may be that their daughters are taking on the fathers' roles. Such questions beg further research. These teenagers have not experienced normal family life back home (prior to 1975), so further inquiry would have to be done with adult and older women; as memories of that era are often suppressed and sometimes idealized, this may be an interesting but difficult task.

Another relationship described here is that between mothers and their small children. Mothers appear to be patient and tender, nurturing, but not overly anxious. Misbehavior may be commented on or not, but it is seldom punished or corrected. Pholla was sympathetic about her toddler's hurt but did not scold the brother. She expressed concern to me that her children got into trouble, but took no action. Mothers keep their babies physically close to them to an older age than American mothers do but also freely allow others to hold them.

One final relationship that I found striking was that of child siblings. Older siblings generally have very tolerant, nurturant, and friendly relationships with their younger siblings. This is particularly true between girls, but is evident for many boys as well. Children carry siblings half their size, dress them, sleep with them, feed them, spend money on them, stay home to tend them, help them in church and school, and generally look out for their welfare. Although this might be partly a consequence of so much family death and of the loss of other siblings, the general pattern certainly fits the traditional values and behaviors described by Ebihara. Nothing I ever observed suggested a trend toward a more American pattern of sibling rivalry or of playmates chosen from outside the home.

The affect that becomes clear in all these relationships is one of warmth, cooperation, docility, support, and tolerance. Adults and young adults display tender and respectful attitudes toward their parents. The slight bridling at parental authority is kept under cover, and minor adolescent rebellions create scandal in the community. Teenagers are solicitous of, obedient to, and generally respectful toward their parents and contribute substantially to the finances, housekeeping, childcare, and literacy needs of the household. Siblings are gentle toward one another and enjoy one another's companionship, both within age levels and across wide age ranges.

Throughout this chapter we have seen that most elements of the kinship system in this community—many of the rules and many of the relationship patterns themselves—are very close to those found in Village Svay in 1960. Despite the tremendous family upheavals caused by the war, the Khmer Rouge, and flight, the structure and values of family culture have changed very little, and traditions remain strong and strength giving. Perhaps a key to such survival is the flexibility of the kinship rules and patterns themselves. The bilateral pattern of descent and the ambilocal nature of residence create a wide range of kin for people to turn to in times of need and may prevent one side of a family from becoming either too domineering or too overburdened. The easy adoption of kin, officially into a family or more loosely into a household or extended family, is a traditional pattern well-suited to a circumstance in which many people have lost close kin; it also allows for the pooling of scarce economic, linguistic, and skill resources. Although American schooling, housing, friendship patterns, economic system, and general social life run counter to traditional Khmer family relations, for the moment, at least, most families are choosing to maintain their broad-reaching, flexible, and deeply important kinship patterns.

Some of these patterns, however, cause conflict with Americans, American institutions, and American values. The very size of the family units puts them in conflict with American architectural style, landlords, and neighbors. Landlords are unwilling to rent to such large families, and neighbors are appalled at the number of children. Strong ties between siblings hinder the development of friendships between Cambodian and American children that might otherwise ease their initiation into American society. Marriage customs such as polygyny, brideprice, arranged marriage, and elaborate weddings are either disapproved by Americans or flatly illegal. The primacy of kinship over school and work creates concern among teachers and annoyance from employers.

NOTES

1. All citations of Ebihara in this and in subsequent chapters refer to this 1971 work unless otherwise noted.

2. This is Ebihara's use of the term, not Murdock's classic, though hypothetical, definition (1965:71) following Robert Lowie's suggestion of the term, which was also hypothetical.

3. "Eskimo—FaSiDa and MoBrDa called by the same terms as parallel cousins but terminologically differentiated from sisters; the terms for the two cross-cousins are usually but not always the same" (Murdock 1967:223). Essentially this system, though rare in the world, is the same as that used in the United States.

4. The terms don't specifically denote "sibling" either, though that is how Ebihara and my informants translated them. My informants said the terms mean "like sister" and "like brother, you know?" and use them also between spouses, cousins, and good friends.

5. The stem family is composed of one nuclear family with the parent or parents of one of the married adults; this is different from the extended family, which comprises one or two elderly parents and all of their children of one sex (usually sons) and those children's families of procreation (Murdock 1967).

Chapter 4

Patterns of Social Organization

While kinship and the family are the most important modes of social organization in Cambodian society, in the refugee community in 1995, as in Village Svay in 1960, there are additional elements which contribute to the nature of social relationships. This chapter describes the systems of gender, age, community leadership, and social class by which the Cambodians in Middle City organize social interaction and relationships and demonstrates that age and gender patterns continue to follow, to a great extent, traditional patterns. Community organization and social class, too, although more elusive to American observers, may also be emerging and functioning somewhat as they did in traditional village Cambodia. Community organization has not developed as it has in many other American cities; there was neither a Mutual Assistance Association (MAA) nor a temple-based organization during the period of research, and neither seemed likely to develop soon.

GENDER AND GENDER RELATIONSHIPS

A father is worth a thousand friends and a mother worth a thousand fathers.
— Ebihara, proverb (1974)

Many aspects of gender relationships have been described in the previous chapter, but there are a few additional points to be made here. First, Southeast Asian cultures are noted for having a relatively high status for women and equality of the sexes, and traditional Cambodia is no exception (Ebihara 1971; Matthiasson 1974). Unaware of this, Americans are surprised at the independence of Cambodian refugee women and the somewhat egalitarian nature of gender relations in the community, and they mistakenly attribute these features to rapid Americanization. Second, gender equality is always a difficult characteristic to measure, partly because there are so many dimensions of equality, such as equality of political or economic power, and partly because equality is so often confounded with sameness (Lamphere 1987; Martin and Voorhies 1975; Reiter 1975). Men and women have some distinct roles in the Cambodian culture of Middle City, but there is also considerable overlap in their roles. Gender role patterns, like other patterns in this culture, can be traced in part to the traditional culture, in part to acquired American customs, and in part to new developments within the community.

Evidence from the kinship patterns would indeed predict an equal status for women, or at least one more equal than in other societies. Societies with Eskimo cousin terminology, for example, typically are characterized by "monogamy [and] independent nuclear families" (Murdock 1967:227), and while ambilocal residence generally indicates "woman's comparative equality with man in property and other rights . . . it is her superiority to him . . . that favors matrilocal [uxorilocal] residence" (Murdock 1967:205). We might challenge Murdock's claim of women's "superiority to him" existing in any culture, but women's position is often higher in matrilocal cultures than in patrilocal cultures. Ebihara reports a preference toward uxorilocal residence within the ambilocal pattern in Svay, and that is perhaps also the more typical pattern in Middle City, but the tendency may be away from that if young couples follow the neolocal patterns of their American peers (and sometimes American spouses), implying a concomitant loss of status for the role of mother-in-law. Following Murdock's analysis, if there is a shift from matrilocal to neolocal residence, this could eventually contribute to a shift away from the current independence of women. It is far too soon to ascertain this, though; this is a situation to measure over the next generation.

Some linguistic patterns, such as the absence of gender-specific pronouns, may also suggest ancient and deeply ingrained gender equality. Although Ebihara does not suggest it, linguistic and kinship patterns, being the more ancient, may indicate that greater egalitarianism existed prior to the Buddhist (14th-century) and French-based (19th-century) legal codes, and thus the occasional male dominance shown in some matters may be a recent and perhaps somewhat superficial overlay.

Ebihara found that despite Buddhist teachings and the French-based legal code, which give men generally superior positions over women, rural women had a number of important rights and that in ordinary village life "male and female . . . [were] virtually equal" (p. 113). Similarly, Khmer women in Middle City own property, have jobs, and manage the family finances. Many women are heads of households, and although they often express concern for their own and their children's safety because of the absence of a male, they do not relinquish authority to adult sons, sons-in-law, or other kinsmen who move in for protection.

Girls sometimes complain that they do more work in the household than their brothers and enjoy less freedom to venture from the home, especially at night, but generally they feel and are encouraged to pursue educations and jobs on a par with the boys in the family.[1] A fourteen-year-old was teasing some boys who were high up in a tree: "What you think you are, monkeys?" I asked her if it was okay for girls to climb trees too. "Of course girls climb trees! My mom say anything boy can do, girl can do! Run, jump, get job, anything!"

And so they do. Little girls and boys play together at rough and quiet games indoors and out. Teenagers associate less across gender lines, but until recently boys and girls have done equally well in school and were equally as likely to begin college. Both teenage girls and boys are likely to have jobs, especially summer jobs, and the girls join in the hard farm labor such as picking fruit or tossing pumpkins and watermelons into trucks. When one man was moving, I was the only one surprised to see that the helper he had hired was a young woman. "She's as strong as anybody," I was told matter-of-factly. "She can do anything."

Boys are given a bit more freedom to roam; at the temple and other Buddhist ceremonies, boys beyond toddlerhood are seldom in attendance during the rituals, preferring to play outside. In the American church as well, boys are more likely to be out of the classrooms and in the halls. Teenage boys have fewer household responsibilities if there are sisters to do the work, are much more likely to drive cars, and have much more freedom around the city.

Summer camp has been a sore point between Ann, the American who has been so helpful to them, and the parents. The mothers say sure, the children can go, but when it comes time to sign the permission forms, they're not at home or have changed their minds. Ann feels the girls are not allowed to go because they are wanted at home for housework and childcare, but the mothers also feel that girls, particularly those nearing puberty, need an older brother there "to take care of them." They're not specifically worried that the girls will come to physical harm or become pregnant; they are concerned that the girls appear, publicly, to be properly watched over by the family, so that there won't be gossip.

Employment in the American sector does not quite reflect gender balance. The larger number of men employed in higher status jobs probably reflects males' better access to education in Cambodia in the 1950s and 1960s, or it may simply be because of the large number of widows with small children, who consequently receive public assistance. In some families, mothers of young children stay home, but most of the time women get outside jobs if they can—if their children are all in school or if they can get relatives to do the childcare. The need for affordable childcare is great; the greater problem is finding a job which will support a large family. Most women want to work and plan to work once their small children are in school.

Many tasks may be considered generally more appropriate to one gender but are occasionally and without shame performed by either. For example, women are typically in charge of cooking, but many men and boys help with day-to-day cooking or even in the preparations for communal events. As in American society, some men spurn "women's tasks" while others perform them cheerfully and competently. Most families have only one car, and when the father is present he is the driver, but many women drive also. Although the skill is new, driving fits the traditional independence and economic importance of women; however, driving also increases the mobility of these women, which is not traditional.

Religion is an area of life in which men's and women's roles are very different, though not necessarily unequal, perhaps again fitting what Carolyn Matthiasson calls a "complementary society" (1974:xviii). Only men are monks, but women can be nuns. There were neither in Middle City at the time of my research, but monks were sought frequently for special events and needs, and people traveled to consult monks in other cities. When I asked, people said nuns were "just the same" as monks, but nuns seem to play a distinctively subservient role in the temple, and people do not consult nuns as they do monks for personal or family problems.

On the other hand, older women play central roles in Buddhist religious ceremonies, such as sponsoring ceremonies, collecting the money (thousands of dollars), parading the gifts, and presenting the important gifts to the monks. This too is consistent with Ebihara's description of village Svay; she saw women's more constant and prominent role in religious ceremonies as a balance to men's brief period of religious service to the monks in youth and monkhood itself later in life. This subject of religious roles is explored further in the next chapter.

Adult men and women tend to associate in same-sex groups more often than in mixed-sex groups. For example, at a ceremony men may sit on one side of a room and the women on the other, or even in separate rooms. When this separation is pointed out, an informant will be surprised and say, "Oh, no, that's just how it is tonight; those men just want to talk to their friends, the women don't get to see each other much, so they want to talk." It's really very flexible, and young men are about equally as likely to sit with their wives, and old men to join the old women. It is quite common to see a group of women engaged in some communal activity, such as cooking, with one or two young men or teenage boys hovering about the fringes, occasionally joining in the conversation or being the butt of a joke, remaining handy to run an errand, but not usually staying long or joining into the main activity.

Although there is much equality, both male and female informants often referred to greater "respect" toward women. They insist that Cambodian women receive more respect than American women also and more than Cambodian men. During the wedding and prewedding ceremonies, the bride need not be present the entire time but may come out only during the more important moments. This was explained as showing "respect" to the bride, so that she doesn't have to endure in their entirety the long and somewhat grueling rituals. One young woman explained that long dresses are an indication of respect: the dresses are more dignified and afford the woman more privacy; men, like children and American women, can wear shorts and bathing suits because they are not respected. "American woman have more freedom, but Cambodian woman have more respect." On observing an age-mate in a long dress that was traditionally styled but slit to her knee, a teenage boy made a face and said, "I hate that!" Surprised, I teased him: "Don't you think she's beautiful?" "Yeah, but I hate that. It's okay for Americans [to dress like that], but not Cambodians. I hate to see Cambodians do that." His disgust was shared by the group of teens we were among, and they said, "Yeah, Cambodians will be talking about her for weeks!"

My observations and interviews suggest that though there are customary differences, there is nevertheless great flexibility in the roles of men and women, great tolerance of variation. One young woman says of an aunt, "She doesn't like men, only women. Well, not she doesn't like men—they get along okay, but she just prefers women." Frequently, marriage is refered to in practical terms: "Otherwise, when she gets old, nobody to take care of her," referring to the necessity of having children. This point leads to the next form of social organization, age-grading, which I feel is more important than gender in the life of the Khmer in Middle City.

AGE AND AGE GRADING

I can't wait until I'm older! When you grow up you can have anything and do anything you want. I can't wait to be eighteen!

—seven-year-old, discussing her older sister

Much has been said about relations across ages in the previous chapter, but two particular points must be emphasized here. One is that relative age is a primary determinant of social relations, and the other is that absolute age and relative age entitle one to respect, deference, and special care.

Although Cambodians were not traditionally organized into formal age-grades, age nevertheless functioned, as it does in all societies, as a primary means of distinguishing and assigning role, rank, and status. The importance of this is exemplified by the common use of the terms *bong* and *p'own* (older and younger). For example, two teenagers, upon meeting, immediately used bong/ p'own. Later they each translated this to me as "cousin" although there was no kin relationship between them, and neither learned the other's name although they lived together for two days. (As noted earlier, personal names would not normally be used in such a situation.) On another occasion, two women friends discovered that they had been using the terms incorrectly—that is, the younger had been addressing the older as p'own (younger). The older woman had known the true situation of their ages but let it slide. When the younger woman discovered that she had been using the incorrect term, the older woman laughed and said, "Never mind, we're in America now; it doesn't matter," but the younger woman was very embarrassed and tried to make the correction. Many times, when people refer to their own children or to mine, or when a child refers to a sibling, they simply say, in English, "the older one" or "my little one."

The attitude of respect toward age was widespread and strong in traditional Cambodia. Although there was concerted effort to destroy this attitude during the Pol Pot regime by classifying old people as expendable, removing children from their parents, and forcing children to criticize or betray older people (Ngor 1987; Criddle and Mam 1987; Sheehy 1987), and although there is certainly pressure against valuing age in American culture, there still is much evidence among the Khmer in Middle City that age has value and is entitled to respect and special care. The elderly are not expected to seek employment, though they often play major roles in childcare. They are given small children to sleep with and older children to look after them. During flight a child may have been left behind to look after elderly relatives, a necessity despite the anguish for the family. Otherwise, the old people would "have nothing, nobody to take care of them. When you're old, you need to be able to say to someone to come and squeeze your legs, arms, anything that hurts; when old people get pains, they need young people around."

Precise age, on the other hand, seems to have less meaning. Although a few people cited exact ages to me, others are vague about age. When I was invited to the birthday party of a child I'd never met, I asked the child's age. "Oh, one or two, I don't know," said his teenage aunt. Confusion has been compounded by the practice of assigning ages in refugee camps, specifically lowering children's ages so they could get more school in the United States; thus a child of fifteen who has never been to school may be placed, as "age eleven," in the fifth grade, and many in high school are twenty. Teachers are aware of this practice and support its intent. Imprecision about ages can cause difficulties, however. One twenty-one-year-old is frustrated because he's not yet officially sixteen, and thus can't drive. When children try to explain their actual ages, Americans may not believe them because it is difficult to judge ages across race. At first I sometimes guessed children's ages to be four or five years younger than they were: girls of eighteen or twenty might appear pre-adolescent and weigh eighty pounds. Inaccurate age records will also become problematic when adults reach sixty-five, entitled to retirement or social security, but have records showing them to be five years younger. Age confusion can also cause conflict with American law. One daughter was denied entry into the United States to join her parents because immigration laws defined her as no longer a "child," having turned, according to their records, twenty-one. It took over a year to convince them that she must be younger than twenty-one because there had been a pregnancy between her and her older sister, who was just twenty-one. While precise age is significant in American culture, relative age has far more relevance in Cambodian society.

Despite the vagueness regarding age and birth dates, people do rise through various age levels. The following sections describe behavior characteristic of and toward people of each age grade or stage.

Infancy

Although infancy is a protected time and newborns are kept at home, they are not secluded from the rest of the family. Many parents make a special infant hammock, with a string for rocking that can be looped to someone's toe. This is set up in the central room, placing the baby in the midst of family life. Siblings clamber about, swinging or patting the baby, and normal household clatter continues, yet the infant sleeps peacefully. If the baby wakens and begin to fuss, it is bottle-fed by anyone nearby. Breast-feeding, though traditional, is rarely practiced by new mothers in Middle City.

Babies are ready to be taken out at two or three months, carried in Western-style plastic infant carriers. They are dressed with much care and are widely fussed over, particularly by children and teenage girls, but to some extent by adults of all ages. They are handed over to siblings, fathers, grandmothers, young aunts and uncles, and to Americans. The appearance of a baby at a New Year or a wedding party occasions a cheerful gathering of women and girls. The baby is likely to spend the evening as the centerpiece of a table, frequently picked up by its mother and other adults and children and finally falling asleep in the middle of this crowd of admirers. Babies are a joy, and children of both sexes and all ages hold them, carry them, dress them, and talk to them. It is common to see a boy or girl of eight or ten with a one- or two-year-old on the hip; both the infants and the mothers are correctly confident that the babies will be lovingly tended. For example, in church one day two little boys about ten and twelve walked into the Khmer service with an infant of about eight months. They proudly sat down with her in the front row, got her out of her snowsuit, and kept her entertained for about forty-five minutes; they were entirely relaxed and competent with her; the mother was not in the room, and the boys did not turn to anyone for help. Babies are also tended very gently by fathers. Adults may tease a baby a little—pulling it away from its mother, rubbing a hand over its face, offering it a banana with the peel still on—but not to the point of upsetting the baby.

The desire for babies and children was expressed well by a teenager responding to the Sunday school teacher who was explaining birth control: "We don't need it. We're not like Americans. Even if we have a lot of children, we can take care of them." Another said, "Americans think children are too expensive, but we love them."

Toddlerhood

Toddlers are also treated lovingly and patiently by people of all ages. During the ESL classes at the Agency, toddlers were on or under the table constantly or swinging on chairs. Occasionally the American teacher would lift a tot off the table to protect the plate of cookies or pitcher of juice, but it was a short-lived measure. In the Khmer-language church service, two toddlers might carry on a conversation across the aisle or play together at the foot of the altar; the minister just raised his voice. At the Khmer language classes for children, the twenty-year-old teacher gave equal and serious attention to a two-year-old as he passed from student to student checking their written work.

By the age of two-and-a-half or three, a baby knows some of the courtesies of respect. Even a baby less than two can *sompeah* (put his palms together) in request for each bite of food. In the temple and at religious ceremonies, a mother will place a two-year-old in her lap and gently fold his legs into the appropriate position and place his palms together in sompeah to the monk. The child may clamber up or even wander off, but the mother may silently correct him several times. At a one-year-old's birthday the child may be out of sight until time for the cake and gifts; the gifts, envelopes of money, are passed up to the birthday child, who sits in her mother's lap. The child's hands, within her mother's, are placed in sompeah to accept each envelope. The baby's expression is somber; the gathered adults grin and "Ahh" approvingly.

Toddlers are less talkative than Americans this age, although they are addressed frequently. Some are physically rambunctious, jumping and clambering on their parents or older siblings, but they're not generally as noisy or as tantrum-prone as American two-year-olds. Some toddlers are very reserved and can sit quietly with a bottle for an hour or two, just watching people around them. This quiet manner should not, as it should not in older children, be interpreted as "shyness"; many toddlers are rather relaxed about going to a child or adult they do not know.

By the age of four, children are much more independent of their mothers and instead associate primarily with siblings and other older children. At community events they play with age-mates. At a wedding or the New Year, it may be the little children that initiate the dancing as the band warms up. At one wedding, a two-year-old was trying to reach the crepe-paper streamers swagged above the dance floor. A four-year-old caught him just in time to prevent his tearing them down, then proceeded to leap and catch at them herself. Others joined in this game, and soon all the decorations were down, trailing after the children as they turned their attention to dancing. None of the three hundred or so adults present interfered. Toddlers are often left at church and elsewhere in the care of siblings. At the temple, toddlers and children play freely out of sight of their parents, in other rooms or outside; they are perfectly adequately cared for and not in the least danger. Like infants, toddlers are used to being carried and tended to by many. Years before Hillary Clinton's book, Cambodians frequently recited to me, "It takes a whole village to raise a child."[2] But such behavior is not accepted in, and perhaps not well suited to, American culture, and it causes worry among the American Sunday school teachers, who feel that children not watched by adults are in danger. The tots' willingness to be picked up by anyone probably increases the danger.

There is an accepting attitude toward child behavior that Americans would consider disruptive and unruly: a child swinging in circles around the podium from which the minister speaks, another trying to open a bottle of lotion he has rummaged from his mother's purse, another trying to pull his mother out of the pew, loudly shouting, "Mae, Mae, Mae!" Generally such a child is ignored or silently mollified, perhaps distracted by a sibling or adult.

Childhood

By the time children are of school age they spend most of their time with other children. They are seldom alone, and when they are, they are lonely. Although they are generally taken wherever their adults go—to weddings, meetings, church, the temple, parties, and ceremonies—and are always in proximity to adults, they are less often in direct interaction with adults. They play and eat separately yet are in and out and under foot enough to pick up correct behaviors. In such situations, their behavior around adults is circumspect and observant.

Despite having little direct adult supervision, children of this age are quite capable. Adults told me that in Cambodia a child of five would be able to build a fire and cook rice, tend cows, fetch water, and watch a baby. In Middle City, children of five spend most of their time playing or watching television, but by the age of ten they can cook a simple meal, go to the store on errands, calculate food stamps and change, interpret for doctors and nurses, and do a lot of childcare. They also can bring in a large tray of food in a crouching walk, kneel on both knees, and place it properly before a monk or other adults. A "good" child is helpful, cooperative, and obedient.

This is not to say that children don't have plenty of energy. Boys can be particularly rambunctious; at community events they play outside late into the night, sometimes with a football or soccer ball, climbing trees, often just running around; some girls join in this rough play, some play their own active games such as jump rope or tag, and others cluster at the fringes of the adults, dancing or watching. At home, both boys and girls play outside, choosing Cambodian playmates if possible. They also spend a lot of time watching television, playing videogames, and drawing.

Despite the apparent freedom little girls have, they're eager to grow up, intensely curious and awe-filled toward sisters and friends on the brink of adulthood. A favorite subject in drawings, the only subject for some of them, is glamorous, long-haired women with long dresses and wasp waists. They talk about weddings and delight in dressing up, eagerly pointing out new earrings or new shoes.

As with younger children, there is considerable tolerance for minor misbehavior. Pholla says she worries that her five-year-old threatens bigger kids; she tells him he is too smart to act like that, but she doesn't really interfere. When her children are playing noisily in the living room during our interviews, she tells them to play in the back room, which they do, not instantly but neither with fuss. They return frequently, to be whooshed out again with a sweep of the arm and a grin. When the toddler cries, Pholla says with sympathy, "Meng made you cry?" and scoops the child into her lap but says nothing to Meng. When they are playing outdoors in the snow and ice barefoot and bare-handed, she grins and speaks to them in a mock-shocked tone; they get on shoes, but not gloves or socks. Children under ten also frequently interrupt adults, who may ignore them. Ebihara points out that although there is considerable tolerance for defiance and unruliness in small children, as children enter adolescence they become more docile, more respectful, and more responsive to family needs (1971:116). Though this seems contrary to the American pattern of increasing defiance and disrespect toward and during adolescence, it certainly was the pattern I observed constantly among Cambodians in Middle City.

There also seems to be respect for the opinions of school-age children, and a great deal of trust is placed upon them. Heng took her second grade son out of school to help his older brother make funeral arrangements. The two made a decision (not to do an autopsy) counter to the one she had already made. Children come home from school and cook themselves a snack and settle themselves right in to do homework without parental prompting; they seem to go to bed when and where they please and dress as they please. In general, they have more freedom of small decision making than American children, but also more responsibilities and more elders (mainly slightly older siblings) around to check them if they do behave improperly. Some of this reliance on young children is necessitated by the parents' not knowing the rules of American culture and not speaking or reading English and so guessing, often rightly, that the children's judgment may be better than their own (about clothes, for example). Problems develop, though, when children decide that notes from school are not important enough to translate to their parents, or when eight-year-olds pack nothing but hairspray and party shoes for a week at summer camp. The American teachers feel the children get neither enough supervision nor enough support at home.

Perhaps because they are somewhat free of adult supervision in their home life, school-age children do not take particularly well to supervision from American adults. Although they're considered well-behaved in school, they tend to look more to the teenagers to tell them what to do and to keep them in line. They "do well" in Sunday school because they like what's going on and find the activities fun, but they converse constantly among themselves in Khmer and ignore the teacher if they can figure out what to do on their own. In the American church service they chatter quietly but constantly, sing or hum softly (not hymns), draw, and play pocket games among themselves. When they get too noisy, the Americans are helpless to shush them; this may be because they do not really comprehend the idea of being quiet in church, since Cambodian adults also talk in normal tones in church and at the temple.

Adolescence

Often in early or middle adolescence boys become even more rowdy and more removed from community activities. They are awkward and embarrassed in school, tease one another, and tend to hang around in gangs (their word—I would say groups). The girls at this age, meanwhile, are becoming more demure and, if possible, even more responsible. The tomboyishness of some ceases, and attention to hair, makeup, jewelry, and clothes increases. Becoming closer to their mothers and other adult women, they seem to enter a kind of sisterhood with all adult women. They participate more fully in traditional ceremonial and communal life by joining the women in cooking, sewing, serving, and other preparations. They are also more involved in the activities run by the American church: helping in the nursery, supervising the little ones, participating in the pageants, serving snacks, and so on. Boys begin joining more in the community life at about eighteen or twenty, serving and clearing away food, driving, running videocameras, and helping with other electronic equipment.

Dating is a sore point for teenagers. Many of the girls feel unfairly restricted by their parents; others believe dating is wrong and gossip about girls they think have boyfriends and are thus, by definition, not virgins. The association between dating and loss of virginity is strong. A young woman explained her wedding guest list: "Some of my friends I wanted to invite, but they have boyfriends; it's bad luck to have a non-virgin at a wedding." Boys, particularly, are considered incapable of controlling their "passion"; girls' passion is considered less strong, but adults believe they are lured into sexual activity by the public flaunting of sexual behavior among American teens and on television. Sexual impropriety is always blamed on the girl, not on the boy.

Some have boyfriends or girlfriends whom they see at school or work, at communal ceremonies, at friends' homes, or in public places such as shopping malls and restaurants. But the official policy is that a boy comes to meet a girl's parents first and asks permission to visit her in the home. Eventually they may be allowed to go "out," depending on the particular parents, but the idea is definitely that they are considering one another for marriage, not just going out to have a good time. There is some conflict here between American and Cambodian ideas of "going out." Ann, who teaches the teenagers' Sunday school classs, tells them that when she was a girl, she was allowed to date (they gasp and grin) but that her mother insisted that she go out with several boys alternately, rather than have a steady boyfriend, in order to prevent her becoming "too serious" at too young an age. The girls giggle and feign shock; it is indeed in complete conflict with what their parents think appropriate for them.

The pressure to find a marriage partner is not overt, as parents tend not to be particularly directive about any of their children's affairs, but covertly it is strong.

Preparations for an engagement and wedding are extensive, lavish, and expensive, and focus a great deal of attention on the girl. The financial sacrifices, though substantial, are met by the family with goodwill. Little girls watch closely as the clothes and other regalia are made or rented, gold and diamonds are purchased, the house is rearranged, guests move in, preparatory ceremonies are held, vast quantities of food are purchased and cooked, bands are hired, halls are decorated, and the other teenage girls whisper and giggle in huddles. In addition to the glamour and grandeur, they see the future bride becoming even closer to her mother and older sisters and sisters-in-law, as this sorority of adult women opens its doors for the new princess. Further, frequently a new young man enters the household, bringing gifts and help to the mother and welcome attention to the little children. All of these highly visible attributes make marriage a very attractive project to the little girls.

Young Adults

Young adult refugees, from about twenty to forty, are the generation most caught in the frontier between cultures, the generation most likely to have a little English and also to remember life in their own country. Old enough to have been enculturated into the values and expectations of Cambodian culture, they find themselves adults in a new land, carrying the full responsibility of their family but without all the family support that tradition prepared them to expect. They must care for their aging parents and grandparents as well as their own children, yet they haven't the siblings, aunts, uncles, and cousins, nor the monks, that traditional life would have provided them as helpmates in difficult times.

Instead, they find themselves in workplaces filled with age-mate Americans who may occasionally have similar problems, but who have been raised and schooled to independent decision making and who of course also have the requisite language, urban, and job skills. Middle City, in contrast to many American cities, is a city of multigenerational residents, so that most young adults do in fact have adult siblings, parents, and other relatives to turn to in times of need. Most Cambodian adults over about thirty, on the other hand, have no older generation. They speak minimal English and have had little schooling, either in Cambodia or in the United States. They can get jobs, and most do; despite the barriers, many have several jobs. They do not seek materially better lives for themselves but struggle with harsh living conditions and monotonous jobs for the sake of their children, whom they sometimes nervously consider to be Americans. They watch the teenagers pick up English and American ways, knowing that they themselves have no real access to that life.

Middle Age

The generation of adults age forty to sixty in 1995 was age twenty to forty in 1975, at the Khmer Rouge takeover, and so spent their youthful, productive years in slavery; it is this generation, particularly, that has so few men. Traditionally, by the time their childbearing years were over, Cambodian women had enough children and sons-in-law to insure that much of the heavy farm and household labor was taken care of by those younger and stronger. In Middle City they may have as many children, but children old enough to be helpful are gone all day at school, and adult children are gone to work or may move out completely. Nevertheless, the young do contribute labor and income to the maintenance of the household, and some middle-aged women find themselves in supervisory positions. A few have jobs, but that does not seem to be required of them, and most speak very little English. Both men and women of this age are respected and are sought for advice and ceremonial leadership; they have not, however, taken more visible roles of political leadership, such as organizing any kind of Cambodian association, temple, or newsletter.

The Elderly

I have noted the high value of both relative age and absolute age. Accordingly, very old people receive a great deal of love and attention as well as respect and deference; in turn, they are the source of much pleasure, having time and patience to devote to small children that other adults may not have. Since elderly parents often live in the house with a married daughter, or children may go to live with a grandparent to tend to the elder's increasing needs, children may become quite devoted and attached to grandparents from an early age.

But in Middle City, many elderly are lonely and unhappy. In addition to the physical stresses of aging, they have no one to talk to and little to do; nothing in their environment is familiar to them. With younger adults off at work, the very old can become an additional burden on the teenagers, who may feel the distress of their grandparents deeply. Old men and women are less likely than any other age group to wear American-style clothes, speak English, or have much mobility. Although they are regarded solicitously as individuals and as a class and are treated with much care and respect publicly, their role in a transitional culture is difficult. They may be much loved by their grandchildren and have considerable responsibility for their care, but as children approach adolescence they begin to find their grandparents' ways too old-fashioned and even incomprehensible.

Unable to drive and afraid to take buses, many elderly spend their days indoors in lonely apartments. Although the younger generations drive their elders when they can, the young are often extremely busy and are beginning to see jobs and school as having higher priority than catering to grandparents. The elderly are sometimes brought to the communal events by their children, but they have few other opportunities to meet with their friends. They are happiest at the temple, where they are surrounded by familiar sights, sounds, and smells, where they can dress and live according to their customs, and where their traditional knowledge brings respect and authority. But the temple, several hours away, is too far for families to go often; some never go. Although the elders are still very much beloved, it is easy to foresee that their role in the future may become devalued and more marginal. Physically removed from the younger generations by schools, housing, and lack of transportation, the elderly are becoming isolated even from their own people; psychologically removed from Americans by linguistic, religious, and other cultural differences, they will never be part of American social life.

Individual characteristics of age and gender direct everyone's behavior and interaction and appear to an outsider, along with kinship, to be the only forms of social organization. But major communitywide events do occur with some regularity and frequency, and many Cambodians interact with one another on an informal daily basis.

COMMUNITY ORGANIZATION

[She] is a real community leader. Not the kind we would choose—she has babies every year and just stays around the house being a mother. But she's a loving mother, and the community respects that.

—American, seeking community leaders

No, I can't do it. I can help, but I can't be president or vice president. I'm too young. Have to find somebody the community will respect.

—young man, on the suggestion that he begin a community association

Community Relations

Relationships among Cambodians in Middle City are outwardly friendly and supportive. Many live in neighborhoods where there are clusters of Cambodian families along a single block or in a single building. This originated because these were neighborhoods where sponsoring agencies could initially find affordable housing. At the very beginning, some new families were simply moved in (by sponsorship of the short-lived assistance association) with other families, sometimes one family to a room, and spent some time being shunted from apartment to apartment.

Some families have moved away from these clusters. One reason is to buy single-family homes—there is a great desire for home ownership. But another, more subtly expressed reason is to move away from the community and to move the children out of ESL classes and into better schools. The out-moving has been possible particularly for families who manage to keep two or more adults regularly employed because of job or language skills, and it is particularly desired by families whose language skills result in constant community demands on their time. Even those who move out look after their "people," often making sure that the apartment they move from goes to another Cambodian, offering assistance in times of illness or death, and attending the parties and events held by people in the city. On the other hand, many people report jealousy, always on the part of others, when one family manages to move to a better neighborhood, buys a house or car, or appears to have been helped directly by the church.

Community Organization

The absence of a Cambodian MAA in Middle City is a source of frustration for the Americans who work with them and for some of the Cambodians as well. The first Cambodian family, which had entered the United States a few years before the large migration in 1981, established an MAA that functioned for a few years, sponsoring some families and helping them by finding temporary housing, food, and other necessities. There was a director with an office, a typewriter, and a few grants, but the workload was immense. Hostilities developed between the leadership and other members of the community, with widespread rumors of favoritism and misappropriation of funds. Ann said, "They just hated him [the director], and she [his wife]was working herself to death."

The Association had unofficially disbanded by the time my research began in the spring of 1987. I often heard people say, "We need to get together," "We need a newsletter," "We need an organization," but nothing happened. Ann was asked to get the Association going again, to make a newsletter, or to start *something*, but she felt it was not her place to do so alone. She obtained a few small grants on their behalf but could not engage Cambodians to carry out the projects with her. I, too, made efforts to find some small grants but, like Ann, was unable to engage interest among the Cambodians themselves. There was no direct sentiment against these projects, but neither was there the level of motivation necessary to carry them out.

There are various possible explanations for this lack of an association. Particular individuals, when asked why they didn't take the initiative, said, "I'm too young, they wouldn't follow me," or "He could do it, but he would want to be paid," or "People take sides." The few Cambodians working with public agencies fear that leading the Association would put them in conflict with their jobs—that people would expect favors and blame them when things didn't work out (this occurs anyway). Americans working with the Cambodians in Middle City have other explanations for the lack of a community organization, such as individual personalities, lack of money, overwork, general laziness, and the experiences under Pol Pot: "There is really no way to make peace among these people who have known so little peace." It also may be that there are few people with leadership experience in Middle City, since it was the educated and the leaders who suffered most under the Khmer Rouge; it is also true that those with leadership and other practical skills feel themselves already overburdened with the informal demands made upon them by their compatriots. In addition, the personal qualities necessary for organizational development in the United States—assertiveness, self-confidence—are not qualities highly valued by Theravada Buddhism or by Cambodians in general. It is inappropriate to put oneself forward as leader, and so those who might do so, who have skills useful to such an organization, are held back by their own values of propriety and also by the certainty that if they did step forward they would lose respect in the community and become the focus of criticism and gossip.[3]

On the other hand, Cambodian communities in many other cities in the United States, even some with similarly small numbers, have established formal organizations, sometimes associated with a temple, sometimes not, which provide many services (North and Sok 1989). Some of these organizations have expanded to assist other refugee groups, and some have folded. The absence of a formal association in Middle City was received with surprise and concern by Cambodian leaders I met in other cities, who felt that an MAA is critical for the well-being of refugees. Although I passed along their offers of assistance, nothing ever came of the offers.

The lack of a community political structure should not be completely surprising. Ebihara found little in Village Svay that she or we would describe as community government: "Social bonds among the community's residents are diverse and relatively unstructured. There are no well-defined groups beyond the family and household, no clear-cut social stratification, and no rigid norms dictating interaction" (1971:92). Villages and hamlets had no chiefs or councils; rather, kinship and other ascribed statuses patterned social interaction and community action. This is just as I found the community behavior in Middle City, and to have found otherwise would have surprised me. On the contrary, the well-organized MAAs in other cities are the surprise, and the very existence of such organizations suggests a fairly significant culture change, the acceptance of a Western cultural pattern that has not yet been, or perhaps will not be, adopted by Cambodians in Middle City.

There is not really an absolute lack of leadership. The New Year party occurs with regularity: the same place, same time, same food, same program. Everything seems to be in order: the announcements get out, a hall and band are hired, the tickets are sold, the food is plentiful, the videocameras run. When a leader for a ceremony is needed, or a translator, or a surrogate parent, someone appears to fill these roles. For some other needs, the schools, the Agency, the church, sponsors, and Ann served for ten years. But now, in 1995, the Agency has newer refugees to worry about, the church has dismantled its refugee ministry, sponsors have long since tired of the relationship, and Ann's position has been terminated. How these changes will affect the Cambodians remains to be seen.

SOCIAL CLASS

The Cambodian political culture developed from a system descended from Hinduized kingdoms; equal access to wealth or authority was not sought nor even perceived as an available social value. Wealth, power, education, and other rewards were distributed unequally without question, according to birth, family, religion, and other ascribed ties. Aside from immediate and slightly extended families, the other primary relationship was between patron and client.

In traditional Cambodia, a patron was someone who had more land or money than others and lent money or gave assistance to them when possible. It was God's incontestable decision who would be patron and who client, and it was the patron's God-given duty to lead and to some extent provide for the client and the client's family, receiving, in return, respect, deference, loyalty, and occasional labor. In thus "doing good," both groups received religious merit for the next life. Since the elite, the patron class, were the very people most often killed by the Khmer Rouge, most of the Cambodians today in Middle City are those whose role and socialization has been for centuries that of client.

Patronage as a system may be in a situation of flux among Cambodians in Middle City. Those few who were urbanized in Cambodia no longer have wealth to distribute, but they have useful advice in their greater knowledge of English and of Western socioeconomic systems (hospitals, welfare, taxes, legal matters, getting loans, etc.). Several of these people act as unpaid translators and cultural mediators, but they resent it—they get called at all hours of the night and weekend to come to the hospital or to give legal or other advice. They, too, have difficult lives in the United States and have suffered great losses in status; this unofficial social work puts additional strain on their own lives.

Americans know these socioeconomic systems even better, and for ten years Ann devoted most of her time to this kind of assistance, as a sort of "superpatron." Many Cambodians turned to her rather than to other Cambodians. They also tried to use the sponsorship system as a system of patronage, but American sponsors and sponsoring institutions have different ideas. The Americans have come to believe that as long as they are willing to act the role of patrons, the Cambodians will continue to depend on them, and thus the Americans have begun to withdraw their support. The stance taken by the Agency, the church, and most other Americans is that withdrawal of patron-like assistance will automatically result in the development of leadership qualities and roles in the current culture, although the circumstances of the Cambodian community do not seem to have improved since this withdrawal began.

Other indicators of social class also exist. Giving large sums of money, particularly at religious events and weddings, where the amount is clearly written on the envelope and recorded in a book or announced over a loudspeaker, still brings prestige in the community. But American culture offers alternative ways of gaining prestige, such as appliances, houses, jobs, cars, and college educations for one's children. It is possible that those who attend Christian religious services and those who are never able to go to the temple may lose track of the Buddhist concern to seek merit for the next life and that reliance on American institutions and individual jobs may replace the system of patronage.

Social class is a topic little discussed in conjunction with refugees in the United States, perhaps partly because much research has focused on the enormous immediate needs rather than on more generalized culture patterns. Another reason may be that almost all Cambodians arrived here desperately poor, and it was difficult for Americans to detect subtle differences of status within that overall general poverty. Finally, assertions or even accidental slips hinting at class privilege were punishable by death under the Khmer Rouge, so people may have consciously and unconsciously buried their class identity. Thus those who had been middle class and lived in Phnom Penh—those few who managed to survive—are cautious about conveying a sense of privilege or superiority and feel that they'll be criticized or resented if they assume roles of authority. There is even a third class, a more privileged and infinitely more lucky class in many U.S. cities: that small elite group who happened to be out of Cambodia, either in the United States or elsewhere, in April of 1975, missed Pol Pot, and are thus not technically refugees. In Middle City, people speak critically, suspiciously, or scornfully of such Cambodians (in other cities) and feel they cannot empathize with the refugees and therefore can neither represent nor be fair with them.

It is possible that as social class distinctions begin to more sharply delineate, older forms of patron-clientship will reassert themselves, either wholly or with adaptations. At the moment, American efforts to foster the development of some sort of organization, or to discover "leadership" within the Cambodian community, seem to be at a stalemate.

SOCIAL RELATIONS IN A NEW SETTING

Although kinship appears to dominate social organization, social action, and social relationships as it did in the traditional Cambodia of Ebihara's fieldwork, other elements of social structure also figure into the daily lives of the Cambodians in Middle City. Of the types of patterns discussed in this chapter—gender, age, community, and class—my observations of behavior and informant comments lead me to believe that age, particularly relative age, is the most salient factor guiding everyday behavior. Terms of address, greetings and other speech patterns, obedience, gestures of respect, and general demeanor are guided by relative age. The relationship of older to younger is not authoritarian but one of tenderness and concern for the welfare of younger siblings and children in general. Reciprocally, young people owe respect, deference, and obedience to their elders. Failure to show such a respectful attitude will not necessarily be overtly scolded or punished, but will be the subject of community gossip and criticism. Little children are somewhat less obedient than older children and teenagers, so that the development of an obedient and respectful nature indicates the achievement of maturity, wisdom, and self-control, thus entitling one to respect from others. The egalitarian nature of this age-based system reflects Buddhist ideology described in the next chapter.

At the same time, gender and community are not to be ignored as factors guiding social behavior. Gender relations may indeed still demonstrate that "happy balance" Ebihara described a generation ago. On the surface, boys and girls play together, men and women converse and work together easily, and old people chat and tease and laugh and argue across gender lines. As in traditional Cambodia, many tasks are gender specific, but not rigidly so.

This gender balance may merely represent the retention of traditional attitudes, or the independence of women may have increased as a consequence of enslavement, the loss of husbands, and the trauma of flight. Many women were on their own in those situations and had to cope or die. The loss of men has continued in this country, where young men have died of SUDS. Consequently, women have had to do things on their own—such as buy houses, learn to drive, and get factory jobs—that they might not have done in Cambodia. The first house purchase in Middle City was by a woman, the original leader of the MAA was a woman, and women seem to have similar employment to men. Women's religious roles are different from men's, but equally important and public. I do not think the independence or strength of women can be attributed to the positive influence of American culture, as many Americans believe.

What is not so clear is whether this gender balance traditional to Cambodians, and readily apparent in their new culture as refugees, will be maintained as they learn American culture. It is too soon to predict, but we might speculate by examining gender roles in the American institutions through which the refugees are learning American culture. It is instructive here to note that, although many of the Americans who work with Cambodians are women, they are often volunteers or semivolunteers; those who are paid tend to be in temporary, low-paid, or part-time positions.

Patron-client relationships and social class would be useful areas for further study. Ebihara's discussion of patronage is brief, but it is such a common pattern throughout the Third World that it would seem important to understand it, particularly as it functions in resettled refugee communities. Possibly such relationships could be intentionally encouraged in order to ease adjustment in new refugee communities. Social class is another fertile topic for future research. Longitudinal research may reveal whether clear social classes develop, whether these replicate formerly held positions, and to what extent Cambodians enter or remain outside of the "American" class system. Recent (Mortland 1993; Van Arsdale 1987, 1993) and future research on MAAs may help us understand what factors lead to the development of helpful MAAs, to what extent a refugee community's eventual satisfaction depends upon the presence of an MAA, and to what extent temples or religious organizations differ from MAAs in meeting the needs of refugees and refugee communities.

NOTES

1. That is, they are so encouraged until the parents become concerned about the risk of pregnancy or gossip.

2. I realize that this is also "an old Chinese proverb," "an old African proverb," etc. Nevertheless, it is recited with ownership by Cambodians, who say, "At home we always say . . . , " and the sentiment holds true in Middle City.

3. For a similar situation, see Longmire's (1992) script of an interview in which the Cambodian applicant is, to an American's eyes, so perplexingly self-effacing as to seem uninterested in, or possibly incapable of, the job.

Chapter 5

Ideology: Traditional Values in a New Setting

Ideology may be the most difficult element of culture for outsiders to study. Less observable than technology and social organization, it is also not easily verbalized by the members of a culture. Active or tangible manifestations of ideology, such as rituals and ritual objects, may be kept from the anthropologist's view or may be difficult to interpret; interview data is often incomplete or contradictory. Nevertheless, human behavior, particularly in situations of culture change, can often be understood only in terms of deeply held values; in turn, behavior often gives clues to cultural values. The arts, as social behavior, are particularly affecting and effective means of communicating cultural values. Rituals and religious celebrations, as multimedia aesthetic events, are important means of illustrating religious history and reinforcing religious and other values. In the Cambodian community in Middle City, the most significant traditional art forms are integral to religious ceremonies, and all ceremonies are lavishly infused with art of many forms. This chapter discusses Buddhism, traditional ceremonies, and several art forms as they embody and convey Cambodian traditional and changing values.

Cambodians often speak of being a "good person," want their children to become "good people," and admit that "some Cambodians are not good people." Ebihara lists the characteristics of being a good person: "generosity and selfless concern for others; warmth and good natured temperament; abhorrence of fighting, drinking, fornication, and other sins; devotion to family; industriousness; religious devotion; and honesty" (1971:197). All of these traits are apparent in either the behavior or the expressed beliefs of the Cambodians in Middle City, and their importance is apparent in comments expressed about others. Themes of selflessness, calm, cooperation, industriousness, cheerfulness, and devotion to family appeared repeatedly in my fieldnotes.

BUDDHISM

> There is no aspect of a person's life . . . which is not affected by Buddhism. . . .
> Buddhism is the heart and mind of the people of Cambodia.
>
> —Welty (1966:296)

Most Cambodians in Middle City are Buddhists, although a few have been Christians since childhood or converted in refugee camps or in the United States. Cambodians practice Theravada Buddhism, which entered Cambodia about the thirteenth century (Welty 1970:292) and introduced a more egalitarian and individual-centered value system than the Hindu-derived religion they had earlier practiced (Ebihara 1966; Steinberg 1959). Theravada Buddhism emphasizes spiritual purification (and thus a better future life) through individual good behavior and meritorious deeds and thus is a significant source of personal values. The official religion of Cambodia, it is practiced by 85 percent of Khmer, is embedded in the national law of Cambodia, and creates an underlying normative code which permeates everyday life and thought (Ebihara 1966:175). Although Ebihara found that most ordinary villagers knew little of the complexities of Buddhism, everyone learned the fundamentals by attending temple services and from hearing and memorizing chants. The basic principle understood by everyone is that a person earns merit toward a better life by being good, by avoiding evil, and by performing specific meritorious acts—usually giving money or gifts to the wat.

The five major precepts defining "good" behavior for ordinary people are to avoid lying, immoral sexual relations, stealing, killing, and drinking alcohol. Ebihara found these precepts followed to varying degrees by the villagers, and so they are in Middle City. Small lies and the avoidance of the whole truth are pretty common, at least toward Americans, officials, and parents; much of this is what we might call "white lies"—for example, giving me information people thought I wanted or giving school officials information the officials know is false anyway (such as age, relationship, etc.). Teenagers avoid the whole truth with their parents, too; doing so may be traditional—the shame of the truth being worse than the lie—or may have further developed in the United States because of generational disagreements concerning teenage behavior. For example, girls typically deny having boyfriends, but teenage pregnancy is not uncommon. The other three main precepts are also followed variously. Theft is rare among the Cambodians in Middle City, and I know of no incident of murder, nor of anyone killing animals (insects, fish, and other small animals are exempt). Most Cambodian men and many women drink beer and occasionally other liquor (cognac, but also vodka as medicine), but public drunkenness is rare and invites public scorn—again, quite as it did in Village Svay thirty-five years ago.

Five further precepts are followed only "by the most devout" (Ebihara 1966:178) in Cambodia and not at all or only by the elderly in Middle City. These include not eating after noon (to my knowledge, only monks observe this or sometimes the elderly on especially holy days), not wearing cosmetics or jewelry, not sleeping on raised beds, not dancing, and avoiding intercourse on holy days. Indeed, the elderly women in Middle City wear little makeup or jewelry; some dance and some do not; a very few prefer to sleep on the floor rather than on a raised bed; most are widows.

Traditionally, Buddhism played a practical role in everyday life as well. The wat contained, in addition to the temple itself, a library, bathhouses, a crematorium, and a school. It was a place where people could come on a daily basis for advice or to share news and visit with friends, travelers could find safe haven, and the elderly could stay for extended periods—indeed "the educational and social center of the community" (Welty 1970:293). Middle City has no wat, and although the Cambodians travel to the one in Riverside on special occasions, there really is no comparable gathering place or haven nearby. I see this as one of the most serious problems facing the community.

Monks are very important in traditional society. They officiate at the community religious festivals such as New Year, Phchum, and Kathen and also at personal and family rituals such as weddings, funerals, and One Hundred Days ceremonies (memorial services held approximately one hundred days after a death). They are called to the home when a person is ill or dying and may be sought for advice and assistance in other difficult situations, such as marital problems or a spate of bad luck. Special etiquette is required toward monks, such as using special language, and approaching, bowing, sitting, and handing them objects in a specific and deferential manner. This too is considered "good" (meritorious) behavior. Men or boys may enter the wat for a few years, receiving some formal education, serving the monks, and bringing merit to themselves and their parents. Young men in Middle City are not making this choice. Women don't become monks but play prominent roles in the temple ceremonies and spend a great deal of time in preparations for them, acts which also bring merit. Elderly women devote increasingly more of their time to such religious tasks and occasionally move into the wat as nuns.[1]

Initially, I thought the preponderance of the elderly at the ceremonies was an indication that the religion might be waning or that uniquely American demands on the time of younger adults precluded their participation. But Ebihara describes the same conditions for village life in 1960: the youth, particularly the men, had too many other responsibilities that kept them from participating either personally or through monetary donations. It was the elderly, freed from the daily exigencies of field labor and childcare and perhaps feeling closer to "the final tallying of merit" (Ebihara1971:396), who could devote themselves more seriously to religious activity.

So it is in Middle City. The young participate to a lesser extent, and their participation is manifested by their efforts to transport the elderly to the wat in Riverside and their help in cooking, serving, and washing up rather than by participation in the rituals themselves. I initially interpreted this peripheral participation to the process of culture change. I asked young men, "Is anyone studying with the monks now?" and "Who will be the monks when these men get old?" They answered with shrugs: "This America now. Nobody want to do that. Got to go to school, get good job." I asked monks similar questions, and was told, matter-of-factly, without the least indication of concern, "No one. They need to go to school. In this country, you need college." Others said young men will come from the refugee communities or from Cambodia, yet I wonder. Ebihara noted that few young men were entering the monasteries in 1959 (none under twenty) and speculated that the young adults were being lured away from religion by secular education and consumer goods. Yet it is just those uninterested young adults from 1960 who have become today's middle-aged generation, supporting the wats in the United States.

The teenage boys in Middle City are indeed preoccupied with jobs and school, and their parents are busy trying to provide for large families in expensive and difficult circumstances. Only long-term study will reveal whether today's adults will continue to support the monks and today's youth eventually replenish their ranks, but it is premature to interpret low youth participation as an indication of flagging religious devotion, Americanization, a shift to Christianity, or even as indicative of culture change in general.

CEREMONIAL LIFE

If many Cambodians in Middle City have never been to the wat in Riverside, nearly everyone goes to community and family ceremonies held locally. People of all ages attend, often as many as four or five hundred at wedding and New Year parties and fifty to a hundred at the ceremonies held in homes. While some of these ceremonies have secular aspects to them and have adopted certain elements of Western culture, they remain primarily and intentionally traditional. Particularly in this refugee situation, even rituals ostensibly celebrating individuals' life events also function importantly as rites of intensification and thus are important mechanisms for the maintenance and transmission of traditional culture.

Rites of Passage

Rites of passage frequently celebrated by the Khmer of Middle City include birthday parties, particularly for one-year-olds; engagement or prewedding ceremonies; marriage ceremonies; wedding parties (comparable to our wedding receptions); thanksgiving ceremonies for the life of a parent; funerals; and One Hundred Days ceremonies. These range from being very secular—birthday parties and wedding parties—to quite religious—marriage ceremonies and One Hundred Days ceremonies.[2] Some seem almost completely American in form, such as a "white wedding," complete with white lace wedding dress, tuxedos, and tiered wedding cake, while others, such as the One Hundred Days ceremonies, appear to be almost exactly as they would be carried out in traditional Cambodia. Most are blends of traditional culture and American culture.

Birthday parties for firstborn one-year-olds may be held in the home or in a rented hall and may include a few or a hundred guests. There may be a band or taped music, but there is always a meal of traditional foods and often an American-style bakery birthday cake with candles. The birthday child is not a focus of attention, except for the moment when the cake is brought out and other gifts (money in envelopes) are handed up. The birthday child receives the cake with palms together and a somber expression. At one such occasion, silence accompanied the arrival of the cake, and I was nudged and told, *"Premarie!"* I put my hands together and waited expectantly for someone to lead a prayer, but soon realized they meant that task for me. "Me?" I squeaked, very embarrassed. "Yeah, pray happy birthday!" So I sang "Happy Birthday" to a hundred somber stares, which I later learned was exactly what had been requested.

Weddings may be very traditional or very American, and some people have both. Most typically, there is an attempt to have a wedding as close as possible to people's memories of traditional weddings. The traditional three days are telescoped into a day and a half (Friday evening and all Saturday), and sometimes even that is shortened to permit an American (Christian) church ceremony on Saturday afternoon. Every effort is made to include the many changes of elaborate costumes, traditional musicians, and several abundant meals of traditional food. The bride and groom's position is more difficult than the usual kneeling (actually sitting with feet tucked to one side): they kneel bent forward with elbows on the ground or on a silken cushion, palms together in front of the face—for hours; everyone acknowledges that this is extremely uncomfortable. The room is filled with ritual objects such as candles, incense, fruit, and beautiful arrangements of fresh flowers. The Friday evening and Saturday ceremonies have many separate ritual segments, such as gong-led processions, haircutting and shower ceremonies, a parade of gifts, the bride eating a banana and the groom grapes, the passing of candles, and many prayers and sermons to the young couple.

Traditionally a monk would perform most of the marriage rituals, with the help of an *achaa*, an assistant to the monk, but in Middle City almost all weddings are led by the achaa only. The parents, other adult friends, and a "sponsor" of a wedding are in charge. Since the traditional wedding does not include the signing of American documents, most Cambodian marriages performed in Middle City are not recognized by the state, although similar marriages performed outside the United States are recognized.

The omission of the marriage license is an interesting example of culture change and adaptation. The first arrivals may have been unaware of American marriage laws, although it would seem that American sponsors might have shed some light. Certainly by the time of my research, young Cambodians, at least, were well aware of the state requirements regarding marriage, and yet few couples actually legalized their marriages. To get a marriage license requires a fee, office visits, and a waiting period. The young people I spoke with believed that the marriages performed by monks and achaas were not legal whether the couple obtained a license or not. They may be right; not only must the couple have a license to get married, but the officiant must also be licensed. The young people I asked did not to feel that the monk had such a license.[3] So there are two hurdles to legal marriage: the problem of getting a license and the belief that a ceremony performed by a monk is not legal anyway.

But there's more to it. The young women have learned that their children will be entitled to Aid to Families with Dependent Children (AFDC) if they have Cambodian weddings, but not if they have American weddings. It's not that they plan to be on welfare or even want it. Most young women are working and intend to work even after they have children. But their lives have been unpredictable, and they know they are still very vulnerable; they prudently protect the possibility of AFDC should they need it. Most of them are not fully aware of the future advantages of legal marriage, such as inheritance, job-related health care policies, social security and retirement plans, and so forth.

A few couples have American-style church weddings in addition to or instead of traditional weddings. These are generally planned, organized, and carried out with the help of a minister and American members of the congregation and are considered by U.S. law to be "legal" marriages.

The wedding party, similar to an American wedding reception, is held the evening of the second day of the marriage ceremony. It is to this that the written invitations refer and for this that the greatest expenditures are made. There are always printed invitations (usually in Khmer and English); a rented hall; silk flowers pinned on guests as they arrive; decorations of crepe paper streamers, balloons, and flowers; tuxedos on the groom and groomsmen and elegant traditional gowns on the bride and bridesmaids; disposable table cloths, plates, spoons, and forks; a hired band with one or two singers; a multicourse meal including soup, many elaborate entrées, dessert, beer, and cognac; a ritual procession by the bride and groom and escorts to distribute cigarettes and to receive good wishes and gifts of money (which are in supplied envelopes and are placed in an ornately embossed silver bowl); and hours of dancing. This is perhaps the most expensive and extravagant event in the life of a Cambodian family. A wedding may cost $6,000 or $8,000, although much of that returns in the form of the cash gifts from the guests and the groom.

Adult children may hold a ceremony to honor their elderly parents when the parents become very ill, especially toward the end of life, "for their future, to open their way to heaven." In Middle City this ceremony is held in the home, with the floor cleared of furniture and covered with mats. The main part of the ceremony is prayer, led by the monk or the achaa, but other features include the presentation of money and gifts to the elderly parents, the placing of cooked rice in the monk's bowls, and the sharing of a communal meal. The gifts include things that the parents will need in their next life, such as food, clothes, and household goods. Physically, the gifts go home with the monks and the cash goes toward temple needs or may be designated for the monks' personal use. Over $1,000 may be collected in money and other goods, resulting in merit for the sponsors, the individual donors, and the elderly parents. These major investments should be called to mind when Americans say of the Cambodians that "they're not future oriented."

Funerals in Middle City have been partly American-style, with a church service led by an American minister and burial in a cemetery. Only a few elements of traditional funeral rites, such as the keening and the wearing of white, accompany this event. There are also several days of mourning rituals carried out by monks in the deceased's home, sometimes beginning before the actual death. A final death ceremony is held approximately a hundred days after a death, although in Middle City such a ceremony may be held much later, particularly if a parent died some time ago in Cambodia or Thailand. These are specifically Buddhist and very traditional ceremonies. They are held in the home of the deceased, are led by a monk or several monks, and involve many of the typical ritual elements such as incense, giving of cash, offerings of rice, much prayer, and ritual communal meals.[4]

Because the life crisis ceremonies are many and extensive, I have chosen only one example, shorter and simpler than most, to describe in detail. However, in this example we can see the blending of American and traditional culture as well as the blending of secular and religious elements.

Prewedding Ceremony

A prewedding ceremony formalizes what Americans would call an engagement, a definite plan to marry. Preparations begin weeks or months before the actual date. Though not as elaborate as weddings themselves, these are formal and expensive events. Preparations involve the purchase of food, ritual food gifts, and possibly special cookware and dishes; new clothes for the bride; the invitation of guests (this should be done in person, though it is now sometimes done by phone); the preparation and cooking of special foods; the removal of furniture and laying of mats for the ceremony; the preparation of speeches; and the purchase of rings and other jewelry.

The groom and his parents approach the bride's family regarding expenses, which are the responsibility of the groom and his family, and someone must query the groom about the seriousness of his intentions, counsel him regarding the responsibilities of marriage, and investigate him and his family background to make sure there will be no embarrassments.

The ceremony takes place in the home of the bride's parents and is attended by fifty or more close relatives and friends of all ages. The day and night before, the bride's mother, friends, and kinswomen, sometimes with the help of young men and children of the household, prepare many traditional foods, wash the dishes that will be used, wrap the ritual gifts, clear the room of furniture, and lay down special mats. Some of the guests, including the bride's close friends, stay all night.

On the day of the ceremony, friends and family gather in the house, the bride hidden in her room with her friends until the appointed time, children playing about, women continuing to cook, and the men and some women chatting. The groom and his friends (if his family and friends are from a great distance and cannot attend, some of the other guests will take this role) take up the ritual foods (mainly cognac and fruits wrapped in bright-colored cellophane) and line up with these outside. Guests are arranged in pairs without consideration of sex, age, or other status, but according to the color of the giftwrap, and parade into the house bearing the gifts, which they place at the men's side of the room in front of the groom.

The bride's group and the groom's group kneel facing each other on the mat-covered floor. Speeches are made by a lay leader about the importance and seriousness of marriage, and each family gives assurance that they really want to do this; after all, "the bride's family can't just take all this money and expense from the groom, then change their minds." If the groom's parents are unable to attend, the leader represents them, explaining their names and occupations, where they live, and why they cannot be present. Most of this part of the ceremony is addressed to the groom. Eventually the bride is led in by her friends to the striking of a gong and kneels before the leaders and the groom. She too is given words of counsel, and then the bride and groom exchanged large, many-gemmed gold rings. They then turn toward the bride's mother, making further pledges to her, and pass the gifts to her. As there are many gifts and space is limited, they are passed out of the room over heads. Later these gifts are opened and guests are given portions of the food to take home, the bride's mother saying, "Here, I have all these gifts, you take a little bit of my richness with you too." At the end of this formal part of the ceremony there is much picture taking (although the entire procedure has also been videotaped, with necessary pauses for the cameraman to move to better vantage points), people gather to chat indoors and out, and everyone shares in a bountiful meal of traditional foods.

Young people have been present during this entire event. They may accompany the adults in the shopping and participate in preparing the house and food; girls, particularly, help with cooking, washing dishes, and wrapping the ritual gifts. A few select young women (they must be virgins) play a role similar to our bridesmaids. Boys are more peripheral, but even if they are playing outdoors they witness the parade and are aware of the events. Children join in the traditional meal and often gather as the inevitable videotape is played later in the day.

These rites of passage serve important functions in addition to marking individual life crises. They are also occasions for communal gathering, for reaffirming leadership and other roles, for marking and publicly displaying the distinctive ethnic heritage, for conveying cultural values, and for the young to observe and practice traditional adult roles.

Rites of Intensification

Rites of intensification specifically celebrate and foster group solidarity and are thus an ideal context for the transmission of cultural values. *Col Cnam*, the New Year celebrated in mid-April, *Phchum ben*, the fall festival honoring the dead, and *Kathen*, a fall festival honoring the monks as they emerge from retreat, are perhaps the three most important traditional celebrations among Cambodians in Middle City. The following sections describe Kathen, a particularly traditional ceremony, and New Year, which, in its Middle City version, seems strikingly modern and secular.

Kathen

Kathen, one of the most important festivals of the Buddhist year, is an occasion to gain merit by donating food, clothing, money, and other ritual and practical items to the monks. Families who are able make the long trip to the wat in Riverside. Families and individuals from several cities sponsor the event by collecting donations from the Cambodians in their own cities.

Gifts include practical items such as bags of rice from Thailand, paper and cloth towels, bedding, cooking pots and utensils, ordinary umbrellas, canes, canned food, tea, and bottles of soda pop, presented in plain plastic or brown paper grocery bags. Ritual gifts may include large, embossed silver bowls of rice, candles, incense, silk flowers, and mats. There are three particularly notable gifts: money trees, orange silk for monks' robes, and ceremonial umbrellas. The money trees are made of wire and decorated with silk flowers and crisp new paper money intricately folded into flowers and other fanciful designs and anchored with florist's wire. The amount of money may not be large, as the denominations are $1, $5, and perhaps $10 bills, but the trees are accorded an honorable place in the parade and on the pile of gifts. The packages of silk for the monk's robes, one for each monk, are presented in their rectangular cellophane wrappers; each has an ornately beaded and sequined felt cover and rests on a heavily embossed silver bowl. The ceremonial umbrellas are about three feet in diameter, have red and gold patterned tops, several layers of edging in bright colors (blue, gold, green, and red), white ball fringe at each layer, scalloped edges, golden spires, and red poles. The entire collection of gifts is placed before the monks in a festive pile about eight by four feet across and two to three feet high.

Money is also an important gift. At one Kathen, $5,000 in cash was collected in addition to the other gifts. Sponsors of the event, usually elderly women, each pledge a certain amount, perhaps $1,000, in addition to other specific gifts. They collect some of this from friends and kin, but what they are unable to gather they will make up themselves. Smaller amounts of money are donated by other individuals and families and are announced over the loudspeaker. This money goes partly to support the daily life at the temple and partly toward a fund to build a larger and more permanent temple.

The temple in Riverside is located in a semirural area with an ample yard for parking and play. The house where the monks live is a modest American ranch-style house. The temple itself, not visible from the street, is a large, low, open-sided, concrete-block pavilion; the open walls are covered with plastic in winter. The architecture of this building, the interior decor, and the use of space are very different from American patterns. For example, the dais upon which the monks sit, the table upon which the gifts are placed, and the altar are all very low, meant to be used or viewed by people seated on the floor. The floor seating allows for greater numbers of participants and also for flexibility of seating arrangement, as people shift, for example, from facing the monks to small circles for eating.

The social dimension of the event mustn't be overlooked. Before the actual ceremony, many adults stand outside talking. Some women are in the house cooking, and some are in the temple itself with the monks or in the anterooms. Other participants, particularly women, the elderly, and a few small children, gather within the temple, kneeling on the mats, chatting to friends and catching up on community news. As the space fills, women lean comfortably on one another, shoulder to shoulder, knee to knee, with toddlers and babies clambering or napping across laps. Five men with microphones sit at a long table collecting and tallying donations of money; they maintain a running commentary, announcing each gift over the loudspeaker, stating the name of the donor, the amount, and the donor's city. Children, from toddlers to teens, are in the parking lot and yard, running, playing ball and jump rope, climbing trees, and talking with their friends. They speak a mixture of Khmer and English and play both American and Cambodian games; most wear playclothes, but a few girls are in very frilly dresses.

Several women and girls supervise the serving of rice into small bowls. Each participant takes a bowl of rice and a spoon to a side table upon which are five large silver bowls of rice, and spoons rice into each of the silver bowls, bowing at each and offering a silent prayer for good fortune in the next life for one's parents, for the monks, and for oneself. This is not an esoteric afterlife such as Heaven, but the next, real, live life. Each of the five bowls is for one of the monks; as the monks consume the rice, the prayers go to the ancestors.

About an hour before noon, praying begins, led by the monks and the achaa, using microphones. The congregation kneels, palms together, and chants aloud with the monks or responsively, with triple bows marking especially important moments. Toward the end of the prayers, large round trays of food are brought in and placed before the monks, who must eat before noon. When the monks have eaten, young men and women bring out more trays of food and large bottles of soda pop. People rearrange themselves into circles of six to ten, spoon rice onto individual plates, and dip into the communal serving bowls. Children and men appear from everywhere, but some children also eat in an adjacent open room.

When everyone has eaten, the young people gather the dishes and leftovers. The young men carry out huge trays of bowls and kettles full of dishes; women and teenage girls wash the huge kettles and the dishes in the yard with hoses. Younger children return to their play, and men to their outdoor conversations.

When the remains of the meal are cleared away, the parade of the gifts begins. The sponsors of the ceremony, in this case all elderly women, head outdoors, they and their daughters or other female relatives each carrying an umbrella, one of the bowls with an ornately packaged robe, or another ornately packaged gift. The bowls are carried on the head, with a shirt or sweater as a cushion, and are occasionally shifted from one head to another with much gaiety and fuss. Other women carry other gifts—a money tree, a bag of groceries, flowers—and everyone parades around the parking lot several times in a wide clockwise circle (social dance is always counter-clockwise). Traditional ceremonial music plays from a loudspeaker, young men busy themselves with cameras and videocameras, and children watch at the fringe in awe. This is a proud and colorful occasion, and as the parade ends there is much grinning, joking, posing, taking of photographs, laughter. The air is festive and a bit relieved, much like the gathering outside a church after an American wedding.

Finally the congregation returns into the temple, and the five sponsors are seated together opposite the five monks, who now are at the altar. There is praying and discussion about what to do next. They are following a book, but there is still a bit of confusion about the proper sequence of events. Eventually each monk is presented a packaged robe by one of the five sponsors. He prays his thanks and opens it, stroking it appreciatively. After more prayers and speeches, the money trees are dismantled and the bills put in envelopes stating the name of the town and the amount of money.

By midafternoon the children are restless and the adults tired. Many have arrived the day before and stayed, not sleeping well, at the temple overnight. Others have left home early in the morning and have a long drive home. The dishes are washed, women change into slacks for the drive home, children are gathered up, and families head home; the elderly sometimes go home with kin or friends from another city to spend a few days or a week.

These gatherings at the temple serve many functions, some perhaps in addition to traditional ones. For some, they are clearly deeply serious religious events, serving to purify one's soul and to bring peace to one's ancestors. Some adults realize the important educational role of these visits in the lives of the children: "So they can be with other Cambodian kids, remember what it means to be Cambodian." Others are more cynical, disapproving of the specific way the monks run the temple and carry out their religious life: "It's depressing to see the monks doing things wrong. I'd rather go to a Christian church doing things right than a Buddhist temple doing it wrong." They may also disapprove the motives of those who attend: "Most Cambodians just go to show off their diamonds and their new clothes; they compete."

New Year

I've chosen the New Year as a third example of community celebration because it is the event I see as most changed from that which informants described as "traditional." As celebrated in Middle City, New Year is quite secular in tone and includes many more Western elements. The only event in the Buddhist calendar celebrated as a community in Middle City, it attracts most of the Cambodians in the area and occasional friends and relatives from out of town. Like wedding parties, it is held on Saturday night to ensure the greatest possible attendance. A more traditional celebration, with the appropriate prayers, games, and other festivities, is held at the temple in Riverside on a different weekend, and a few Middle City Cambodians attend that as well as the local party.

People arrive at the hall (a city recreation hall) about 8:00 P.M. and join friends and kin at long, bare tables. The tables fill as family and friends gather, and, since there are never enough seats, men gather in clusters around the edges, in a side room, at the entry, and out in the parking lot. Children come in and out, the more active staying outside for most of the evening, running around late into the night. Food is sold by the piece—eggrolls, meatsticks, individual servings of fried rice and spicy shredded cabbage, soft drinks, beer, small bags of chips, ice cream—but families sometimes bring food as well, to the annoyance of the organizers, who are trying to recover some of their costs through food sales. There is a band with a singer, and dancing begins at about 9:00, often initiated by the younger children. There is little formal agenda; eating, drinking, dancing, conversation when it can be managed over the music, and outdoor play by the children all go on simultaneously. The evening ends about midnight, families gathering up their sleeping babies and exhausted children. The entire evening has been videotaped by several families.

We see more evidence of American culture in this celebration of New Year than in the other ceremonies. The charging of a fee and the use of tickets is new; traditionally the event would have been held at a wat. Although some adult women wear traditional festive clothes, increasingly more are wearing American dresses and slacks; teenage girls and young women have come to dress almost entirely in American party dresses; men, boys, and children are dressed, as usual, entirely in Western style. The setting—the hall, the building, and the tables and chairs—are American. There is no attempt to decorate, so there is not the customary Cambodian profusion of color and flowers. Some of the food is traditional but some is American, and the eating is done Western style—at tables, on individual flat plates, with forks. The videotapers and the musicians use Western equipment.

Despite these innovations and despite the complete absence of reference to Buddhism, this remains nevertheless also a clearly Cambodian event. The main foods and the music are essentially Cambodian, the language spoken is Khmer, and the entire gathered participants are Cambodian (fewer than ten Americans out of four or five hundred people present). In fact, this event is an excellent example of the increasing cultural mosaic evident in the Cambodian community in Middle City. Food, clothing, dance, and music are actually varying blends of traditional Cambodian and contemporary American styles. Gender patterns remain typically Cambodian, similar to those seen at the more traditional and more religious events. There may be a difference in age behavior, however. Since participants purchase their own food at a window, the young people are not in their more traditional serving role but are busy dancing instead; the elderly, though treated kindly and respectfully, are not the focal point of attention as they are at the temple ceremonies. In fact, as I watched over the years, the elderly seemed to participate less and less, and the event has come to be increasingly dominated by (somewhat rowdy) teenagers. In recent years there have been fights, drunkenness, threats, and gangs from another city, causing many families and elders to leave early. The middle-aged and middle-class families that sponsor the event are disturbed by this turn and worry about the future. It's possible that the young men of the band could organize the event on their own, and families and elders might lose interest entirely. Secularized as this event already appears to be, loss of this most important Buddhist holiday of the year, the one celebration which brings the entire community together, could seriously threaten the maintenance of traditional social, religious, and aesthetic values.

Community Celebration and the Future

The ceremonies described in this section can be seen as forums for ethnic identity and group cohesion, maintaining and transmitting traditional culture. They also all have some elements of American culture and thus also serve as forums for gradual adoption of elements of American culture. The typical separation of the ages allows the children to communicate about American things and ideas (such as school and their current romances) while the elders derive status and comfort by practicing their religious traditions. At the moment, the simultaneous constant presence of all ages at these events means continual exposure of the young to the traditional customs and values of the elders, while the elders, momentarily released from the household, witness the youth, as a body, adopt American ways. There are mixed feelings in Middle City regarding the temple in Riverside. Many people don't attend, for varying reasons: it's too far, they don't like the monk, they feel a need to Christianize, they feel unwelcome among the Cambodians of Riverside (an attitude similar to the wariness felt between villages in rural Cambodia), or they feel a lack of seriousness in the atmosphere, a lack of ceremonial propriety; there is also a question of financial impropriety in the management of the temple. The absence of a temple in Middle City itself results in a decrease of community religious events and the secularization of those which remain; it may eventually result in an absolute reduction of community events and the erosion of ethnic solidarity.

ARTS AND AESTHETICS

Art shapes and is shaped by the cultural system which produced it, and thus is a unique record or trace or reflection of that system. Through their art, we can come to know other cultures in a special way. . . . [Art] objects are records of cultural process, and they provide *direct*, unmediated access to the values and experiences of their producers . . . direct testimony. They are not filtered through somebody else's consciousness (biases, preconceptions) as are data on social systems, for example. (Rubin 1989:12)

Although anthropologists are often loath to discuss aesthetics or even to describe art objects, an understanding of their arts is particularly important to understanding refugee culture because the arts provide one of the few means refugees have to express their traditional culture and to demonstrate to their children the richness of their heritage. Cambodians in particular have a rich history of the arts, and though much of their tangible art was destroyed and many artists killed during the Khmer Rouge regime, aesthetic interest and aesthetic values abound in the daily and ritual lives of the refugees. Arts thriving in the Middle City community include clothing and body adornment, textiles, interior house and temple decoration, the presentation of food, ritual drama and religious paraphernalia, classical and popular music and dance, and children's drawing.[5] Some of the artistic expression derives directly from the homeland, such as music tapes and textiles made in Cambodia; some is specifically American, such as the clothing of most teenagers and videotapes rented from American stores; much is a blend of Cambodian, American, and other cultures such as Chinese, Indian, and Thai (as, of course, classical Cambodian arts were cross-culturally influenced); and some may be developing during this period of exile. The following sections describe a few of the more readily observed and widely practiced arts.

Personal Adornment

Most people, women particularly, are highly conscious of clothing; they buy and rent expensive traditional garments of silk with gold threads and buy American clothes. Middle-aged and older women, some men, and young children often wear color, pattern, and texture combinations very different from choices made by Americans. For example, in wearing the traditional skirt and blouse, a woman might wear a bright pink lace blouse with a burgundy and yellow ikat-patterned skirt. When wearing Western-style clothes, women may wear two different plaids or two different flowered prints; men may wear differently patterned shirt, jacket, and slacks. Teenagers and young adults, on the other hand, have quickly adopted more restrictive American ideas about combining pattern and color, at least for their school and job clothes. Even when wearing traditional clothes, such as at wedding and temple ceremonies, teenage girls seem to be restricting their range of colors and patterns—gold blouse with burgundy and gold skirt, for example, or single-color rather than multicolored sequins on a long gown. While the cut of the dresses and the textiles themselves remain traditional, the rich color and pattern combinations worn early in my fieldwork have ceased to be aesthetically desirable to young women who have been under the influence of American peer aesthetics.

Interior Decoration of Homes

Interior decoration is another area in which culturally distinct aesthetic expression is clear. Cambodians love flowers and color, and even people with very low incomes do their best to have silk, plastic, or real flowers about the house, in rich combinations of red, pink, gold, and turquoise. Lace, ruffled, or beaded curtains hang in doorways. Other decorations include colorful satin pillows, tiny blinking lights, crepe paper, fringed foil streamers, tinsel garlands, and bright posters of rock stars or Angkor Wat or Buddha. Plain American furniture may be covered with brightly patterned cloth from Thailand. Even when some of the items are American-made, the rich patterning of light, color, and texture is an expression of their own aesthetic. As families become more settled and more financially stable, new items appear in their homes, such as satin bedspreads and pillowcovers of deep color, richly quilted and appliquéd, purchased from Asian shops. To an American, the first glimpse of a Cambodian home may appear chaotic, but an understanding of the style of temple decoration shows that home decor actually follows a very specific and religious aesthetic pattern.

Temple Decoration

The decoration of temples and altars provides vivid models to the young and reinforcement for the elders of traditional aesthetic values. Though details may vary from city to city, the aesthetic is the same, and the temple in Riverside is fairly typical. Inside the main open space (the *salaa*) of the temple itself, the floors are covered with woven plastic straw mats in red, green, blue, yellow, and white. The ceiling is draped, tentlike, with striped fabric from which hang swags, bells, and flowers of crepe paper and strings of small triangular pennants in red, yellow, and blue. Support posts are covered with giftwrap or wound with multicolored crepe paper streamers. The main wall, before which sit the monks, is hung high above with 18" x 24" framed pictures illustrating important events in the Buddha's life, about five or six different pictures repeated and hung side by side to border the entire length of the wall at ceiling height. The pictures show a soft, slender, youthful Buddha robed in orange, standing, seated, and reclining against a tranquility of brilliant blue skies and water, lush verdant grass, graceful trees, snow-peaked mountains, flowers, and golden sunlight. Before the monks is a long, low table with vases of real and silk flowers. To the right, away from the central altar area, hang three bulletin boards completely covered with hundreds of snapshots, lapped and glistening like fish scales.

The altars themselves are even more richly decorated. The main altar, in the salaa, is backed by a wall-size poster of Buddha framed by strings of tiny colored lights, glitter stars, and garlands of tinsel. The centerpiece of the altar is a large, simple, seated Buddha of white-painted plaster with a saffron-painted robe. Like the Buddha of the pictures, he has long earlobes, black hair in a topknot, delicate eyebrows, long

Michael M Birch

Buddhist altar

lashes, softly rounded, somewhat feminine facial contours, and a serene, beneficent expression. Above the Buddha is a canopy fringed with white lace, and around him hang appliquéd brocade banners of various colors, built of rectangles and triangles and reminiscent of many-tiered pagodas. Each piece is edged in metallic gold trim, and the series is topped by and ends in long triangles. They flutter and glint gently in the air. The canopy is supported by slender poles covered with red wrapping paper patterned with black phonograph records, brightly colored balloons and streamers, and the words "Rock and Roll." On the altar are ten vases of flowers (red, turquoise, pink, yellow, orange), eight candles, a foil pinwheel, a brass pot with sticks of incense, several boxes of stick incense, and a short stack of telephone books. The altar is composed of three tiers covered in printed fabric, with each level outlined in multicolored foil fringes and tiny, blinking, colored lights. The altar decorations change occasionally. The ambiance is of rich color, profusion, motion, light, and gaiety.

Inside the house itself there is a smaller altar. In this room, too, are floor mats and silken cushions, but of simpler color and design. The walls are nearly covered with the repeating Buddha pictures. The three-tiered altar is of black marble, and the large central Buddha, raised on a bronze dais, is of gleaming bronze and wears a robe of orange silk. From the ceiling hang the triangular banners and a macramé plant hanger with cascading red silk roses. Beneath the Buddha are a slender golden canoe with nine candles, a small oil lamp, a few brass bowls, seven vases of flowers (real, silk, and plastic), and several votive candles, including one with a jack-o-lantern on it. Though still lush and ornate, this room has a darker, richer, and more somber atmosphere.

Even the style in which the community gathers is visibly and symbolically different from that of the congregation in an American church. Shoes are removed to indicate respect and to protect the mats. People come and go without causing disturbance. They sit directly on the mats, so there is flexibility of seating arrangement and individual posture (although legs and feet are always neatly tucked to the side). People join friends and kin in little clusters, chatting softly and sitting close, touching. Children come in and out as they wish and are not disruptive. During the prayers most people join in the chant with raised palms together, but again, except during the most important moments, quiet chatting and silent communication continue. People shift positions freely and drop in and out of participation. When the prayers end, people shift into small circles to eat, reaching for a spoonful of food, passing soda pop, smoking. It is a scene of densely arrayed, brightly shifting color, much like the photo montage, the profusions of flowers, and the colorful banners fluttering above the altars. The overall aesthetic of the temple compound and the ceremonies held there is of richly varying color and pattern, brightness, graceful motion, and cheer. The Buddha himself is portrayed as soft, calm, glowing, benign, somewhat androgynous; nature is lush, tranquil, vibrant, idyllic.

Dance

A mother sits at a wedding party, three-year-old on her lap. They watch the dancing in silence. The mother holds the little girl's hands in hers and puts them through the graceful swirling gestures. She does this for a few moments, checks the child's face, does it again for a bit, checks again, then chuckles and stops. The child is passive throughout.

Of the various art forms practiced by the Cambodians in Middle City, dance may be the one with the most potential for drawing American public interest, appreciation, and support. There are several forums in Middle City within which traditional dance could be taught and displayed to Americans, such as a large international folk festival, various folk-dance organizations, and recital halls. At one time the church helped, but both the youth and the church have lost interest; a local dance organization invited participation in a public recital; and I have located grant possibilities for financial support but could not garner interest. Those youth who arrived with dance skills and might be today's teachers have grown and have family, job, and school responsibilities; today's teenagers also have competing interests.[6]

The most formal teaching of dance has been via a young woman who had classical dance training in the refugee camps. As a high school student she formed, with the encouragement of some American teachers, a small troupe of teens who practiced regularly, choreographed their own dances, made costumes, and performed on community and public occasions. This young woman owns videotapes of traditional dance and occasionally shows them to guests, but the troupe itself disbanded, partly because of her more pressing obligations and partly because of a lack of community interest and support; she says, "The kids don't want it. They're lazy, and the parents won't make them come."

Social dance is an art passing on to even the youngest children and provides a vantage point for the process of cultural transmission and culture change. Informal teaching goes on at home and at parties. When I asked children how they learned to dance, some would say, "I don't know, just learned it," but others acknowledged lessons from older siblings. It is actually rare for an adult to teach a child as in the fieldnote cited earlier.

Less intentional teaching occurs at the communal events such as New Year and wedding parties, the main attraction of which is several hours of social dancing. On these occasions the dancing may be initiated by the toddlers, sometimes while the adults are still eating and the band is just warming up. A small group of little girls ages two to about ten, and perhaps some very young boys, not usually over six or seven, take to the otherwise empty dance floor, dancing in a circle or line. The oldest girls in the group direct the others by leading or physically manipulating their hands or pushing them into place. The children stay when the adults enter the dance floor, joining the circle of adults, sometimes on the fringes, sometimes in the center of the circle, and sometimes each directly behind some adult model. At this point the older children join in too, either with toddler siblings or with age and sex mates. Children seldom dance with the opposite sex. It is not unusual to see a teenage girl dancing with a toddler, or dancing with an age-mate but with a toddler holding on to her skirt.

Young men, too, may dance with an infant or toddler in their arms or holding their hand.

The floor pattern of the traditional social dance is a counter clockwise circle of couples with men on the inside and women on the outside, in front of their partners. The couple does not touch or particularly look at one another. The foot pattern is a forward stepping with the feet, long-short-short, alternating the beginning foot (right-left-right, then left-right-left). There is a slight twisting at the waist, shoulders leading, as the lead foot alternates, but the body and head are held very erect. The main motion of the dance is a sinuous movement of the hands and forearms, which are held slightly above waist height and moved from side to side with the step, first the right hand leading to the right for three steps, then the left hand leading to the left for three steps. The forearms are kept nearly horizontal, but the hands, traditionally, are bent upward, palms out. This particular gesture is difficult to do without training and is not often seen in the dancing in Middle City, but it was demonstrated to me by an elderly man reputed to be a "very good dancer" and also by the young woman teacher. Many simply hold their rounded hands palm up in a softer, relaxed position. In one popular dance, the leading hand is turned at the wrist out-in-out. The music breaks about halfway, from more traditional music into popular rock music, and the circle breaks into face-to-face couples doing standard contemporary dancing: no progression across the floor, more movement of the torso, and great personal variation in foot, arm, and body movement.

The youngest girls, from about the age of two or three, know the major elements of the dance structure and movement: without adults they dance counterclockwise, body and face erect and serious, with the foot patterns and arm movements basically correct; by about four or five they have the hand and finger movements and the very subtle body movement correct. Little boys are more likely to tag along at this if urged by older sisters; school-aged boys generally join only in the fast portions of the dance, at which many of them excel.

A striking example of culture change occurred one summer over a series of communal events. At the first party, a American man and a Cambodian woman danced the first dance of the evening in waltz position. For a while, no one else joined them on the dance floor; then another American man tried to get another Cambodian woman, Sothea, to dance with him in that position. Although usually fun-loving, bold, and accepting of American patterns, Sothea was embarrassed and would not put her hand on his shoulder, and they ended up dancing face-to-face with palms flat toward one another but not touching. She laughed, and others laughed, but there was an air of minor scandal as the entire crowd kept their seats and watched. Later that season at another event, a few young married couples began the dancing in waltz position. Sothea, older, danced in that position with Cambodian men and was roundly criticized: "She's just showing off. She's trying to take other women's husbands." Finally, at a wedding toward the end of the summer, as eight little girls and two toddler boys moved onto the empty dance floor and began their play and dancing, four of the girls started to negotiate the correct postures for the waltz position. They paired off, then struggled with embrace, hand holding, waist holding, then finally settled into the pattern of one hand up and one hand down. No one else

Dancing at a New Year party

seemed to notice these girls, and no one corrected them. And so the position passed from a posture practiced only by Americans to one tolerated for the young, somewhat acculturated adults to a posture little children were picking up naturally as they practiced the art of dance.

Music

Cambodians in Middle City have several forms of music. In homes, Asian popular music plays on tapes and videotapes. At religious ceremonies one hears traditional ritual chanting and classical music both live and on traditional instruments or tapes imported from Thailand. The children have a general familiarity with American popular music and can sing along with the radio. In the Khmer Christian service at the church, the adult congregation (mostly women) sings hymns from Khmer hymnals, without accompaniment. The singing is clear, very feminine, metallic, thin but strong, full-voiced, sometimes warbling but unhesitating, with clear, confident slides. Although there are often only about eight women present, the sound is full and rich.

Popular Asian music plays in homes much of the time, either as audiotapes or as background music on videotapes bought, shared, or rented from Cambodian and Thai stores. This often features a woman singer in a high voice that Americans might identify as nasal or metallic. I once awoke in the middle of the night to hear a teenager singing to her young sisters. Although she was singing them back to sleep, she was singing clear and full. Her voice was rich and sweet, and she sang nonstop for forty minutes. At New Year and wedding parties, a local Cambodian band plays drums, electric guitars, electric keyboard, and synthesizer, with a modern speaker system. They may have a male or female vocalist or both; again, the singing style is quite distinct from American singing.

Traditional classical music is played on tapes or by live musicians at religious ceremonies and sometimes at wedding ceremonies. Unfortunately, few instruments are available, so a complete ensemble is impossible. The ensembles I've seen in Middle City include a *skor*, a drum of wood and leather held under the left arm and played with both hands; a *kheum*, similar to a hammer dulcimer, with thirteen sets of three strings each, played with two metal hammers; a *takay*, a kind of picked three-stringed lute having small, round feet and a metal covered soundbox; and several cylindrical or hemispherical, long-necked, vertical, two- or three-string instruments played with a bow. Certain songs are specific to certain parts of certain ceremonies; for example, there is special gift-giving music at a wedding.[7]

Several children have said they'd like to take music lessons, and some of them fiddle at the piano in the church, but I met none who were being formally trained in either Cambodian or American music, though the dance bands do not seem to lack for members.

Children's Drawing

Children's art can be remarkably expressive, and the drawing of the Cambodian children in middle City is revealing of both traditional and changing cultural values. Many of the children appear to be quite interested and talented in drawing. I always carried extra pencils because little children rummaged my purse for them. In the Sunday school at church the teenagers were encouraged by the teacher, Ann, to draw. She bought good supplies—oil crayons, paints, pastels, charcoal, high-quality paper—and plenty of them. She didn't give instruction but brought in sample pictures for them to copy or made suggestions based on biblical themes, gave lots of praise, and pinned their work on the walls, which were covered with their drawings and paintings. They used some of the religious pictures offered as models but drew their own ideas too. Several of the older boys were particularly skilled at drawing the human figure and had a good sense of anatomy, perspective, shading, and so on. They also drew idyllic pastoral scenes of Cambodia: mountains with the sun shining between, lush green ricefields, streams, blue skies, palm trees, and flowers, sometimes with a small figure walking down a road or serenely bent in the fields, themes reminiscent of the temple pictures of Buddha's life.

Young children draw too and have their own standard themes, rehearsing an image over and over. Little girls draw glamorous young women with long hair in elaborate hairdos or ponytails, with long formal gowns, spike heels, bright red cheeks and lips, and flowers and jewelry on the waist, neck, wrists, and hair, reflecting what I have come to refer to as a "glamour aesthetic." This differs slightly from American girls' fantasy play with Barbie dolls since in this case they are drawing images of real teenagers they really see and actively emulate. Little boys draw cars and airplanes.

Young children spend most of the church service drawing, kneeling on the floor and using the pews as drawing boards. They also watch the older kids draw. As an example of the capacity of some of the children to concentrate on a matter of interest, I offer here an excerpt from my fieldnotes on a Sunday school classroom. Seven-year-old Rim and fifteen-year-old Long are alone in the room, Long recognized by his peers and by Ann as artistically talented and Rim a child the Americans consider unusually active and difficult to manage, one of the few who is a discipline problem at school.

Rim stands beside Long, not quite leaning against him, watching intently as Long draws. Long shows no notice. For three minutes Rim watches, frozen; then he leans forward, actually against Long's left arm, and continues watching for three more minutes. Long draws silently. Rim leans away, studies some drawings other kids have made on the paper tablecloth, follows them with his finger for a minute and a half, then turns back to Long. He leans, forearms on the table, face about 12" from Long's pad. Kim enters the room and sits; Rim does not look up. He reaches for a box of pastels, sits down on a chair beside Long, reads the back of the box, glances at Kim, watches her for a moment as she draws. Rim picks up a marker, draws briefly on the tablecloth, then turns his attention back to Long, watching immobile for another three minutes.

Generally, drawing was a more active and social process: in the living room amid a crowd of family or in groups at church, drawing on and commenting on one another's pictures, drawing on my fieldnotes, tracing household objects, showing the pictures to adults in the room. Often a child would comment, "It's not very good" or

"I'll draw it better." In the Sunday school room, too, drawing was a social process. One adult persisted in trying to get someone to draw a rainbow on her paper, finally simply shoving the paper in front of a teenager, who politely and carefully complied. On another occasion a teenage boy worked for a while at a drawing I had momentarily laid aside. Many of the teenagers get good grades in art, but none go to the city art school or take art lessons.

PRESERVING TRADITIONAL VALUES

At present, the arts are the most visible manifestation of tradition among the Cambodians in Middle City. Of all the various forms, religious ceremonies at the temple, with their choreography, music, ritual objects, rich silken fabrics, colorful settings, costumed participants, and pageantry, are the most vital forum for traditional art. There, in a protected environment, completely free of Americans, where every act is infused with symbolism and every object and sound and aroma evoke memories of the homeland, the temple ceremonies draw young and old together, temporarily, back into the vibrance of their traditional Cambodian life. But Middle City has no such forum, no similar setting in which the young can so fully experience the enactment of traditional values. As time passes, fewer and fewer make the journey to Riverside, and fewer and fewer speak of trying to build a temple in Middle City.

As for the more secular arts, although much talent is in evidence, no one except the band has parlayed any of the arts into an income-producing activity or made inroads into the American market, producing goods or performances for American consumption. The teaching of the traditional court dance seems to be at a stalemate and no one makes the musical instruments or weaves the fabric.

Many of the religious, social, and aesthetic values of the Cambodians in Middle City are in flux. There is concern on the part of adults that children will adopt American values rather than learn the traditional Cambodian values of being a "good person." Parents worry about the children learning misbehavior, disrespect, and disobedience at school, and older adults worry that the young parents are ignoring their children, letting them grow wild like Americans. They see some good in America, but they worry that the right choices will not always be made. One woman said to me,

I tell the kids, I get mad at them and I say, "You learn everything from Americans, you learn all the bad things from the American kids, but there's one thing you don't learn: you don't learn to admit. American kids, they do the bad things, but they admit it. You do it, but you don't admit it. When you going to learn that?"

The focus of these four chapters has been upon the Cambodian community and its maintenance of the traditional culture. The next chapter carries the description beyond the boundaries of the Cambodian community itself and examines the relationships between Cambodians and Americans and between Cambodians and the American institutions in Middle City with which they interact.

NOTES

1. Although some scholars say Cambodian Buddhism does not actually have nuns, this is the term my informants used to refer to elderly women who live at the temple for short periods of time.

2. One traditional rite of passage that is not practiced in Middle City, and which is even rare in the memory of my informants, is the seclusion of girls at first menses.

3. According to my reading of the licensure laws, a monk would probably qualify but an *achaa* probably would not. Neither the lawyers I consulted, including the one supplied by the Agency, nor the licensing bureau in the state capital were able to clarify this.

4. For more on funerals and care of the dead, see Pan 1986.

5. I realize that children's art is not ususally considered "art." Here, however, children are doing what they see as art and what, when their elders do it, is called art. More important, the children's drawing, like that of adults, vividly portrays their values and ideals and so, like adult art, is a window into the culture's ideology.

6. For more on traditional dance, see Cuisinier 1927.

7. For a brief overview of this subject, see Sam-Ang Sam's "Khmer Traditional Music Today." He describes the devastating loss of musicians, music, and musical instruments because of Pol Pot and makes a particularly interesting point about change in traditional ensemble music: because of the deep respect for the elderly, "we cannot tell our older musicians . . . not to play just because they do not know how to play [the appropriate instrument]" (1994:45). This results in unconventional combinations of instruments and perhaps other innovations. For more specifically on traditional music, see also his dissertation, *The Pin Peat Ensemble: Its History, Music, and Context* (1988).

Chapter 6

Agents of Culture Change: Individuals and Institutions

While recognizing that virtually every facet of Cambodian culture in Middle City is to some degree affected by its American urban context, the foregoing chapters have dealt primarily with Cambodian culture within the social institutions of the Cambodian community. In much of their daily life, however, Cambodians must interact with Americans and within the structures of American institutions—with sponsors, health professionals, landlords, neighbors, teachers, social service providers, salespeople, and employers. Some of these are of special interest because their primary orientation is sociocultural change. The first section of this chapter briefly describes some of the patterns of relations between Cambodians and American individuals, and the second section discusses the roles of two particular institutions of social change, the social service agency I refer to as the Agency and the Protestant church I refer to as Hillside Church.

RELATIONSHIPS WITH INDIVIDUAL AMERICANS

Sponsors

Cambodians were permitted to leave refugee camps and enter the United States only if some individual or organization agreed to sponsor them. Sponsorship doesn't require a major financial responsibility, but it does entail a legal and moral responsibility to care for the refugee and thus involves some expense and time. More than most refugees, the Cambodians were in very precarious health, a situation that discouraged individual sponsorship. Consequently, most were sponsored by churches or, later, by the hastily established and short-lived MAA. Often sponsors were given only two days' notice of the arrival of their family. The sponsor was to meet the family at the airport and provide immediate clothing, food, and temporary shelter. Most of the refugees arrived very ill, not only from their long-term hardship but from exhaustion, jet lag, air sickness, and the effects of Dramamine, so the immediate need was sleep. Sometimes unexpected things, like the smell of cigarettes or the sound of lightening, would trigger frightening memories of bombs. Even car sickness was a problem, since they weren't used to riding in cars.

Information provided to the sponsor was scant and often inaccurate, so sponsors learned not to buy clothes or rent housing until the family had actually arrived. One of the first sponsors gathered a collection of dresses and dolls for a four-year-old, only to discover upon her arrival that the child was fourteen. Sometimes groups arriving as nuclear families were found to be related only distantly or not at all, so the sponsors felt obliged to revise housing arrangements.

The first Cambodians, from about 1979 to 1982, although they were often in very desperate physical condition, tended to be more educated, from more urbanized backgrounds, and often had some English. It was they who receive the first, more eager sponsors and the most concerted efforts from agencies and individuals. In the best situations, sponsors took their tasks seriously, augmenting the services provided by other agencies. In addition to their primary assignment of finding apartments, they showed people how to use money, pay bills, shop in stores, use appliances; they helped children one-on-one with schoolwork, ferreted out jobs, found doctors, and, too soon, arranged funerals. One young woman says of her sponsor, "He's like a father to me. Every time I got trouble, he's the one that comes first. He really cares about us." A good sponsoring relationship can be a major factor in an economically successful adjustment process. I once observed to an Agency worker that a more recently arrived group of refugees, Eritreans, seemed to be doing better; they just looked healthier, and they had better housing, better clothes, better jobs, went to more reputable schools, and were learning English faster. Her immediate response was, "Oh yes, they have much better sponsors!" In recent years a few have continued to provide help and friendship by advising on matters such as mortgage arrangements, car insurance, or minor legal matters. But most sponsors have pulled back: they've grown old, have acquired new responsibilities, have moved, or they simply feel the refugees should be on their own now.

It is important to note that good sponsors have been the exception. When more Cambodians,[1] in larger numbers, came in 1982 and 1983, they were more likely to be sponsored by organizations rather than individuals, and thus personal relationships were less likely to develop. Some were sponsored by the fledgling MAA, which disbanded shortly afterward. Others were sponsored by churches, which also eventually withdrew, either because their efforts to proselytize failed or because the refugees just had far greater needs than they were prepared to deal with. Consequently, most Cambodians now turn to other Cambodians for help, even though those others may also lack the requisite skills or knowledge.

One might expect the traditional patron-client relationship to have developed between sponsors and their refugee families, but this seldom happened. Such a relationship may have been expected by Cambodians, but it surely was not what Americans expected. Americans continually spoke of "helping these people become more independent" and "developing leadership within the Cambodian community." The committee at Hillside Church expressed constant frustration that Cambodians did not take charge of some of the events the church organized for them, and that they continued to be so "dependent."

Landlords and Neighbors

It's been difficult to find landlords willing to rent to Cambodians. Landlords say the refugees have too many children, cook in unacceptable ways with unacceptable spices, and are generally noisy and dirty. As a consequence, the Cambodians often end up in housing where such things as noise and dirt don't matter to the landlord. On the other hand, a few landlords have grown to know them and appreciate their virtues: in fact they're quite clean, they pay their rent on time, they are quiet and family oriented, and the children are rather well behaved. One landlord in particular has befriended some of them, helping in times of crisis and offering advice about and sometimes help with cars, shopping, and small legal matters. He's one of the few Americans who occasionally appear at New Year celebrations.

Neighbors, however, are seldom friendly. There seems to be a range from quiet tolerance to overt hostility and violence. In the first neighborhoods where the Cambodians were placed, violence was routine. Car windows were broken, the paint gouged, tires slashed. Children couldn't be left outside unsupervised because the neighbors threw chairs and garbage at them. One child had a pencil jammed up his nose by an American child at the school bus stop; others were chased by dogs and teenagers. One summer, garbage cans were overturned, windows smashed, used syringes and human feces and urine were thrown into the apartments (in one case a syringe was found in an infant's crib near a window) and into the smashed cars. Those who have moved out of the first, most desperately impoverished neighborhoods into more generally working-class neighborhoods find relationships less dangerous, but not particularly friendly. Only rarely have I seen American neighbors attend Cambodian events, and these were primarily special dinners given by one family specifically for Americans.

The Cambodian Cluster Project, the initial resettlement policy, was designed to settle Cambodians in clusters, often in the same neighborhoods, where there were not presently other refugees. The intent was to protect regions such as the West Coast, which already felt overburdened by Southeast Asian refugees and, secondarily, to form ethnic groups into communities, which had been demonstrated to enhance chances of successful adaptation (Stein 1986). For the Cambodians in Middle City, it meant isolating them from Americans who could have offered basic help with strange appliances, shopping, transportation, and so on. It also meant they found themselves in a city with little experience in dealing with refugees.

Friends

Few adult Cambodians have American friends other than those originating through the ties of sponsorship or church. This is evidenced by the absence of Americans at such community events as New Year and wedding parties and in more ordinary home situations. Even as Cambodians have moved from the original neighborhoods, this has changed little. A few married-in Americans attend the large celebrations such as New Year and weddings, and in the early days the minister of Hillside, a few teachers, a sponsor, or someone from the Agency might attend these events, but otherwise there are seldom Americans other than Ann and myself. There have been few adults I could identify as *just* friends. The children and some teenagers have begun to make friends with Americans, but since this worries their parents, Americans are seldom brought home or invited to community festivals.

The American

Throughout this book I have referred to Ann, the American who has devoted more time to the Cambodians in Middle City than any other individual. Ann was a member of Hillside Church when the first Cambodians arrived, and her interest in them eventually led the church to pay her to direct activities that involved what the church called their Cambodian Ministry. She taught the teenage Sunday school class, which was all Cambodians, and answered requests for help of all sorts, particularly with illness, hospitalization, birth, marriage plans, death, minor legal problems, and house purchasing. She was a liaison between the church, which wished to help but did not always know how, and the refugees, who did not know other ways to get help. Ann was the American whom Cambodians called at 2:00 A.M. and the one the hospitals called, too. She was also the one American at all the weddings, the parties, even the births, and she has probably been to almost all the homes. She acted as a liaison with the Agency and the schools as well, so she was really the central linking figure among the various systems. Many other Americans—at the schools, the church, and the Agency—wished to help but only in a more tangential way.

Cambodians have said, and my observation supports, that Ann was the one person who knew more about everybody than anybody else did. I kept a calendar of her daily activities for two months, and she spent thirty hours a week directly involved with Cambodians, for which she was paid half-time. Occasionally she was able to attend national conferences for refugee workers, but she had little time for scholarly reading. What she accomplished she did by virtue of her large capacity for empathy, her respectful attitude toward cultural differences, and her genuine love of people. Ann was in many ways caught between the two cultures: between her job as culture change agent, which included teaching Christian Sunday school, and a sincere interest in their traditional culture and a genuine desire to see certain elements of it maintained. As the years went on, she was also caught between her own desire to help people she saw as desperately needy and the church's increasing desire that the Cambodians be self-sufficient.

RELATIONS WITH AMERICAN INSTITUTIONS OF CHANGE

There are several institutions in American society with which refugees and immigrants regularly come into contact, whether they particularly choose to do so or not. These include immigration and sponsoring agencies, schools, medical facilities, employment agencies, job sites, stores, welfare agencies, and churches. For the following discussion I have selected two, the Agency and Hillside Church, as examples of institutions that have made concerted and explicit efforts to help the Cambodians learn American culture. The following chapter discusses the relationship between the schools and the Cambodians, which of course encompasses the schools' role as change agent.

The Agency

The Agency was the institution officially designated to provide immediate assistance to the incoming refugees, and over the years it has continued to serve them in various ways. The Agency provides services to immigrants, refugees, and foreign visitors; these services include citizenship classes, ESL classes, employment counseling, interpreters and translators, and advice about immigration status issues, but at times it has also offered limited day care (while the children's parents were in classes at the Agency) and training in childcare. At the time the first Cambodians were arriving, the Agency was well funded and was able to provide considerable help, including resettlement (which includes finding housing, furniture, etc.), but since 1984 the funding has been cut by about 60 percent and many such services have been discontinued.

I observed two series of classes at the Agency during the summer and fall of 1987 and occasional classes in subsequent years. The first was a class funded by a federal grant, intended to train refugee women (in this case all but three were Cambodian) to become licensed childcare providers in their homes. The other class I attended regularly was an ESL class requested by the women in the childcare class. There were occasionally other classes on how to go about obtaining jobs.

The Agency had decided that childcare classes would provide a good means for the women, particularly the widows, to become economically self-sufficient without having to leave their own small children; in addition, other women would have childcare available so that they could pursue outside jobs. The initial assumption was that American neighbors would also use the service provided by these women, and that in fact some of the Cambodian women might eventually be employed by regular day care centers.

I felt from the first that this project was doomed to failure. The homes were not certifiable by the state for physical reasons such as refrigerator temperature, dangerous stairs, fire hazards, and so on, and I expected American neighbors would be put off by the general disrepair, crowding, lack of English, and absence of telephones, although, as the teacher said, socially and emotionally the homes were probably ideal and the women very loving, tolerant, and gentle toward children. In fact the teacher later expressed misgivings to me about any attempts to put the Cambodian children in outside day care, a project the Agency had been encouraging on the principle that the children would be better prepared for schooling and the mothers would be freed for employment; she felt "a problem with putting these kids in day care; these kids are in good loving environments. . . . Taking kids out of this environment is questionable."

The other question, whether the women would find appropriate employment if they did have day care, wasn't raised. On the economic level, the minimum-wage jobs the women might get (without health insurance or other amenities) were unlikely to support their two or three preschoolers in day care; certainly such income could not match their AFDC payments. On the societal level, we must question whether the general public is better off having these women tie threads or glue labels while someone else, perhaps less competent, parents their children. But I never heard such issues discussed, at the Agency or elsewhere.

The classes proceeded anyway, despite the teacher's misgivings, on the principle that at least the women would get some tips about caring for their own children. Again, no one considered whether these mothers might already know how to take care of children. At any rate, the women understood little of the material. Though some was quite basic—elementary American nutrition, home safety, maintenance of immunizations—much was completely beyond the experience of the women and irrelevant to the context in which they lived. For example, they were told to put kiddie locks on their medicine cabinets; I saw medicine on televisions, open shelves, coffee tables, kitchen counters, but not in medicine cabinets. Nor were these women likely to see kiddie locks in the Oriental groceries and minimarkets where they shopped, nor would they have asked for them. There was a session on CPR and the Heimlich maneuver, but the women, generally pretty freely physical with one another, were terribly embarrassed; they just grinned and shut their eyes or looked down at the table and wouldn't practice.

Once a fire-safety instructor gave a talk on making a "fire escape plan"; she told them to be sure to have a written plan posted in the home for everyone to see and to arrange a "family meeting room" in which to gather in case of emergency. These women, who lived in two-room apartments with six or eight children, understood this well enough to laugh aloud at such ideas. They were also told to make sure to do regular safety checks on their furnaces, and the procedure for this was described at length, but the instructions were incomprehensible to me.

There was a young Cambodian translator, but not everything got translated. She was often busy in conversation with one person or group and missed what the teacher was saying. Sometimes a guest speaker went too fast, so that translation was impossible, and sometimes it was clear that the translator could not follow what was being said. Sometimes she simply refused to translate: "They know all that already," or "No, I'm not going to tell them that; they don't want to come to class another night," or "Go on, they understand."

Babies and toddlers played underfoot and on the table during the classes, a constant distraction. They were fed and conversed with, passed from woman to woman, and occasionally taken out. When there were not enough materials (workbooks, for example) the tots would have them, and the mothers would do without. The women spent much of the time chatting and laughing softly with the children and among themselves, fiddling with one another's hair, going through one another's wallet pictures, and so forth; the teacher had no way of knowing when they were talking about the lesson and when not. They sometimes watched the teacher, but when she asked questions or asked them to demonstrate, they got embarrassed and giggled. I later came to see that much of this as culturally appropriate audience behavior, similar to the women's demeanor at the temple or the church, but it didn't match the teachers' expectations, causing teachers to get flustered occasionally and the lesson to fade out toward the end of the hour as the teachers' sense of control deteriorated. The teachers were actually very patient, and I never saw them lose their tempers, but they looked frustrated and expressed hopelessness to me occasionally in conversation.

The Agency also provided language classes, sometimes specifically at the request of the refugees. For example, early in the childcare class the women were asked what they would like to learn about. The overwhelming answer was "English!" so a special class was set up in conjunction with the childcare class. In these classes, the women recited chorally and helped one another with answers. They took the lessons with good cheer, but some felt the pace was too fast. The teachers came to feel that for many this was simply a chance to get out of the house; as one teacher said, "It's a social hour for them, a chance to get together; maybe they learn a little English, maybe they don't, but they come, so they must enjoy it."

Since the language classes were taught by volunteers, they were usually held at night, problematic because some of the women had no one to leave the children with at night. The agency provided bus tokens, but many of the women were afraid to ride buses, particularly at night; they didn't know their way around the city, and they didn't know enough English to ask for help. One woman told me she couldn't go because if she began classes and then had to quit when the weather got cold, she would lose her welfare check. I assured her that she must have misunderstood, and told her I would check on this for her. I did; she was correct. For a time the Agency hired a Cambodian driver to take the women home at night, but attendance nevertheless dropped off as the weather grew colder and the nights darker.

At other times there have been classes to help them seek employment, such as lessons on filling out applications. The teacher made efforts to actually find employment for the women in the class, but the paperwork was complex. For example, the women had to provide verification of their husbands' employment, thus necessitating another trip; there were time limits within which the forms must be sent, so that if someone missed class one week (as was often the case), the whole procedure had to be started again. The teacher felt there was racial or ethnic discrimination at some of the job sites she sent people to, but she didn't know how to pursue that legally and was afraid that doing so might close doors for future employment opportunities.

Although I found this particular teacher extremely patient and painstaking in her lessons, even these classes were sometimes difficult. After one such hour-long class, they had not even gotten through the first six lines of a job application (name, phone number, date, etc.), and at the end the women seemed confused. They didn't know their phone numbers, their addresses, their Medicaid numbers, nor how to calculate the number of the month. At the end of class, when the teacher asked them to write the date, someone asked, "Last name?"

The Agency used to provide other services, particularly to individuals, such as transportation to doctor appointments or translators for hospitalization, but funding cuts had greatly reduced such services by the time of my research. Many people consequently tried to find other means, saying of the Agency, "They just drop you, leave you there by yourself, no way to get home."

Prior to the beginning of my research and continuing until very recently, the

Agency had a series of directors and other administrators, and many temporarily funded and part-time workers. The lack of funding and the ephemeral nature of the positions was a constant problem. One woman hired on a grant said,

I came in cold; I didn't know what to do, no experience, nothing about the people or their culture or what their needs were; by the time I figured out what would work, the grant [period] was almost up. I could try to get it renewed now that I see what's needed, but frankly, I've got two college degrees and I'm making four dollars an hour.

Although people were friendly and willing to be supportive of my research, I was never able to get such basic information as a census, the kinds or number of classes held over the years, attendance figures, employment figures, kinds of jobs held, or the extent of literacy or English ability among the original arrivals or at the present. Over the years, records were in shambles or nonexistent.

In all their efforts, the goals expressed by the Agency and its employees have been "to help families become self-sufficient," "to try to develop self-esteem," "to educate the women, largely a motivating process." The first of these goals certainly reflects federal guidelines (Tollefson 1989; USDHHS 1982, 1993), but it is unclear whether any of them are shared by Cambodians. I was never aware of any survey of the Cambodian population to discover their own needs.

Hillside Church

Hillside Church served a social, rather than religious, function for the Cambodians. For them, it was primarily a helping agency, and they sought a patron-client relationship with it. For a time they attended as bidden, but as the patrons slowly withdrew services, the Cambodians' participation also ceased. The church's stated intent was to help the refugees in their adjustment, and its official stance was to accept the Cambodians as Buddhists, but eventually the members came to question why they should help people who were not church members and not even Christian. The Cambodians' simultaneous acceptance of both Buddhism and Christianity was not understood. At first the church made genuine efforts to assist the Cambodians in maintaining certain of their traditional practices, such as the dance and food, but the church's concern was not purely to offer friendship, as they often said. They did not, for example, simply hand out money as the Cambodians might wish; they gave specific loans for specific needs, such as for college tuition or home purchasing, and would not have supported more traditional needs, such as brideprice, wedding costs, bringing in a monk for a family emergency, support for the wat, or traditional medicine. Thus, although the church perceived itself as having a purely altruistic relationship with the Cambodians, it was actually a major active force for social change.

Hillside provided a variety of services to the Cambodians as a special ministry when the first Cambodians arrived in Middle City. It made efforts to provide a gathering place for the community and to encourage community responsibility for community needs and issues. The special ministry activities—the youth group events, grandpa dinners, Khmer-language Christian services, Sunday school—were open to all, Buddhist or Christian, and indeed church going was a social event for those who attended. Although few Cambodian adults attended the American church services, they arrived early on Sunday mornings and gathered in the halls chatting and exchanging news with one another, with Ann, and with the Sunday school teachers, sometimes getting help with transportation, talking about an upcoming wedding or other community event, exchanging information about who was sick or needed help, getting advice about immigration, and so on. It was this hallway chat or comments from teenagers that cued Ann to many of the needs of the community.

There was some conflict over loyalty. Some of the refugees were originally sponsored by other churches and felt obligated to those churches and more specifically to individuals at those churches who had helped them at the beginning or were continuing to do so; but some members of Hillside felt that they were doing more for the Cambodians, so all the Cambodians should attend there. For example, one American tried to convince a family that they should attend Hillside rather than their sponsor's church because the service was in Khmer and they would therefore understand it better. "Religion is very difficult," he told them more than once; "You can understand simple things in English, but religion you have to hear about in your own language." The mother replied, "What you want is breaking up my family. I will give you my boys, but no one else." This was not a religious issue; it was a matter of her loyalty to the minister's wife, who (as a good patron) had befriended her and was teaching her English. The mother wanted her whole family together but was torn by the competing demands of the churches.

This conflict was exacerbated as Cambodians began to move out of the original core neighborhoods near Hillside. For several years, the church hired a Cambodian youth to collect the children for Sunday mornings and the special events such as picnics and Easter egg hunts. However, this became difficult as some of the families managed to move away. When I called, at a little girl's request, to see if someone at Hillside would pick up her family for an Easter party, I was told by the minister, rather petulantly, "No. They belong to another congregation now." In fact, they had moved rather far, too far for the minister to want the bother of transporting them; the mother, understandably, had been attending the neighborhood church, which was her sponsor and which was renting a house to the family, but the children missed the activities at Hillside. Most of the time the church was frustrated in its desire to draw Cambodians in; in this instance, its own competitive nature caused it to lose an opportunity to retain a family that wanted to come. Thus if parents made a move to improve their housing (and generally their safety as well), they not only removed their children from the important support network of Cambodian playmates, but also from the acculturation support of the church events and some adults who were particularly interested and understanding of them.

Despite its stated aims, at times the church was not all that inclusive. There was often discussion whether to include nonmember Cambodians in a project—a small allowance for college students, for example, or free circus tickets. They grew annoyed that the Cambodian parents were not coming with their children, but they offered little to adults after the brief period of Khmer language services. At one time they discussed holding a social event for the adult Cambodians, but knowing that for the Cambodians that meant serving beer, they gave up the idea.

For about ten years there was a committee whose task it was to oversee the Cambodian ministry. The committee wanted a Cambodian member, partly to provide a clearer direct understanding of the community and its needs and partly to encourage "leadership" in the community itself. They never succeeded in this because the meetings were always held in the daytime, when most Cambodians worked; of course the meetings were conducted in English. The church never grasped that English-speaking adults were rare, employed, and *very* busy with requests from their own people.

One program provided specifically for the Cambodian adults was the Khmer-language Christian service conducted for a time by a Christian Cambodian minister. This, too, offers an interesting example of cultural blending. About fifteen women attended, with a half dozen or so babies and toddlers; one young man occasionally came with his wife and children. The services were held in a small, plain chapel consisting of pews, a small podium, and a shelf with a vase of flowers. The women gathered and greeted one another much as they do at the temple, chatting quietly, passing babies and toddlers and sometimes small packages. They sat close, though there was plenty of space. The minister read the service from a book in a clear, straightforward voice, and hymns were sung in Khmer from hymnals. There was a collection, and most women put in a dollar. People entered and left quietly during the service, sometimes to take out a particularly obstreperous child. The gentle chatter continued irregularly throughout the service, the minister simply speaking loudly enough to be heard, but not really raising his voice or responding directly to the undercurrent. Small children wandered from adult to adult, rummaged through purses, climbed under pews and up the steps to the podium, hung on the podium, and were fed little treats. This audience behavior was very similar to that in the Buddhist services at the wat—behavior Americans find annoying in church and shocking if it comes from adults. This could also be an important cue for those providing services for Cambodians: Cambodians do not expect an event such as a religious service or language class to be unidimensional. Whereas an American can enter a church in silence, observe a ceremony, and then walk out having spoken to no one, Cambodians' idea of a religious event is much broader, and social interaction is an integral feature.

There were several programs, varying over the years, which included all children but particularly attracted the Cambodians. Sunday school was a constant, but there were also at various times and for various periods a sort of "opening" gathering, junior church, a nursery, a youth group, (American) holiday parties, and Khmer literacy classes taught by a young Cambodian volunteer. The Sunday school classes were regularly attended, but special events brought many children that did not usually come to church. For the younger children there was a standard Sunday school lesson from a prepared series; they read aloud, did projects in workbooks, and gathered together in a large room afterward for a snack and an art project.

The art projects provided a social time. The projects might relate to the church season or other American holidays or might simply be something Ann felt the children would enjoy, such as painting butterflies or making sun catchers. The teenagers from Ann's class joined the children to help out, and sometimes the toddlers came in from the nursery too. This was a time for the preschoolers, who generally tagged along with slightly older siblings, to learn to sit at tables and to hear plenty of English. They knew enough about language differences that children over three knew which language to use for which people. Most of the children worked at the projects with seriousness, though they chattered in Khmer and English constantly as they worked. They seldom looked up at the teachers and seemed to pay no attention at all, but they accomplished the projects according to the instructions nevertheless. This was also a time for teenagers, particularly the girls, to gather and discuss such things as makeup, clothes, their own Americanization process, and what their mothers would and would not let them do. Sometimes an American girl or two joined them, so most of this discussion was in English.

Ann's class usually began with a religious theme but usually turned to such topics as dating, AIDS, teen-parent relationships, and other problems of adolescence. Sometimes she initiated discussion with videotapes. The kids were often silent during these discussions, but they came and they listened. Since she knew the families, she often knew what issues might be of concern at the time, such as pregnancy, cancer, or death. She felt it her responsibility to raise these subjects because she felt they didn't learn about them at home. When the first children went off to church camp, she taught the girls about menstruation because none of them knew; "The mothers were grateful, relieved they didn't have to do it."

Ann also often had an art project for the teens, some of whom display remarkable drawing talent. They chatted softly as they worked, more in Khmer than in English, and sometimes a Cambodian adult or two joined the group, perhaps to consult with Ann or to get a teenager to translate something. Sometimes the younger children came in for a film or just to hover over an older sibling. The room was hung with their work, which they praised and criticized rather freely, though gently. For those who came, Ann's room was a gathering place for community exchange, a place where American and Cambodian cultures met in a relaxed atmosphere and where the customs of each could be discussed or challenged with impunity.

The church, like the other American institutions upon which the Cambodians depend, had difficulties with finances and personnel. At the Cambodian committee meetings much time was spent discussing the budget, and Ann devoted considerable time to writing small-grant proposals. More directly problematic for the Cambodians was the frequent changes in personnel. In the less than five years I attended, they had three ministers. The first was much loved by some of the Cambodians; when he left they felt abandoned. There was also a variety of other short-term assistants who worked with the children or the adults. One woman who had lived in Asia had a good understanding of cultural differences and the accompanying intergenerational conflicts, but she stayed only a year; a beloved youth minister who organized a youth group and many activities for the older kids stayed only six months.

THE PLACE OF CAMBODIANS IN THE CULTURE OF MIDDLE CITY

Except for these few individuals and institutions (and schools, which are discussed in the next chapter), Cambodians in Middle City are virtually invisible. Most city residents do not know there are Cambodians in their midst and know nothing about Cambodia or the experience of these refugees. If they notice Cambodians at all, they assume they are Vietnamese.

As for the few Americans who are aware of the Cambodians, they feel their term of assistance is up. They expected the project to be shorter and the Cambodians to be more expressively grateful. During the first years the Cambodians allowed themselves to be pressed into dictating little articles for church bulletins or giving videotaped interviews in which they expressed, over and over, how thankful they were to all the wonderful Americans who had helped them, how grateful they were for their new lives, how good Jesus was to send them here, and so on; but they, too, now feel they have done enough of that.

For their part, Cambodians in Middle City participate little in the life of the city. They do not participate in city or neighborhood politics or social events, school meetings, or parent-teacher organizations; they do not join voluntary associations based on arts, sports, professions, or social action; they do not take classes in skills or hobbies; they do not vote. They also benefit little from the amenities of city life: they don't attend free concerts, plays, or sports events nor use museums or libraries. Even when a Cambodian dance troupe came to town, I could press few into attending, and no one came when a visiting Asian classical dancer specifically asked to meet them.

As David Haines (1982, 1993) and others have pointed out, changes in U.S. policy regarding refugees have shaped the conditions of refugee adjustment here. I refer specifically to the shift away from policies designed to help refugees and toward policies designed to render them economically independent as quickly as possible.[2] This emphasis on immediate employment meant that adults were given little recovery time upon arrival and only very brief English-language training. We have seen that Cambodians were far less likely than other refugees to have had prior education, urban or job skills, or knowledge of English and more likely to still suffer serious consequences from trauma; yet they were whisked into low-paying, dead-end, often dangerous jobs, most of which offered little contact with English speakers (since these were jobs specifically chosen *because* they required little English), little training, no health care, and little contact with educated or upwardly mobile Americans who might have acted as friends or mentors. In Middle City, these jobs were specifically cleaning and dishwashing jobs in hotels (isolating), and meat cutting (dangerous).

Despite good intentions and sincere efforts on the part of some individual Americans to ease the process of culture change for these Cambodians and to help make life better for them, there are evident in this chapter many instances of culture clash. One of the difficulties in Middle City is that various people wish to see the Cambodians organize in some way and for various purposes, but neither Cambodians nor Americans seem able to get this started. Probably very few of the Cambodians truly have the wherewithal—skills, social following, age, physical health and emotional stamina, money, and time—to develop, from scratch, a self-help organization. Most of the Americans and the American institutions would like to see this occur, and they all have major resources—skills, money, facilities—to contribute to such an endeavor, but they each see their own task as more focused than providing a general self-help or cultural organization. The church is interested in serving spiritual needs, but not to the extent of bringing in and supporting a monk, temple, and so on, even if it could afford to do so. The Agency is charged to help people with general "resettlement" needs, but not to the extent of providing English classes in the neighborhoods where people live or childcare so that mothers can get jobs. No one has offered to get a newsletter going so that these rapidly scattering people can maintain contact with their own culture as they move into neighborhoods that are safer and more conducive to upward mobility for their children; no one provides adequate health, mental health, and dental care to these people who so desperately need it; no one has offered to set up an office and pay a salary so that an MAA can operate.

There seem to be three kinds of social institutions in which the Cambodians participate: specifically Cambodian, such as the family and Buddhism; specifically American, such as most of their jobs and neighborhoods; and those which seek a relationship in order to change the Cambodians, such as the church, the schools, and the social agencies. There is no institution in Middle City whose interest is primarily, or even largely, to meet needs as Cambodians see them, and few people, with the clear exception of Ann, have much interest in learning about Cambodian traditional culture or recent history. Thus, despite what Americans may say and believe about "learning from one another" and "cultural pluralism," the process of cultural transmission here is dichotomized and decidedly unidirectional.

It is important to recall that I describe here a single city, one quite different from the coastal cities and certainly different in its deficiency regarding refugee support. Yet Middle City is not really an unusual city, and the refugee situation there may actually not be so different from that found in other cities, and in fact may be common where refugee populations are small.

NOTES

1. The word "wave" here would be an exaggeration. The Cambodians did not arrive in completely distinct groups at two different times, but as an uneven but continuous flow over a period of about five years. Nevertheless, some of the social distinctions between the "waves" of Vietnamese also pertain to the Cambodians, though to a lesser degree.

2. For complete details on this, see the *Report to the Congress* for 1992 (USDHHS 1993). Nearly every page of this 157-page report refers to the major focus of the various services, which is "early employment" and "early and permanent self-sufficiency." The report for FY1993 chronicles the steady reduction of funds for refugees. In this volume, the recurring phrases are "appropriation has been insufficient to cover these costs" (USDHHS 1994:16) and "reduced the eligibility period" (p. 17). This report also reiterates the focus on self-sufficiency: "The program's goal is to help refugees attain self-sufficiency within four months after arrival, without access to public cash assistance" and "All services are directed toward the twin

objectives of the Matching Grant program: the immediate goal of keeping refugees out of the welfare system for the first four months after arrival in the U.S. and the long-term goal of early and permanent self-sufficiency through employment" (p. 27).

Chapter 7

Formal Education: Cambodian Children in American Schools

The whole Huoth family was missing from school all last week; does anyone know why?"

"Yeah. Sambath was suspended."

"So—why were all eight of them out?"

"Because when he translated the suspension notice to his parents, he sort of interpreted it as a special holiday, so the parents assumed all of the kids were off."

—teachers' meeting

Anthropologists of education[1] have long called for a holistic view of education, encompassing the whole cultural context in which people live, in order that we may understand the broad patterns of children's lives of which formal schooling is but one facet and into which formal schooling must fit. Gail Weinstein-Shr's study of new literacy among Hmong adults exemplifies the possibilities of such research; she finds that the Hmong's rapid pace (one afternoon to several weeks) and high rate of new literacy is related to their own traditional kinship and other social systems: "By helping to make explicit what social as well as educational resources . . . students bring to education, we make it possible for them to build on what they have, and to therefore have more successful and productive learning experiences" (1990:19). The present work has aimed to build on such a model by presenting the "simple routines" and "overarching conceptualizations" (Kimball and Burnett 1973:xiv) of this refugee community; this chapter turns to specific relationships between that broader culture and the school culture, noting areas of conflict and suggesting ways of building upon those home-based simple patterns.

Most readers are aware of the fallacies in the "whiz kid" stereotype[2] of Asian children in America: first the implication that all Asian cultures (and hence all Asian children) are alike and second that all Asian children have met with success in American schools. In fact, Cambodian children in particular have had difficulty with American schools. This chapter attempts to address two questions: how can we account for the difficulties and what can the educational institution do to better meet the needs of these children?

As anthropologists, we seek answers in culture. In this case, we must consider both cultures in which the children move—the culture of the home and the culture of the school—to discern areas of incongruence or conflict. For minority children, conflicts between the cultural patterns of the home and those of the school can lead to confusion, distress, and ultimately failure. Perhaps a consideration of such conflicts can suggest ways to reduce school failure—that is, failure of our educational system to successfully educate the children.

THE PERCEPTION OF FAILURE

Just what do we mean by failure? As noted earlier, although research has documented the general success of Southeast Asian refugee youth (Caplan, Choy, and Whitmore 1991), other research has also found that Cambodian high school students typically have lower grade-point averages, lower achievement scores, and lower job-status aspirations than do other Southeast Asian students (Rumbaut 1989; Rumbaut and Ima 1988). Middle City students fit this pattern; a high school teacher said to me, "All but one of our Cambodian males are failing; they don't do homework, they cut classes, they skip school."

Generally, the little children appear to do well in Middle City elementary schools. The middle-class teachers, used to fairly tough inner-city kids, are attracted to and respond warmly to the charming, reasonably quiet, extremely polite, and respectful little cherubs entering kindergarten. The children do what they are told and are inordinately cooperative; they are seldom absent and get good grades. By junior high, the story is changing. The material becomes more difficult, requires more study, more memorizing, and more homework. More assumptions are made about children's background life experiences—their knowledge about current events, sports, the city, and so on. In addition, Cambodian teenagers aren't developing what one teacher calls "student behaviors," such as habits of taking notes in class, doing homework, and studying. Attendance begins to drop off, and their grades fall. By high school, the teenagers are in serious academic trouble, often irretrievably. A few still work hard and continue to do well, but they're the exceptions. For the most part, attendance becomes erratic, homework is seldom done, and many youth say, openly, that they "don't understand anything that is going on." Those who get even average grades do so because they are still in ESL (English as a second language) classes, where content is less challenging. Many of them drop out sometime after age sixteen, even though that may only be ninth or tenth grade for them. Those who do graduate often try college, but they find themselves hopelessly unprepared, even for junior college. They take and retake remedial English and fail science and history classes. Some of them persist for a few years, but most drop out after a year or so. The girls marry and get jobs or have babies, the boys get service or factory jobs. The teachers say, "The parents just don't care. They're not future oriented."

Cambodians are not of one mind about this. The few Cambodians in Middle City who have received good educations at home and are thus generally adequately employed (but still underemployed) blame the parents. "They're just country people, they don't know. They're my people, good people, but they're ignorant. They don't know about education, so they don't care." Or another, "The parents, they just let the kids run wild; they don't encourage them. You've got to praise kids, keep them going to work so hard." Jean Moua, a Hmong educator, has echoed this last sentiment, urging that unschooled parents need training in order to know what is expected of them and how they can help and support their children in school (Moua 1994).

Parents in Middle City who haven't been to school themselves say with sincerity that they would like their children to do well in school, but that the children just don't want to study or read. When a school counselor told a mother that her daughter needs to spend time reading, the mother chuckled and nodded agreeably, but she later said to me, "Yeah, she has library card, but she doesn't like to read." She saw no connection between reading storybooks and getting an education for a job and thought the suggestion absurd. Several times I offered to find tutors for children, but the parents said, with bemused smiles, "I don't think he'd like that."

The children themselves also differ in their attitudes about school. The little ones like it; they are cheerful in class, accomplish what they are supposed to in school, and whip through their homework; "It's easy," or "It's fun," are frequent comments. On the other hand, teenagers who drop out or are doing poorly say, "It's boring, I just want to get a job. School doesn't teach you anything to get a job"; others say, "It was too embarrassing; you ask a question and the teacher just says, 'Read the directions,' but I didn't understand the directions; I never understood any of it." The few who attempt college find the classes huge, the pace impossible, the teachers remote. They drop out. Cambodian college students that I interviewed in California said that the biggest problem for them in high school was lack of parental support and understanding; they said their parents just didn't know how much they had to work at their studies and didn't give them time to do their homework, confirming Moua's statement regarding the need for parent classes.

Thus whether we consult Americans or Cambodians, children or parents, teachers or researchers, we encounter dissatisfaction with both the process and the results of the education; no one's expectations are being met—neither the parents', nor the schools', nor the youths'. Both the schools and the Cambodian youths attribute the difficulties to lack of parental support; the parents say they want their children to go to school, even college, and they understand the need for education in this culture. In order to understand why many Cambodian parents may not appear to be supportive of American schooling in concrete ways, we need to recall certain elements of traditional Cambodian culture and values, focusing on cultural characteristics and themes that are at odds with current American school culture.

TRADITIONAL CULTURAL FACTORS

Rather than be surprised that Cambodian children do not do as well in school as Vietnamese or Chinese children, we should consider the very different cultural traditions and quite different recent history. In Cambodia, only the capital, Phnom Penh, was a Western-style city, and few people traveled there from the countryside. The rural life was simple, perfectly self-sufficient, and fulfilling. Most Cambodian adults in Middle City were farmers, and many continue to regard that life with nostalgia, nurturing the hope of someday returning. Boys went to temple schools for a few years, but traditionally most girls didn't go. Literacy was for reading Buddhist texts, for aesthetic and moral purposes. Since it had little practical value, little place in everyday life, and was considered quite difficult as well as esoteric (Needham 1991, confirmed by my informants), it was not pressed upon children who were not interested. Only in recent years had education become somewhat more common.

Life in Phnom Penh was very different. Boys and girls went to French schools, some through lycée level, and sometimes to college or to France for college, resulting in a sharply divided society: a small, urban, French-speaking, educated elite, and a vast, uneducated peasantry a bit suspicious of the colonially influenced elite. In the rural areas, although education was respected, it was also somewhat tainted by its association with the elite. As we have seen, it was generally these rural people who survived Pol Pot and came to the United States, and their children who found themselves in American schools as unprepared as can be imagined. Many have gamely adopted our styles of clothing, food, transportation, and so on; but ideology is not so malleable, and it is the stark contrast between the values of Americans and the values of rural Cambodians that pose barriers to American-style schooling.

What exactly are these values which are in such contrast? In the earlier discussion of Cambodian ideology, I noted two institutions, the family and Buddhism, which permeate both the everyday lives and the special ritual lives of Cambodians. Despite many adaptations to American culture, these two institutions are still strong and highly influential even in the lives of the young. In addition, three character values—selflessness, cooperation, and respect—seem most clearly to define the Cambodian ideal of being "a good person." These five themes function, and must be understood, as an integrated system; the values are expressed within the institutions, which in turn support and reinforce the values.

We have seen that the foundation of daily life and society is the nuclear family, both in traditional times and today in Middle City, where a family shares a dwelling, pools income, and spends its leisure time together. Time and energy are due first to the family, particularly as respect to elders, but also to the unit as a whole. Children learn to help at minor household tasks at a very early age and seek to participate in family life in this way. Teenagers who seek time away from family and with outsiders are going astray, becoming selfish. Girls, particularly, demonstrate their goodness and worth by keeping the house tidy and the little children under control. The focus is always on the good of the family, bringing honor to the family, rather than on bringing honor and good to the self. Schools challenge this by encouraging adolescents to spend more time alone in study and with peers in school-related activities.

Despite this centrality of family, it must be recalled that the Cambodian kinship system is not rigidly organized. In the absence of clans, other customs serve to maintain family connections, such as long-term visiting, moves to live near married sons or daughters, and marriage arrangements through kin. One consequence is frequent changes in children's residence. When youth move to marry kin in distant cities their high school careers are interrupted, sometimes permanently. Frequent and long-term visits to distant kin similarly result in school interruptions for children. The common practice of a child or teen paying extended visits to an adult sibling works well for the young bride or young mother glad for a teenage helpmate, but it does not work well with American-style school routines: the children miss school for a few days or a few months, or they must shift schools midyear as they move from household to household. It's not that anyone is trying to foil the child's education; in most cases, the parents are simply following tradition without fully comprehending the difficulties caused by such discontinuities in schooling.

"Respect" is a theme central to the concept of "a good person." Children respect everyone who is older, particularly family members, and the degree of deference accorded increases with age. Respect is manifested by unquestioning obedience, by not contradicting or challenging. To disobey by choosing one's own activities (play, for example, or schoolwork) is to reveal oneself not only as childish (and therefore unworthy of respect), but as not a good person, not a good family member. Thus, when parents call upon a child to do a task, no one, including the child, should think whether the child might have other things to do. The prime consideration is the good of the family, and this is the important lesson for the child to learn.

On the other hand, while obedience is expected in family matters, young people are free to make many choices regarding their own personal lives. Thus parents are unlikely to suggest or urge particular activities on children, such as reading a book or joining a school club. Children may be forbidden to associate with certain peers or perhaps even to go out at all, but these prohibitions are necessary for the reputation of the family, not because of specific danger to the individual child.

Similarly, parents are unlikely to try to "make" their children study. Ability to learn academic subjects is viewed somewhat as Americans view artistic talent—a wonderful blessing but not something that can be forced. A parent whose child is not doing well in school is likely to smile and shake her head with resignation: "Yeah, he's not smart. He's like me—hard to learn English!" The issue is certainly not worth controversy within the family.

The importance of age may also affect schoolchildren. Old people who have never been to school receive a great deal of love, attention, and respect. Treated with honor and awe, the elders are important and attractive models for the young, resulting in a somewhat conservative effect on the youth.

Finally, it is important to recognize the importance of the virginity of daughters to a family's honor and to the marriageability of the other girls in the family. Thus, although little girls have a lot of freedom and are encouraged to run and play actively, girls approaching puberty are supervised more closely. They should not be out at night, should not be alone with a boy, should not be around boys at all unless closely supervised by a parent or older sibling. Traditionally, many parents felt girls shouldn't learn to write because they would write love letters—which those in Middle City certainly do! Since loss of virginity is considered an inevitable consequence of a boy and girl being left alone, American-style dating is unthinkable. If a girl is suspected of having a boyfriend, she may be swiftly married. American school personnel object when worried parents protect their daughter's and their family's reputation by insisting on marriage, but parents see the schools as causing the problem by creating situations in which boys and girls are expected to interact and also by encouraging students to think and act independently (which of course includes independently of their parents' wishes).

If family is the most important institution in the daily life of Khmer society, Buddhism also figures significantly in forming values. We have seen that for the ordinary person the essence of Buddhism is to be a "good person." The values most evident throughout my research and noted by Ebihara are selflessness, cooperation, and respect. Industriousness is good in itself and as it contributes toward the well-being of the family or others; it is not valued as a means toward the achievement of material wealth, personal wealth being neither particularly admirable nor an indication of a "good person." Thus simply working hard is a positive virtue in children, but working hard at schoolwork has no more inherent value than working hard at family tasks, and it's certainly less visible.

Cambodian children, as they mature, should be developing character, becoming quiet, gentle, respectful, and accepting in their demeanor; traits that Americans value as assertiveness or independence are considered childish, disruptive, and selfish. Selflessness and quiet cooperation, on the other hand, are adaptive values in a small community where everyone is in daily interaction. Equality is more important than "getting ahead" because inequality would result in jealousy and unease. Efforts to outdo others are essentially antisocial, aberrant. In Cambodian pedagogy, the teacher praises the accomplishment of a whole class, not of an individual. Thus when the refugees first arrived in Middle City, the children worked together to ensure that each of them was achieving at a school task at about the same pace, leaving no one behind. Similarly, questioning elders such as teachers is a challenge to authority and society and is thus also a sign of immaturity. Girls are expected to mature a little earlier than boys, and those who are "good" (helpful to their mothers and grandparents and kind to their little siblings) are viewed by the community as good potential wives. Teens of both sexes who devote undue time to selfish pursuits such as school and friends are regarded as a little wild, as poor marriage prospects. Teenagers' demeanor and helpfulness toward the family are under constant public scrutiny at community events and daily in the neighborhoods; school grades, less visible, are less likely to receive public notice or approval.

A moment's reflection on these qualities suggests that while these values are certainly admirable and surely contribute to pleasant cooperative community life, they are not effective in the American school system, where personal success is valued and rewarded above all else and is achieved through competition with one's peers.

Because monks were the traditional teachers, parents avoid visiting the school or questioning teachers, for to do so would be a challenge to the monks' authority over the child. Parents described typical school discipline: "stand out in the hot sun all day or maybe stand on one foot all day." Parents were not to interfere unless "the teacher breaks something," meaning bones. Following this pattern, Cambodian parents in Middle City seldom question teachers or decisions made by school authorities and don't query their children about their schoolday or their homework. Although the schools read this as lack of interest and lack of support, for the parents it is simply the proper demonstration of respect. Parents often say the children "belong to the teachers," much in the way children were "given to" the monks in the old days. Some parents also say that it's pointless and embarrassing to talk to their children about school; since they are unlikely to understand much of the discussion, it presents another situation for inversion of the parent-child hierarchy and contributes to the undermining of parental authority.

I've commented earlier on what I call an "aesthetic of glamour." Though perhaps not a central value, it is broadly evident, and it is one that meets disapproval and opposition in the schools. It may seem only a minor issue when little girls of six wear stockings, lipstick, rouge, eye makeup, and party shoes to school; but to the extent that teachers feel parents are dressing the girls "inappropriately" or "provocatively" and respond (with words, actions, or looks) to that feeling, it represents a cultural conflict between the Cambodian children and the teachers. Teachers may need help addressing their own biases. There may be more to it, however. From the earliest age, this very attractive aesthetic of glamour is everywhere and constant in the girls' lives. The ideal of glamour is perhaps more naturally appealing to young girls and also more readily available and easier to achieve than, for example, academic prowess. Like helpfulness in the family, it is also more likely to attract community attention and approval than the more invisible academic success.

THE EFFECTS OF THE KHMER ROUGE AND THE REFUGEE CAMPS

The experience of life under the Khmer Rouge must be considered a powerful factor not only for the children who actually lived it, but also for children who have since infancy heard stories of those times and who are parented by adults who experienced the atrocities. Earl Huyck and Rona Fields and others have pointed out that the experience of "violence inflicted on 'significant others' is personally and developmentally damaging" (1981:247). Being parented by adults who are physically and psychologically traumatized is also likely to be an important factor in children's development. I've emphasized the importance of family in Cambodian culture. The enormity of the effects of family destruction by the Khmer Rouge is probably incomprehensible to Americans: everyone lost family members, and nearly everyone lost children, parents, or grandparents. The disintegration of family was not only devastating on a personal and emotional level, but was the disintegration of the very social fabric itself.

In addition to the extensive killing and suffering, the Khmer Rouge were determined to undermine any elements we might call modern, Western, or urban—in other words, qualities that might have fostered adjustment in the United States. Specifically, the Khmer Rouge sought out for special torture and killing anyone with education, including anyone who spoke French (since it was learned only in school and represented education), monks (as dual symbols of Buddhism and intellect), and schoolteachers. Playing upon the historic unease between the ruling and the peasant classes, the Khmer Rouge told people repeatedly that the educated were leaches, foreign spies. Thus to be educated was suddenly both reprehensible and dangerous.

The experience of flight, too, was generally worse for Cambodians than for other refugees, since most of them simply ran from horror rather than toward some chosen haven. They had no idea what they would find in Thailand, and the trip itself took them through dangerous jungles and mine fields and exposed them to robbery, murder, and rape by both Khmer Rouge and Vietnamese soldiers.

Once in refugee camps, things were not always better: guards and soldiers continued to victimize women and children. In the best cases there was only minimal health care and very poor education (Tollefson 1989). My informants said they were not really taught English, "just a-b-c." There was no way to earn a living, no way for adults to assert themselves toward improvement of their family's situation. Torn families languished in despair and fear, and the pattern of helplessness and dependence on others, initiated by the Khmer Rouge, continued. For many, severe depression set in, which has lasted up to the present. When opportunities came to go to a third country, there was a further filtering on the basis of education. Those who had some higher education knew French, not English, and so often chose to go to France; consequently many of those who came to the United States were often those with less education or less choice.

Thus they arrived in the United States. They came with a low level of literacy in their own language and almost no English. Few adults had any Western-style schooling, and many had had no school experience at all. Many children had never been to school because of constant war after 1970. Worst of all, although parents knew that education would be necessary for their children in the United States, there was also a subtle wariness about education, both a generalized discomfort with the educated elite of their own country and the specific recent experience that education brings death. This was the framework with which these Cambodians came to face American schools.

During the entire refugee process—from the slave camps, through Thailand, and in the initial months in the United States—those who were educated were not better off in any apparent way. Since the survivors of the upper classes had been schooled in French rather than English, they had the same initial difficulties here as the uneducated peasants. (It is true, on the other hand, that those from the urban elite have eventually had more success than the others; the adults have eventually found better jobs, and more of the youth have graduated from high school.)

EXPERIENCE IN AMERICA: SCHOOLING IN MIDDLE CITY

Arrival in the United States did not bring an end to adversity. The pressure for immediate employment meant parents had little time with their families at a particularly critical time in the lives of those families. Parents who may have wanted to help their children with school had no time to do so, and instead, of necessity, placed heavy responsibilities of housekeeping, childcare, and translation upon the older children. The press for immediate economic independence also meant that Cambodians were placed in the most impoverished, dangerous, and decaying neighborhoods, which also meant the worst schools, schools already impoverished and suffering racial conflict. The teenagers fell into the speech patterns and the school behaviors of their underclass neighbors and schoolmates. Both Cambodian parents and American teachers in Middle City feel that the bad influence of American peers has corrupted the Cambodian teens and lured them out of school and into ganglike activities.[3]

The dialogue at the beginning of this chapter occurred toward the end of the eleventh year the Cambodian children were in the Middle City schools. I ran into similar situations from the first days of fieldwork. When I first began, I naively sought parents' permission to interview children, so I wrote out a consent form, asking the Khmer-speaking aide to translate it. She refused, saying she wasn't going to send home any more notes; even in Khmer, many parents couldn't read them, and it placed a strain on the family for the children always to be reading notes to their elders. I heard similar accounts all during my research. The teachers, including the native-language aides, are aware that the children sign their own permission slips and report cards and mistranslate notes from school.

Parents don't visit schools for many reasons in addition to their tradition of respect. Initially they were sick, had babies at home, and spoke no English. Now they may also have daytime jobs. The generally unfamiliar (and uncomfortable) physical layout of schoolrooms and the unfamiliar social system can also be intimidating to adults who have had no schooling. A visit to school puts parents in one more situation where they must depend on their children to mediate between them and another adult and in fact to explain the general nature of the social system.

Several schools have ESL programs, and the Cambodian children were the dominant group in these at first. The programs shifted from one school to another over the fifteen years the Cambodians have been in attendance, and there has been considerable personnel fluctuation. Because the influx of Cambodians was large and sudden, the teachers were unprepared: most had no knowledge of the culture, no ESL training, and no Cambodian cultural or language materials for the students. Some teachers pursued special summer training or weekend workshops after the program began, but federal support was brief and the teachers already overworked. At times there have been two or three Khmer-speaking aides either connected with specific schools or working with the district.

During their first years, most of the children are together in an ESL class for half the day, then are "mainstreamed" into regular classes for the other half. Federal funding supports this for a maximum of five years, so the children who are not "up to level" after five years enter the high school unprepared to function well in regular classes; as the teachers say, they just don't have "student behaviors": they don't take notes in class, they don't write down assignments, they don't study for tests, they don't read directions, they don't do homework, and they are frequently absent. The teachers feel the five-year limit unrealistic for children who hear no English at home and have no patterns of literacy or schooling in the family; they feel that such children, or some of them, may need as many as seven or nine years in special classes.

The teachers are concerned about the more "successful" students as well. Occasionally they find a particular child they think should be encouraged to apply for college, but the parents often say no for reasons the teachers find unsatisfactory. They acknowledge the role of "cultural differences" here and explain to one another that Cambodians are not future-oriented, that these families need the income now that the teenagers can earn better than anyone else in the family, and that life under Pol Pot and in refugee camps and here on welfare has discouraged planning for the future. But still, the teachers are frustrated, defeated. They do not see that "future" orientation to these families means a longer (in fact, infinite) future than Americans recognize, and that in Buddhist culture doing good for others is more important than obtaining good for oneself.

The children who left city schools and ESL programs for suburban schools without special programs seemed at first to do a little better, although a comparison is not really possible because of the reasons they were taken out: the family was wealthier, had more English, valued education more, had better sponsors, or was more motivated than others to Americanize. Any of these factors could foster school success, so the success of certain children without ESL doesn't mean they would all do so well. This is an important point because those who took their children out view their success as proof that ESL is unnecessary. In recent years, however, neither those children nor others who left later have shown notable achievement in American terms. The ESL teacher and the Cambodian aide are reluctant to release the children officially out of ESL for other reasons: first, once out, the children cannot reenter the program (the funding is lost) so that some students remain on the ESL rolls even though they may be entirely mainstreamed; second, the teacher and aide believe the children are not really up to par and will be lost in a regular classroom; third, the teacher and particularly the Cambodian aide feel that the children are better protected when they are all together—protected from picking up the misbehavior and bad habits of the Americans in the inner-city school.

The primary classes focus on teaching the children the patterns of English speech. The teacher shouts out to the cluster of children gathered at her feet, "The truck is red!" and the children chorus back, "Duh truh ih reh!" She tries again, even louder, "The. truCK. iZZ. reDDuh." A few of them shout back, "Da tru-ck-ck-ck ih REY-AH!" and tumble into a laughing heap. She doesn't mind the joking; she's happy to have gotten these "shy, quiet Asians" shouting at her and hopes that a few will eventually become comfortable with the final consonants. It's unlikely. She's teaching "white" middle-class English to children who won't hear those patterns anywhere else in the school, their homes, or their neighborhoods. What they do in fact pick up in the neighborhood, on the playground, and from their other teachers is Black English Vernacular, and they learn to speak it quickly and fluently.

By many measures, these children may be termed "successful" in school. They're liked by their teachers and by the other personnel. They win awards, usually based on attendance and good behavior, but sometimes for academics too. As might be expected, they often do better in math than in more verbal-dependent subjects, but they do not do as generally and strikingly well as the Asian children from other countries who have earned for all Asians the reputation of "whiz kids."

The high school students rise through various levels of ESL according to their abilities and take varying amounts of regular classes. Because they have begun formal schooling late in life (for some of them, their first formal schooling was ninth grade in Middle City) and because language learning is a slow process, many of them reach sixteen with graduation still several years off; at that point the temptation to drop out is great, for them and for their families. Many do drop out, to marry or to get jobs or just because they don't like it. Others marry and have babies but remain in school. At first, because of the adjusted ages, the teachers encouraged them to remain in school to graduate, even if some were twenty-two or twenty-three. Now, state laws prevent students over twenty-one from attending, so that even if they are one month from graduation, on their birthday they are out.

At first, some of the high schoolers graduated with high grades. In the first year of this study, eleven were accepted into local colleges. Some went and some did not, but by December they were all out of school, finding themselves hopelessly unprepared. They disliked the large classes and the anonymity: "Too big, you're not a person there. No one to help you, no one care about you." Even at a small college, they felt their special needs were not understood. A hardworking young woman struggling with a physics class said, "One hundred and five questions, fifty minutes! Mary, I know the stuff, but I can't read that fast. I told the teacher I can't read English that fast, asked for more time, and he said, 'Everybody in my class is American. If you're here, you're American. No exceptions.'" One girl went away to school and did well but came back after a year to marry; others juggle full-time college, jobs, and babies; still others support elderly parents or clusters of siblings but still try to take a class or two.

I've pointed out that in Middle City the little children seem to do well in school, and the teenagers do not. How can we account for that difference? On the surface, it's easy to understand why the older children had a difficult time initially: they began their first schooling as teenagers and entered high school with no English. Also, simply being older, they had suffered longer the physical, mental, and emotional trauma of the Khmer Rouge. If those were the only problems, we might predict school success to increase over time, with those arriving as young children doing much better in high school than their teenage siblings have done before them. Unfortunately, this is not the case.

The little children do well in school for a number of reasons. Because of their youth, they learn English fairly easily. As young children, they are still well ensconced in families where, despite financial and other difficulties, they are generally secure and tended by a number of caring adults and siblings. Because of their families' values about comportment, they are generally quiet, well-behaved, and obedient, traits pleasing to middle-class teachers and reflected in school grades. Furthermore, although many of the parents are uneducated, they understand the importance of reading and writing in this country, and some encourage or praise their children along these lines.

But as children enter adolescence, they begin to do less well in school. Grades become less dependent on demeanor and more dependent on competitive achievement, a quality alien to Cambodians. Young teens see their older peers and siblings choosing jobs or marriage over school; since older siblings are greatly respected, the younger ones often adopt these patterns too, even if they themselves are experiencing more success in school. Another problem is that, as teens, they naturally are trying to be more like their peers. Since the American peers tend to violate Cambodian parents' ideas of "good" teenagers, interaction brings the teens into serious conflict with their parents and dampens parental support of schooling. Sometimes the conflict becomes so unbearable the teens leave home, generally resulting in their dropping out of school in order to support themselves. An alternative in situations of serious family conflict is to accede to parental wishes by turning away from peers (and school) and marrying or getting jobs; this is a common solution for girls in Middle City.

If the little children are sometimes able to find an adult in the family to help with basic reading or arithmetic, teenagers are far less likely to find someone to help with American history, chemistry, and algebra. Even the occasional sponsor who may help a youngster with schoolwork may be reluctant with high school subjects, so the teenagers are much more on their own.

In addition, although parents may see the benefits of basic literacy, there is less in a high school curriculum that can appear necessary to refugee parents. As teens become older, the value of their practical contributions at home begins to gain precedence over the uncomprehended and impractical subjects they are studying at school: they are important as translators and cultural mediators for their parents; they begin to take on responsibility for important decisions such as school choices for their younger siblings, house buying, banking, and insurance; and their potential income increases.

A related, but less conscious, factor may also be at work here. Cambodian families have lost so much and suffered so much trauma that for parents and teenagers who remember, the need to rebuild may take precedence over all other life goals. Today's youth have had life-and-death responsibilities for young siblings—carrying them long and dangerous distances, giving up their own food to them, nursing them from deadly diseases, and so on. It may be that teens, as well as their parents, feel a need to reestablish family through new births. Since much joyful fuss and attention is directed toward babies and new mothers, girls gain community recognition and establish themselves as "good" adults through marriage and childbirth, the social rewards of which are more evident than the uncertain benefits of more schooling.

I began this chapter with the premise, based on the research of others and myself, that many Cambodian refugee children do not meet with success in the American educational system. The following is a summary list of some the factors which I believe contribute to that lack of success, and which I feel school and educational systems must address when planning for the education of refugee children. Some of these factors are specific to Cambodians, but many apply to other cultures and other refugee situations:

1. Rural Cambodians do not have a tradition of universal literacy and schooling; literacy was highly regarded for its aesthetic and spiritual roles, rather than for practical use.
2. Most parents were farmers and continue to view a farming life with nostalgia; many still hope to return to that life.
3. Socially directed personality traits such as kindness and generosity are more valued than purely self-directed traits such as knowledge and independence; competitiveness and material gain are not admirable values.
4. Marriage and motherhood are socially approved and socially rewarded life goals for girls.

5. Academic abilities are considered a special gift or talent rather than the result of time and effort.

6. Torture and enslavement during the Pol Pot era led to serious physical, emotional, and spiritual problems, which have largely gone unaddressed; as a consequence, many adults and teens experienced depression and other symptoms of post-traumatic stress. These problems do not simply fade with time but can intensify if untreated.

7. Many families, the foundation of social life, were ravaged under Pol Pot.

8. A child's individual inclination should be respected in personal matters (such as schooling).

9. Parents were not given time or support on first arrival to learn English or job skills.

10. Lack of employment opportunities and underemployment result in lack of employed role models for students.

11. Poor working conditions and low-status jobs require many parents to work at night, when children are home studying.

12. Children surrounded only by nonstandard English speakers will learn nonstandard English, adding to their linguistic problems.

13. American high school subjects do not have readily apparent utility or relevance to the families' present situation or life goals.

14. Many parents, unschooled, cannot help teenagers with schoolwork.

15. Since parents can't read notes sent home, children make many serious educational decisions for themselves or for their younger siblings, thus further distancing the parents from the educational process.

16. Children carry many necessary home responsibilities.

17. Parents are concerned about the negative influence of American youth.

18. Parents are concerned about unsupervised cross-sex association among youth in American culture.

19. Schools are physically and culturally unfamiliar and forbidding to parents.

20. Much time, money, and emotional energy are devoted to family reunification and the need to bury the dead in Cambodia.

21. Many adults have a reality-based sense of victimization and hopelessness.

22. Students who cannot devote a full day to high school must drop out and thus lose all chance at further education.

23. Available General Education Diploma (GED) programs are not suited to students with low English skills.

WHAT CAN SCHOOLS DO?

It is most important here to convey the complexity of the issues involved and to highlight the difficult *match* of various American and Cambodian cultural practices and value systems, rather than to judge any of them. Perhaps little can be done about conflict of values: it may be inappropriate for a teacher to urge children to excel if those children's deepest and most elemental cultural values teach them that they should *not* excel; and it may be presumptuous for an American who has never seen her own babies or siblings die to try to dissuade a Cambodian teenager from having a baby.

But there is little point in schools saying, "The parents don't . . ." or "The parents must . . ." or "Their culture doesn't. . . ." These are loving parents doing what they see as best for their children to the extent that their situation permits. They will undoubtedly make the adjustments that they can and that they consider important. It is up to educators to envision ways by which teachers, schools, school districts, educational planners and policy makers, and teacher-training institutions can adjust programs to provide good educations for Cambodian and other refugee and immigrant children. Since American schools are struggling anyway and finding themselves in conflict with many ethnic groups, it is incumbent upon the the educational establishment to examine alternatives and to make changes that will improve schools not only for Cambodians but for all students.

Some of the ideas I offer here are simple, and some are in practice in California and other areas; but they are not practiced in Middle City nor in other cities with small groups of refugees. Other of my suggestions may be so broad or radical that they may seem impossible. But it is useless to decry all the refugees on public assistance without stretching our imaginations to consider novel approaches. The suggestions here are directed to five constituents: classroom teachers, schools, school districts, the national Department of Education, and colleges of education.

The Classroom Teacher

Though major changes must be initiated at higher levels, teachers can make small adjustments to enhance the chances of success for Cambodian children, beginning with simple physical features of the classroom itself. For the youngest children, classrooms can be rendered more familiar and comfortable by seating children on the floor (as at home) and joining them there. Since this is probably where they'll do their homework, they might as well learn to write in this position (as well as at desks). Visiting parents, too, can be provided comfortable matted or cushioned floorspace. Walls should display maps and pictures of Cambodia and Cambodian people—all the time, not just for special units on "foreign cultures." Khmer script should be visible around the room and all children encouraged to try it; a parent or teenager can be invited in to demonstrate and to pronounce the letters. Familiar items can be used when teaching young children new concepts, such as rice or chopsticks for math, familiar words for early spelling and reading. As far as the "aesthetic of glamour," teachers can provide parents with pictures of sturdy shoes and might simply request that girls not wear elaborate earrings; makeup itself is not really hazardous. Teachers concerned about the broader implications of a glamour aesthetic can see that appealing pictures are available of women in a variety of professional roles, while assuring that girls are not teased for their own style of dress.[4] Cambodian children are used to some personal bodily freedom, so teachers might avoid unnecessary regimentation of such things as using restrooms. These suggestions are fairly rudimentary, and implementation would involve minimal effort.

Other adjustments, such as in teaching style, are more difficult to make but may have more long-term significance and may be beneficial for all children as well as for minorities. Since Cambodian culture, like most non-Western culture, is more group oriented than American culture, teachers should develop group projects and cooperative learning activities rather than individual and competitive learning situations. In Cambodia and in Khmer-language schools in the United States, children learn through group recitation, which reinforces the correct patterns until the slower children learn them.   Quicker students may recite alone if they choose, but shame is avoided by not requiring recitation of anyone not ready (Needham 1991). Group recitation encourages effort by the less advanced students and fosters a sense of helpfulness among the advanced students.   In addition, since students are neither praised nor reprimanded by name, their efforts and success become group achievement (Longmire 1992).   As I noted in the description of the Sunday school classes, and as I also observed in schoolrooms, Cambodian children accomplish quite a bit by observing one another, relying on little verbal direction from teachers.   These teaching and learning patterns support important Cambodian values of cooperation and selflessness.   Such cooperative values could be advantageously encorporated into classrooms by rewarding group effort with group rewards, such as extra playtime, rather than rewarding individual achievement individually (with, for example, grades, certificates, or toys).

Since evidence from primate studies and hunter-gatherer cultures shows that children learn best and most naturally from slightly older peers (Washburn 1971), teachers might encourage students to bring siblings (older and younger) into the class occasionally.   Even toddlers (brought in with their mothers of course!) can help older children develop responsibility and patience, important lessons for American as well as immigrant children.

The School

Some adjustments can be made at the level of the individual school.   Since children learn more from slightly older peers than from adults, and more by doing than from being told, the establishment of multi-age classrooms can benefit all children.   In such environments, young children readily mimic those who are only slightly more capable, while older children strive to do well because they know they are role models.   These expanded age groups can encompass school-age siblings, who, as we have seen, are especially important in the lives of Cambodian children. More interaction with older peers and less focus on adults provides a more familiar learning situation for Cambodian (and many other) children.   Another advantage of multi-age classrooms is that children can remain with the same teacher for several years, resulting in more continuity and better understanding between teachers and pupils.   For children who have undergone traumatic uprooting in their past and who may have language problems, such continuity can be significant.

Parents who have had little or no schooling cannot be expected to help their children either with schoolwork nor in adjustment to school culture.   Classes for parents can include English-language lessons, but can also provide general explanations of school policies and expectations, educational theory, and subject matter.   Parents can be given specific suggestions on how to help children with school in general (by limiting television, for example, or encouraging reading), and with specific assignments.   Parents may need to be taught that good grades depend on doing homework rather than on having talent and that bad grades may indicate that a child has not spent enough time on a task, not that the child has misbehaved.   If parents are given little samples of the subject matter before the children come home with it, at least they will have some sense of what the child is doing. If parents are not comfortable coming to school for such classes, the classes can be taught in the neighborhoods and should be ongoing, since new children enter school each year. When there is no possibility of parents' helping children with schoolwork, American children the same age or a little older can make excellent tutors, at the same time enhancing their own self-esteem and broadening their cross-cultural experience.

Schools must take the initiative in promoting better understanding between schools and the refugee community. Administrators can make efforts to establish relationships with ethnic organizations such as MAAs or temples. If there is a wat, a class visit can be instructive for all children and a source of pride for the Cambodian children. Community association leaders and monks can serve as mediators between school personnel and parents. (This is being practiced to some extent in some cities, such as Long Beach, California, but not in Middle City; naturally it depends upon the existence of an MAA or a temple.) Schools can enhance their accessibility to the community by holding schoolwide or communitywide celebrations for New Year and other important holidays, encouraging teenagers to teach the traditional games played and inviting parents to bring traditional food. The elderly, particularly isolated, might welcome space for gathering during nonschool hours. English language and Khmer literacy classes for adults and discussion groups on the difficulties of parenting in the United States could be offered as well, led by Cambodian-American teams. By making the school a familiar and welcoming place for Cambodian adults, adults may come to view the schools as less inimical to their cultural values.

Since poverty and transportation are common problems for new refugees, schools might arrange transportation for school-based activities such as parents' nights or award assemblies; refugee parents are more likely to attend such events in a group than when invited alone and are more likely to respond to a personal invitation than to a note. Mothers can be encouraged to bring their small children to meetings, so that they don't have the worry of leaving them home and also so that toddlers become accquainted with school.

Even simple changes can make schools a little less forbidding. For example, rice, the main food of Cambodians, is seldom served in Middle City schools; it could easily be offered daily as a nutritious choice. Uniforms, used in some cities, assure that children will be dressed according to teachers' standards, help children feel they fit in, and foster group orientation rather than individualism.[5]

Local and State Departments of Education

Major adjustments in educational programs and major policy changes can be made only at the school district or state level and require serious reconsideration of the role of schools in American society. If the goal is to have a society well-educated enough to run a democracy and to fill the expanding occupational and professional demands of the future, schools may have to do more than merely teach in order to retain students. At the same time, schools must be sure that they are themselves getting the teaching, all of it, done, and not leaving some of the tasks for parents or children to struggle with at home.

One of the most frequent complaints of Cambodian teenagers and parents is "homework," that part of schoolwork that spills over into the "home" part of the day. Parents sacrifice the teens' potential income and household help by sending them to school for the day; it is unreasonable that the youth should be gone all day and then want time alone in the evening to do more schoolwork. Particularly for refugees and immigrants, home time is needed for learning home skills, for maintaining the language and culture, and for maintaining the strong family. Cambodian parents in Middle City, skeptical of the value of school learning anyway, feel that children get enough during the day and should not bring school home. General districtwide or statewide policies to complete academics in the school within the school day would allow all children, Cambodian as well as others, to spend more time with their families or at other important activities. Equally important, if schoolwork stays at school, the work can be supervised and a suitable environment assured. Teens from nonacademic households are more likely to develop academic skills in an academic environment, with role models, encouragement, and fewer distractions. Since it is sometimes impossible for homes to provide academic role models and academic help, schools should provide them. Even children with extraordinary self-motivation may be prevented from studying at home because their parents place other responsibilities, such as child or elder care, housework, driving, and translation, on them. By opposing parents' views of what their children should be doing at home, schools may further alienate the adults and foster more dropping out. For students who are behind and for those who seek extra help or extra work, schools can provide educationally nurturing environments after school hours—for example, a quiet classroom with desks and older students or aides available as tutors. Such an environment would also encourage reluctant children to develop habits of seeking help, a serious problem for older Cambodian students.

If learning is accomplished at school, less school time will be necessary for testing. In American schools, tests serve two purposes: to motivate students to study at home and to assess learning. If studying at home is not expected and students do all they possibly can during the schoolday, then testing can be reserved for actual assessment and thus may be needed less frequently, allowing more time for actual teaching. Such a plan places more responsibility on teachers to see that learning is accomplished in the classroom and is more humane than punishing children for things they are not able (or even permitted) to do at home. The schoolday should be as long as necessary to accomplish the necessary work. If some children need more time, they also probably also need more help than they can get by studying alone at home; if some children need less time, they can be given enrichment activities, can become peer tutors, or, if older, can be given a slightly shortened day.

For older children, dropping out before graduation is a common problem. Cambodian girls are more likely than boys to drop out of school because they often marry earlier and have babies earlier than Anglo-Americans (and earlier than Cambodian girls in Cambodia; see Smith-Hefner 1993). They may regret the decision once they have children and find employment difficult. Schools should welcome this reconsideration and should ease return to school by providing school-based childcare with easy access by the mothers. In addition to keeping the girls in school, this childcare could serve multiple purposes if it employed Cambodian adults to care for the babies: it would provide experienced and culturally appropriate care for the babies; it would assure the girls and their parents that the babies were being well cared for; it would provide employment for some Cambodian adults; and it would draw at least a few Cambodian adults into the school, a place where they are hesitant to come.

Among the most burdensome features of public school systems is the rigidity of schedules, both the daily and the yearly schedule. The schedule of the high school day is not accommodating to working teens or mothers. In order to encourage young adults who have other responsibilities to also stay in school, schools must not demand that youth be present the entire day; part-day schooling would enable more youth to attend. Girls, especially, would have some time with their own children and could still perform their household responsibilities. At the same time, the schoolday could be extended into the evening, so that youth could choose to attend classes when their younger siblings are home to babysit. Thus high schools would have flexible hours and extended day schedules as colleges do; this would give teachers, again as in colleges, a variety of options for their schedules.

In the same way, the nine-month, single-term system is not flexible enough for youth with complex lives. A short term of, for example, eight or ten weeks, would enable students who do poorly or drop out briefly to pick up again soon, rather than wait a whole year. For example, a student who failed the fall term could begin again in January. Classes could continue right through the summer, maximizing space and providing employment for teachers who wish. This system, like that of many colleges, would also offer a second chance to students who drop out to get jobs, then regret the decision after a few weeks or months. It would also enable students old for their grade to finish high school more quickly. Such a system would have advantages for younger children, too, who often fall behind during the long summer months. For children with working parents, summer days might be better spent at school or school-based activities (perhaps a combination school and camp program) than alone at home watching television.

One of the major problems for Middle City refugee youth is that they are required to leave school after they are twenty-one. No matter how conscientious they are, there is no place else for them to go. General Education Diploma programs offer little support, few of the amenities of regular schools (like science laboratories), and no ESL components; it is doubtful that they can prepare students completely and broadly for facing life in a new country. Rather than forcing students out, society benefits by permitting students to attend as long as they make progress.

Schools could make two further adjustments in response to research findings. Helga Jockenhovel-Shieke (1986) found that if children have developed their skills of thought and learning in their native language, then further development of those skills will be retarded if no provision is made for continued native-tongue education (see also Huyck and Fields 1981). Therefore schools should provide native language classes. If there are only a few such students, a native speaker can serve as a tutor.

A part-time tutor ought not have to fulfill all the requirements of a regular teacher, so a literate adult from the community might serve adequately. Even in such a small community as Middle City there are several adults who could fill this position well.

When I interviewed successful Cambodian college students in other cities, one of the most frequent points they made was the importance of sponsors in their positive school experience. A few lucky students had sponsors who met with them frequently when they first arrived, tutoring them, teaching their parents English, helping them shop and negotiate other institutions, helping the parents understand American styles of childrearing, mediating on their behalf between the schools and the parents, encouraging and praising the children in their schoolwork, helping the children find extracurricular activities that would not conflict with parental values (and helping the parents understand the benefits of such activities), and helping the older teens plan for college or realistic careers. Although most students were more likely to attribute their school success to other factors (such as that they just tried harder, or wanted to learn, or that their family was of a better social class that valued learning, or that other kids were just lazy), the factor of faithful, helpful sponsors always came up and it merits notice. In Middle City, the earliest families tended to have the better sponsors (particularly individual American families rather than churches, organizations, or kin), and it is also those children who seem to have been most successful in schools. If this is true, school districts would do well to find interested sponsors for families who have lost their sponsors or whose sponsors have not been helpful. Such sponsors can be specifically chosen as good role models for the children and can be specifically expected to help the children and families with educational matters.

Finally, the mental health situation is one which, while perhaps not the school's responsibility, causes problems for students in school. Children who have witnessed extreme violence and family death and children who are parented by depressed and anguished adults need culturally appropriate counseling. The educational community, as a primary advocate for children, must see that the larger community (city, county) provides such care for the children and their parents, since mental health is clearly fundamental to learning.

The Federal Department of Education

Many of the suggestions above may sound fiscally impossible for single schools, school districts, or even states that may feel pressured by large percentages of immigrant children and feel they cannot fund special materials and programs; but such things as foreign language textbooks for students, culture-training programs and books for teachers, native-language literacy programs for adults, and ESL classes can be developed at the national level and sent to specific states or cities as needed. The development of national curricular standards would mean less disruption when all children, not only refugees, move across states in our increasingly mobile society, and equitable funding throughout the nation would prevent some states from feeling overburdened by immigrants and would assure all children of an equal chance at education. It's important to recognize that refugees are not in the United States because of the actions of local communities, but because of political actions and decisions by the national government. We are no longer a society in which children grow up and spend their lives in a single community, and the federal government must take some responsibility for helping refugee children to become productive members of this nation. Furthermore, if programs such as I have proposed here are implemented on a national basis, secondary migration to states that do provide better programs will become be less necessary, and problematically large ethnic enclaves will be less likely to develop.

Colleges of Education

All these proposals are premised on a community of teachers and administrators aware of the particular circumstances and special needs of refugee children. Thus changes must begin in colleges of education, which train not only teachers but also administrators and educational researchers. I have three suggestions. The first is for teacher training to focus more on successful *teaching* methods, so that teachers will consider the teaching itself, and not the assigning of material, their primary responsibility. Prospective teachers can be encouraged to see the classroom, rather than the home, as the place for academic teaching and learning and to accept the full responsibility of teaching on themselves, rather than placing it upon parents, children, or the home environment. Teachers can also be taught to provide cooperative, group-oriented learning environments.

The second suggestion is to require of all prospective teachers coursework in basic cultural anthropology to familiarize them with such principles as cultural relativism and the integrated, holistic nature of culture. Education students can read ethnographies on the cultures present in their local schools, of refugee communities in the United States, of refugee education, and case studies of culture change. Such courses, though taught by anthropologists, can be specifically designed with education students in mind.

The final suggestion for teacher education would give prospective teachers real-life experience with refugee and immigrant families.[6] In this project, the students are introduced to anthropological research methods such as participant observation and ethnographic interviewing. Then each student does ethnographic research with a single refugee or immigrant family, preferably daily, to observe the family's life. The research focuses on the activities, attitudes, and knowledge that are a part of that family's culture, with special attention to patterns of parent-child interaction and communication, family methods of teaching and correcting, and the interactions of siblings. At the end of the term, each student writes and presents to classmates a mini-ethnography based on that family's culture. Such a project would prepare prospective teachers to be more open to and respectful of the home cultures and would encourage them to begin planning culturally appropriate teaching materials and methods. It would improve classroom education in several ways: it would foster teacher recognition that the family has culture; it would enable the teacher to introduce facets of that culture into the classroom in meaningful ways; it would enable teachers to see students in situations where they are quite capable and may carry much responsibility (as opposed to the school situation, where they may seem shy or incapable); it would help the teacher recognize and take into account children's home responsibilities; it would help the teacher understand adult-child communication patterns in that culture; it would put the parents in the role of preceptors and demonstrate the teacher's respect for the culture; and it would be an initial point of parent-teacher communication and understanding.

EDUCATING CROSS-CULTURALLY

I hope some of these suggestions will seem interesting and some practical. Because culture is a complex phenomenon and the interaction of several cultures even more complex, there is no single reason that Cambodian children appear to be unsuccessful in American schools, and there can therefore be no single or easy solution to the difficulties of cross-cultural education in general. Yet we cannot simply ignore the education of children whose life experiences have been different from those of the idealized American middle class.

It may be that the real task for educators is to ask exactly what kind of education is really needed and for what purposes. Cambodian parents want their children to grow up to be pleasant, cooperative, kind adults, as well as loving and responsible parents. While being responsible adults may entail reading and writing and basic math, we might question whether it entails being able to recite the dates of Civil War battles or to solve quadratic equations. We must reexamine exactly what constitutes an appropriate education for people whose foremost concerns are with being good citizens and parents and who are content with ordinary jobs. Perhaps we also ought to consider what we can learn from Cambodian culture and concern ourselves with how we might incorporate their values of cooperation, family cohesiveness, gentleness, and respect into our own educational systems.

NOTES

1. See, for example, Kimball and Burnett 1973; Gearing 1975; Hansen 1979; Ogbu 1974, 1981; and Pitman, Eisikovitz, and Dobbert 1989.

2. For examples in the popular press, see *Time Magazine* 1985, 1987.

3. The boys speak of "gangs," but these have not been like the seriously troubling gangs in larger cities—they have been just groups of boys who hang out (and skip school) together.

4. Young women and teens (high school drop-outs) were horrified at my job suggestions: electrician's or plumber's helper, yardwork, truck driver, etc. I knew they would be, but was trying to test the breadth of their horizons. They grinned, "No, no! Desk job! Reception!" They weren't balking at the difficulty of labor nor had they any idea what a "desk job" entailed (none of them could type, use a computer, or really even communicate effectively by telephone); I believe it was merely the image of women dressed in rough clothes and getting dirty that repelled and embarrassed them. A "good job" meant high heels, makeup, fashionable clothes, and plenty of jewelry; the actual tasks to be performed were not of concern.

5. When I made this suggestion in Middle City years ago, educators laughed—kids would never tolerate uniforms, parents couldn't afford them, it would be illegal, etc., despite the use of uniforms in the city's well-attended parochial schools. When I saw newly introduced public school uniforms in Long Beach, the teachers were delighted and there was no problem from parents or children. In the presidential campaign of 1996, the idea has gained political interest.

6. This idea derives from discussion with Norma González regarding the Funds of Knowledge for Teaching Project in 1993. The Project has since been implemented with considerable success and the results reported in *Educational Innovation: Learning from Households*, a special issue of *Practicing Anthropology* guest edited by Norma González (1995).

Chapter 8

Braving a New World: Maintaining Tradition, Transcending Barriers

This book has had two goals. The first was to provide a simple descriptive ethnography, to develop a broadly detailed portrait of the life and culture of the Cambodian refugees in Middle City in their ordinary daily life, in their special community events, and in their interaction with the American institutions whose purpose it is to serve them. I hope this portrait may provide a framework of understanding for teachers, social workers, clergy, health care professionals, and other Americans who sincerely desire to ease the adjustment of refugees to their new life, as well as for those who develop social policy and programs serving refugees and others.

My other aim was to provide a foundation for long-term study of culture change; thus I have focused to some extent on the processes and contexts of learning in the Cambodian culture and the Cambodian-within-American culture, in order to develop a holistic view of learning. This focus has revealed a complex and shifting mosaic of cultural maintenance and adaptation. Unfortunately, my research has also revealed many barriers both to the maintenance of traditional culture and to the learning of new culture. Many of these barriers may be unique to Cambodians or to Middle City, but many are probably also common to the experience of other refugee groups who find themselves in the United States.

CAMBODIAN CULTURE IN MIDDLE CITY

In this glimpse of a Cambodian refugee community we see the suffering, the achievements, the beauty, anger, compassion, love, tolerance, jealousy, patience, loyalty, solicitude, and joy that form the texture of everyday life. This is a multi-voiced community whose members neither speak nor live as a static entity. Their present patterns of behavior and beliefs are shaped by variations of ancestry and ethnic heritage, gender, age, social class and educational levels in Cambodia, different kinds and degrees of loss and suffering during the Khmer Rouge era, different lengths of time in different refugee camps, and different economic and occupational opportunities in the United States. Such complexity results in myriad variations of adaptive patterns—not merely points along a continuum of traditional to American but a multiplicity of combinations of adherence to tradition, adaptation of tradition, adoption of new, adaptation of new to ethnic purposes, and innovation, within the material, social, and ideological realms of culture.

In their material adaptation to life in Middle City, Cambodians seem to be learning much of American culture, or perhaps what might be best termed "international urban culture"—they cook in microwaves, dress like Americans, aspire to home ownership, drive cars, have their babies in hospitals, and use videocameras. But they also cook in woks and huge imported kettles, dress in traditional Cambodian styles, live in two-room flats, fear buses, and practice coining. American technology is adopted if it makes life noticeably easier—electric stoves and cars and Tylenol 3, for example; or if it enhances the ability to maintain and pass on their own traditions—sewing machines to simplify the making of the traditional clothes, videotapes to preserve the ceremonies and classical drama, and cars to maintain long-distance kin ties. Learning new technology, therefore, is not a problem; the problem lies in the availability of and access to that technology.

Social organization is less amenable to rapid innovation or change (White 1949, 1959). Predictably, then, Cambodian kinship, gender, age, and community patterns remain in Middle City much as they were in traditional Cambodia. Small children learn these patterns within the community long before they go to school or have much exposure to American customs. In the first few years, the maintenance of the ESL classes for the primary children and the presence of an adult Cambodian aide in the school allowed some of these general patterns and the values upon which they are founded to persist, at least through the elementary grades. It is at high school, where the adolescents get a greater exposure to American peers, that some of these patterns and values begin to be questioned, particularly those which impinge on the freedom of the teenagers to associate freely with their friends of both sexes. Some of them, particularly the girls, break away, either literally, by running away from home, or by maintaining friendships of which their parents are not aware or do not approve. Nevertheless, at this time it seems that the basic kinship patterns—monogamy, community exogamy, ambilocal residence with common uxorilocal or amitalocal residence, bilateral inheritance, Eskimo kinship terms, and the stem family—are maintained to a large extent in Middle City, only the current strain between generations suggesting a future increase in neolocal residence. Relationships within the family also seem to follow traditional patterns where they can, although they have been clearly disrupted by the loss of kin, particularly husbands and fathers, during the Khmer Rouge period.

Outwardly, gender relationships are much as Ebihara described them in Village Svay and are unlikely to change much here, being not too unlike patterns Americans claim. Cambodian women, although they manifest a veneer of docility and even occasional deference toward their husbands, are nevertheless, out of tradition and out of present necessity, remarkably determined, independent, and assertive. Although little girls seem entranced with the image of glamour and enthralled with babies, young adult women aspire to jobs or careers outside the home and to small families.

Age patterns, too, are outwardly traditional but are undergoing rapid change because they conflict with American patterns. Obedience to elders, respect for the aged, and reverence for ancestors are patterns that all of today's adults have brought with them and so are instilled in daily family patterns, in the religious ceremonies at home and at the temple, and even to some extent in the ESL classroom. But as school- and churchgoing children are exposed to different values—of independence, self-assertion, material achievement, questioning of adults and authority in general—they are becoming teenagers whom parents have difficulty managing, and they may become adults with less sense of deference to and responsibility toward the aged and the ancestors.

At present, community life goes on but community organization is in limbo. There is no temple to serve as the community focal point in Middle City as there was in traditional Cambodia and as there are in other refugee communities in the United States. Over the years, various efforts to establish an MAA have been unsuccessful. Few people have become citizens, and few participate in other forms of American community organization, such as neighborhood councils or parent-teacher organizations. But "community" exists, if only in the friendships, in the sense of shared history, and in the network of gossip that monitors and mediates social behavior (see Mortland and Ledgerwood 1988).

Finally, ideology may be the area of culture least likely to change. Ironically, the agents of social change in Middle City that have been perhaps the most forthcoming with help on a daily and personal basis are ideological structures—churches. Buddhism, the heart of traditional Cambodian culture, is a very strong factor in the life of Cambodians in Middle City. Lacking a temple of their own, they make arduous trips to another city at a significant sacrifice of time, trouble, and money. Even people who originally said to me, "We used to be Buddhist, now we're Christian," or "Before I believed Buddha, now I believe Jesus" tempered that a bit after seeing me go to the temple. "We're like you—believe both. Both the same, Jesus, Buddha, say the same thing: don't kill, be good person." It may be that they really do support both religions together, or it could be that Buddhism is their source of ideological strength and Christianity merely offers more practical earthly rewards. There is a sense of obligation to churches who have helped. One woman says, "I go to Christian church because they help my family so much when we come. They give us everything, now I want to give back to them"; but she also advocates the building of a temple in Middle City: "I want my people to feel they have a place, something of their own."

Whether this coexistence of Buddhism and Christianity supports the anthropological tenet that ideology resists change or suggests instead that this domain too will adapt is still unclear. Whichever is the case for the adults today, the fact is that the children who go to Sunday school and sometimes church get at least five to ten minutes of intentional teaching about Jesus or the Bible or Christianity each week, more than they get of formal instruction about Buddha or Buddhism; but formal instruction may be not be central in the cultivation of ideology. The distance to the temple and the difficulty of transportation means that many children have never been there. It may be that barriers such as lack of transportation will cause an eventual change that the parents don't desire for their children, such as the loss of Buddhism as community worship, or perhaps a form of syncretic or Americanized Buddhism may develop. The possibility of their own temple in Middle City seems remote.

Ideology seems to be more clearly resisting change in the realm of the arts. It is primarily the traditional aesthetic values which are being taught to and learned by the children. Again, elements of American culture are adopted—spandex for clothes, VCRs for drama, stereo systems for music, dollar bills on the money trees, and Halloween candles on the temple altar—but these are absorbed into the overall very Cambodian aesthetic of richly shifting color, light, and pattern.

MAINTAINING TRADITIONAL CULTURE

Cambodian children grow up in a richly complex, varied, and constantly changing community and culture, the major actors in which are their families and their peers. The traditional primacy of family has remained. At the dawn of the Khmer Rouge regime, people's first thought was to seek their families, and descriptions of life in the slave camps are filled with painful references to lost family. Today in Middle City, too, the family is a constant referent—love for, pride in, respect for, reliance on, and responsibility for family members are frequent themes in conversation. The environment of the very young seems especially warm and secure. Since adults spend much of their time at floor level, small children are at eye level; babies and toddlers live in a world of laps and sleep in the security of parents and older siblings. Older children spend less time directly with their parents, but still a great deal of time with siblings. Siblings of all ages enjoy one another's companionship, and pairs of sisters and pairs of brothers form bonds not necessarily broken by marriage.

The peer group is the other major social context of learning for children. Because families tend to be large and because at least in the old neighborhood children spend a lot of time outdoors playing together, children are constantly in the company of Cambodian peers, including siblings, cousins, nieces and nephews, and neighborhood kids; they run, dig in their yards, play in mud and water, draw, climb trees, play soccer and jump rope and videogames. They also work, though: they spend some nonschool time doing housework and schoolwork, and of course, compared to the traditional patterns, they spend a great deal of time in school itself.

Finally, although children spend much of their time together, they're seldom out of range of adult activity. On weekends and evenings, when adults and children are home, adult social interaction takes place in front yards, on porches, and in the living rooms of homes, with children constantly underfoot. Older children may be outside, but are continually coming in and out of the adult sphere. Teenagers also gather in groups on porches or living rooms, in close proximity to adults and children. During special events, infants and toddlers are again on laps, and again older children maintain a more tangential and sporadic presence but are not excluded from adult activities and are encouraged to participate fully (cook, eat, dance, pray) when they are present. Teenagers (particularly girls) and small siblings seem to enhance one another's status and security at such events. Since teens and adults are tolerant of mild disruptions by small children, the children are seldom made to feel unwelcome.

Much exposure to traditional culture takes place in social contexts that are emotionally charged, such as the communal ceremonies, which are often preceded by tension and excitement readily visible in the faces of childlren and adults as they participate in the elaborate preparations of food, ritual gifts, ceremonial costumes and paraphernalia, and the rituals themselves. Emotional bonds are important even in ordinary daily events; because of the strong and deep bonds within the family and across age lines, modeling and motivation is inherent in the daily family process. Little children desperately want to be like their older siblings, whom they adore and attach to whenever possible. As teens develop more self-control, obedience, and responsibility, the little children witness these traits as goals for their own behavior, even as their less reserved behavior is tolerated. The learning context, then, in terms of the social environment of this community, comprises people of various ages and genders, encompasses the complexity of their entire culture, and is swathed in the emotions of anticipation, love, and respect. By comparison, the hours in school may seem rather more spare.

Two features stand out in these "ordinary contexts for learning culture" in this community. The first is the attitude toward age. Cambodian culture presents age and maturity as positive values. People at each age level are respected and cherished by all of the age levels below them, so that just as one gains religious merit by good deeds, one also gains increasingly more love, respect, and worth as a natural reward of the maturing process. Ordinary daily life and ceremonial life provide ample opportunities for practicing and motivation for learning this important theme. Even tasks with no apparent inherent appeal to children, such as housekeeping, are symbolic of that maturing process which itself has appeal, so that one finds a seven-year-old flamboyantly wiping her brow and sighing dramatically, "Oh, there's so much work around here! Every day I have to sweep the floors, wash the dishes . . ."

The second feature is the importance of community ritual. The heightened atmosphere surrounding ceremonial occasions is experienced by everyone, and teenagers, although they couldn't always explain the meaning of the rituals, could always tell me what to do. Rituals are major contexts for the maintenance and trans-mission of traditional culture and the primary occasions that identify Cambodians to themselves, to one another, and to outsiders *as Cambodians*. It may be that future survival of traditional culture, and perhaps ethnic identity, will depend upon the maintenance of strong families and community ceremonies. It may also be, as I have argued elsewhere (Hopkins 1992), that maintenance of traditional culture may depend upon some degree of acquisition of American culture; for example, it may be that the better-educated and better-employed will be the ones able to read home newspapers, travel home occasionally, and finance cultural traditions such as a temple, monks, a dance troupe, and full-scale ceremonies.

I don't mean to paint an altogether rosy scene here. There are many barriers in the culture of Middle City and of the United States in general that hinder the maintenance of traditional culture. The northern urban location prevents the maintenance of farming traditions; the legislated small size of the Cambodian population hinders the development of ethnic stores or restaurants, a temple, or an MAA. American stores don't sell the items necessary for maintaining ethnic cuisine; they don't stock

Cambodian books, newspapers, or other media that would permit maintenance of cultural and political ties; import restrictions have prevented use of Cambodian ceremonial items, music, and goods in general. The school curriculum does not include their language, history, or culture, so children will become illiterate in their own language and history. After-school programs for children to learn their language and culture are lacking, as are programs for adults who wish to improve or maintain their Khmer literacy. The agencies that offer assistance are actually primarily culture change agencies; the help they offer is limited to that which meets their own goals of Americanization without a real understanding of the Cambodians' perception of their own needs. Finally, Cambodians' sense of gratitude and dependence may lead them to take on American ways, such as religion, that they do not really desire.

BARRIERS TO AMERICAN CULTURE

Though Cambodians often show a surprising flexibility and willingness to Americanize some aspects of their life, many barriers hinder their learning of and access to American culture. These barriers are themselves complexly interrelated, so that any one problem untended leads to the exacerbation of others.

Some barriers, or difficulties, came with the Cambodians as consequences of the political events of their country's recent history. These problems include their illness and generally poor physical conditions, their experience of physical and emotional trauma during the slave years and flight, the sudden and chaotic circumstances under which they fled, and the loss of kin; it would be difficult to exaggerate the depth, the extent, and the continuing importance of these conditions.

The stay in refugee camps in Thailand often exacerbated problems and also created new ones. Not allowed out of the camps to live or even to work, people lost personal autonomy and control over their and their families' lives, circumstances that led to increasing anxiety and despondency as time wore on. Many camps were dangerous —reports of theft and rape by camp guards are common. Years in camps meant lengthy postponement of seriously needed health care. Finally, the fact that many people in Middle City still have kin in Cambodia and Thailand means a great financial drain on the community to send money back to family members, as well as a constant guilt, for both the living and the dead.

Other problems originate with the American immigration procedures and laws. For example, families are separated, sometimes even sent to different countries, because they do not fit the American ideal of "nuclear family." Many are prevented from reuniting their families because they themselves are not U.S. citizens, but citizenship requirements often makes citizenship difficult or impossible to attain. Changes in refugee status and changes in quotas have also prevented family reunification.

Urban resettlement has created barriers for many who might have found appropriate employment and made better adjustments in rural situations. Middle City posed other problems as well, such as unaffordable and inadequate housing, dangerous neighborhoods, and resentment by similarly impoverished neighbors. Failure to educate American students and teachers about the Cambodians' experience resulted in what was seen as "special treatment" for them. Rumors spread among other minorities that the Cambodians were given free houses, free cars, good jobs, and highly paid "special teachers brought in from out-of-state"—although none of this was true. Official policies of dispersal, such as the Cambodian Cluster Project, resulted in separation of family and friends and may have hindered the development of strong MAAs; they have also led to much secondary migration, often away from sponsors.

Other barriers seem to derive from simple cultural differences, differences that cause Americans to feel that the Cambodians are "lacking" things basic to normal life: they "lack" English, literacy, schooling, job skills, and experience with urban living. After nearly fifteen years, many Cambodian adults still have only minimal English, partly because English classes are infrequent, distant, and taught by volunteers, partly because the newly arrived refugees were in no condition— physically, mentally, or emotionally—to undertake study of a foreign language, and partly because they were so quickly hustled off to employment. Lack of English in the monolingual United States leads to a plethora of barriers: to good jobs, to safe and adequate health care, to participation in their children's schooling, to friendships with Americans (who of course "lack" Khmer), and to general participation in American social and cultural life. In addition, non-English-speaking adults often must rely on children as interpreters (and misinterpreters) and on teenagers who, because of their English ability, are often the most employable members of a family.

Middle City is lacking in other conditions that might foster successful adjustment. The absence of suitable employment opportunities and underemployment of people who do have useful skills leads to problems with self-esteem and family relationships. Even those who find some employment may be unable to earn as much as welfare pays, and they lose the medical care for their families. Menial jobs often require considerable strength, a barrier for some who were ill, for some women, and for the elderly. Lack of suitable employment caused Middle City to lose several capable adults who might have become community leaders.

The lack of income caused by high unemployment makes unaffordable many other basic needs, such as health care, transportation, and childcare. These problems themselves lead to other barriers: lack of immediate, appropriate, and thorough health care can create long-term health problems that keep children out of school and adults home from work, keep people tired and in pain, and often lead to greater expenses later. Lack of adequate transportation keeps people from jobs, from English classes, from doctor's appointments, and from participation in their children's school life, as well as from other social and cultural activities that might enhance their adjustment to American culture; it also keeps them from the rural jobs that many could do and some do happily when they can get rides. Lack of affordable childcare prevents women from attending English and job-skill classes or from seeking employment; it also keeps siblings home from school occasionally to do childcare.

There are many barriers to adequate health care. Many of the health problems refugees have are not covered by public or employee insurance. When people do seek medical care, they don't know how to make appointments, are often unable to keep them because of other problems such as family obligations, can't get there, are afraid of the doctors, don't understand the instructions, don't know how to get prescriptions, misuse the medicines, and don't retain their health records. For their part, hospitals and medical personnel are monolingual and lack translators, are ignorant of or misinterpret traditional health practices, direct their instructions to American companions rather than to the patients, lack knowledge of and respect for the refugees' past experiences and trauma, ask inappropriate questions, give written prescription instructions to people who can't read, expect patients to appear with documents no one has told them to retain or to bring, misinterpret what they are told, and blame the patients for their illnesses.

Mental health care, often not covered by insurance plans, is particularly problematic. Given the traumatic experiences, mental and emotional problems are to be expected but are difficult to diagnose because mental health care in America depends upon verbal communication and shared understandings of what constitutes "normal" behavior. Because Americans treat psychological issues as health, rather than spiritual, matters, people tend to expect quick solutions; since first visits typically do not result in a cure, refugees are hesitant to return.

Some of the institutions that I found most willing to help Cambodians themselves presented, and were confronted by, barriers. For example, the schools, the Agency, and the church all had constantly shifting personnel, partly because of their own financial problems. Schools in American society expect parental literacy and expect parents to monitor children's schoolwork and to appear at the school on certain occasions to show that they "care." Parents who can't read, can't speak English, and are unfamiliar with school culture are left out of important decisions affecting their children. Rigid school calendars prevent children who must work from continuing their schooling. Schools lack migrant officials to help work out cultural and legal difficulties with foreign children, and teachers who take on these tasks are untrained to do so; in fact, in Middle City they generally lacked ESL training as well.

Sponsorship also, though designed expressly for helping with adjustment, often itself creates barriers. Multiplicity of funding agencies, frequent change in organizational structure and personnel, variation by state and locale, inadequate initial federal funding, and the intentionally brief sponsorship period are factors that hinder the adjustment process. Admission of refugees in irregular and enormous waves led to inadequate screening or training of initial sponsors, which in turn led to economic exploitation and frequent expectation of religious conversion by sponsors. Sponsors also have unrealistic expectations regarding the rate with which refugees can recover; underestimate the enormity of their own task; lack knowledge of the refugees' language, culture, and recent experience; and lack experience with the social service institutions which might help the refugees.

But sponsors may be a key factor in adjustment. To be helpful, sponsors must be truly dedicated to the long-term project. Looking at school success and failure, I considered all the usual factors: ethnic origins, religion, family system, economics, race, knowledge of English, health, "wave," and "voluntary" vs. "involuntary" status. Clearly some of those factors presented barriers to school success for the Cambodian children: poverty, minority racial status, lack of English in a monolingual society, the appalling state of their health, being at the tail end of the "wave" of Southeast Asians, and their "involuntary" status. Indeed, most school success stories included *some* of the following: urban origins, facility with English, some parental education, shorter time in refugee camps, less severe mental or physical torture. But they almost *all* included something else: sincere, capable, and generous sponsors with the resources to give the necessary attention and assistance to the refugee family from the beginning *and on a long-term basis.* Such sponsors helped by personally finding clean, safe housing; meeting with the family on a regular basis, daily at first, to take them shopping and elsewhere; tutoring them in English and physically taking them to English classes; monitoring the health care they received, getting them to appointments, talking to the doctors, and so on; tutoring the children through their first few years of school and occasionally after that; personally employing or monitoring the employment situations of adults; sometimes financing the children through private or parochial schools; and mentoring the children through school—talking to them regularly, encouraging them in their efforts, helping them find scholarships, and helping them choose colleges. Many of these families still, after fifteen years, have some contact with their sponsors, who still help—not financially, but with advice—in financial, educational, legal, and other matters. These families are not on welfare and the children are not in trouble, and the relationship has slowly evolved from one of patronage to one of friendship and mutual respect.

American ideology poses its own barriers. For example, steadfast belief in "bootstrap" success (despite the ironic impossibilitiy of the metaphor) and the efficacy of individual effort leads Americans to feel that the refugees will do fine if they're just left alone and to blame those who can't seem to achieve fast enough. The enormity of the problems faced by the Cambodians becomes buried under our belief in unlimited upward mobility. This bootstrap myth may underlie the official federal goal of immediate economic independence for refugees, a policy that I have noted before as shortsighted, undermining adequate preparation for truly fulfilling and successful lives in this country.

Another feature of American thought patterns that may exacerbate refugee difficulties is our tendency to think in dichotomies, mutually exclusive dualisms of possibility: one is in school, full-time, or one is out of school; one is married and thus independent of parents, or one is a dependent child; one is Christian or Buddhist, mentally ill or perfectly fine, a citizen or not, American or not. We leave little room in our social and ideological structures for individuals and states of ambiguity and transition, yet most refugees are in states of transition and need intermediate statuses to recognize and assist with that transition—for example, labor laws to protect children who do in fact work for family income; dual citizenship categories; school programs that enable teenagers to take a class or two and also work; medical practices that incorporate family, religious, and community factors; temporary but adequate financial support to provide safe housing for families; neighborhood schools offering adult ESL classes, job training, and childcare; health insurance which covers all of the medical problems and does not cease if parents get jobs; mental health counseling that takes culture and history into account; and workplace conditions that permit parents to parent their children at work.

A third fallacy in American thinking is that everyone wants to be American and that the reason people come here is to become American. In fact, few Cambodians in Middle City *chose* to come to the United States, and once here, few *choose* to become American; rather, they fled a deadly situation. This is not at all the same thing. The American teacher's comment, "If you're here, you're an American," exemplifies the attitude that refugees should want to become, and must be becoming, American. The Cambodians in this study always referred to themselves, as individuals and as a group, as "Cambodians"; they only used the term "American" in special cases, to make a specific point such as, "I have to do it; I'm an American now," or "these kids are becoming Americans"—never as a true means of self-identity. They want to be who they are, and they want to be able to do that where they are—where ill-fate has landed them.

IMPLICATIONS FOR THE FUTURE

We don't have to look too far into the future to see the impact these barriers are having on the Cambodians in Middle City; after ten to fifteen years in this country, many of them are still having a very hard time. Perhaps the most important thing for those who wish to help or interact with refugees to understand is that these barriers cannot be considered in isolation but must be understood as a constellation. For example, ill health, multiple jobs, and enormous family responsibilities prevent those most likely to become leaders from having the time to develop a community self-help association to assist families who are having an impossible time learning English, finding employment, and adjusting to the new life. Thus the development and support of a stronger, more united and active Cambodian community would probably result in a more viable adjustment to American culture. At the same time, total health care, adequate housing, full-time language and job training, and more realistic financial help in the beginning would probably have enabled more families to have become, by now, financially independent. If children did not have to make major contributions to family incomes, more of them would remain in school. Because the conditions in which urban Cambodians live are so difficult, those who are able to do so move out of the inner-city neighborhoods, removing from everyday community life those most able to help others, those with the most potential for leadership.

Those involved with refugee planning in the future must recognize the long-term nature of the adjustment process, and they must also recognize the critical role that sponsors can play in that adjustment. Refugees may lose a generation. Those who watched as their entire lives were destroyed may never truly recover from that loss. But with friendship and adequate supports provided over a period of time long enough to be effective, parents may at least be better prepared to guide their children toward happy and fruitful futures.

References

Agar, Michael
  1986 Speaking of Ethnography. Beverly Hills: Sage.
Aronson, Louise
  1987 Health Care for Cambodian Refugees: The Role of Refugee Intermediaries. Practicing Anthropology 9(4):10–11, 17.
Barron, John, and Anthony Paul
  1977 Murder of a Gentle Land: The Untold Story of Communist Genocide in Cambodia. New York: Thomas Y. Crowell.
Becker, Elizabeth
  1986 When the War Was Over: The Voices of Cambodia's Revolution and Its People. New York: Simon and Schuster.
Bohannan, Laura
  1991[1966] Shakespeare in the Bush. In Annual Editions: Anthropology 91/92. Elvio Antelone, ed. Guilford, CT: Dushkin.
Briggs, Lawrence Palmer
  1951 The Ancient Khmer Empire. Transactions of the American Philosophical Society. N. s. vol. 41, part 1. Philadelphia: American Philosophical Society.
Brown, Katherine H., Kitty Corbett, and Sarah Freeman
  1987 Refugees in the Health Care System: A Staff Training Workshop. Practicing Anthropology 9(4):12–13.
Burns, Allan F.
  1993 Maya in Exile: Guatemalans in Florida. Philadelphia: Temple University Press.
Cady, John F.
  1964 Southeast Asia: Its Historical Development. New York: McGraw-Hill.
  1966 Thailand, Burma, Laos, and Cambodia. Englewood Cliffs, NJ: Prentice-Hall.
Camino, Linda A., and Ruth M. Krulfeld
  1994 Reconstructing Lives, Recapturing Meaning: Refugee Identity, Gender, and Culture Change. Basel, Switzerland: Gordon and Breach.
Caplan, Nathan, Marcella H. Choy, and John K. Whitmore
  1991 Children of the Boat People: A Study of Educational Success. Ann Arbor: University of Michigan Press.

Caplan, Pat

    1988 Engendering Knowledge: The Politics of Ethnography. Anthropology Today 4(5):8–12 and 4(6):14–17.

Chandler, David P.

    1983 Revolution and Its Aftermath in Kampuchea: Eight Essays. New Haven: Yale University Press.

    1990 Reflections on Cambodian History. Cultural Survival Quarterly 14(3):16–19.

    1991 The Tragedy of Cambodian History: Politics, War, and Revolution Since 1945. New Haven: Yale University Press.

    1992 A History of Cambodia. Boulder: Westview Press.

Cohon, J. Donald

    1981 Psychological Adaptation and Dysfunction Among Refugees. International Migration Review 15:255–275.

    1986 The Refugee Experience and Its Relation to Psychological Adaptation and Dysfunction. Unpublished manuscript. San Francisco: Indochinese Mental Health Project.

Criddle, Joan D., and Teeda Butt Mam

    1987 To Destroy You Is No Loss: The Odyssey of a Cambodian Family. New York: Atlantic Monthly Press.

Cuisinier, Jeanne

    1927 The Gestures in the Cambodian Ballet: Their Traditional and Symbolic Significance. Indian Arts and Letters 1(2):92–103. Reprinted in Selected Readings in Cambodian Language and Culture, Anthropology 620. Minneapolis: Hamline University.

DeVoe, Pamela A., ed.

    1992 Selected Papers in Refugee Issues: I. Washington, DC: American Anthropological Association.

Donnelly, Nancy

    1994 Changing Lives of Refugee Hmong Women. Seattle: University of Washington Press.

Donnelly, Nancy D., and MaryCarol Hopkins

    1993 Introduction. *In* Selected Papers in Refugee Issues: II. Arlington, VA: American Anthropological Association.

Ebihara, May Mayko

    1960 Cambodian Kinship Organization. Paper presented at the 59th Annual Meeting of the American Anthropological Association, Minneapolis, Minnesota.

    1964 Khmer. *In* Ethnic Groups of Mainland Southesast Asia. F. M. Lebar et al., eds. Pp. 98–104. New Haven: HRAF Press.

    1966 Interrelations Between Buddhism and Social Systems in Cambodian Peasant Culture. Anthropological Studies in Theravada Buddhism. Manning Nash, ed. Pp. 175–147. New Haven: Yale University Press.

    1971 Svay, A Khmer Village in Cambodia. Ph.D. dissertation, Columbia University.

    1974 Khmer Village Women in Cambodia: A Happy Balance. *In* Many Sisters: Women in Cross-Cultural Perspective. Carolyn J. Matthiasson, ed. Pp. 305–347. New York: Free Press.

    1985 Khmer. *In* Refugees in the United States: A Reference Handbook. David W. Haines, ed. Pp. 127–147. Westport, CT: Greenwood.

    1990 Return to a Khmer Village. Cultural Survival Quarterly 14(3)67–70.

Ebihara, May M., Carol A. Mortland, and Judy Ledgerwood, eds.

    1994 Cambodian Culture Since 1975: Homeland and Exile. Ithaca: Cornell University Press.

Erickson, Frederick
1973 What Makes School Ethnography "Ethnographic"? Council on Anthropology and Education Newsletter 4:10–19.
Fishman, Claudia, Robin Evans, and Eloise Jenks
1988 Warm Bodies, Cool Milk: Conflicts in Post-Partum Food Choice for Indochinese Women in California. Social Science and Medicine 26(11): 1125–1132.
Francis, Sandra
1988 Maintaining an Ethnic Identity in Dayton, Ohio. Paper presented at the Central States Anthropological Society Meetings, Notre Dame, IN.
Gearing, Frederick
1975 Studies in a Cultural Theory of Education. Council on Anthropology and Education Quarterly 6:1–9.
Germer, Lucy
1986 The Food Their Families Eat: Cuisine as Communication among Cambodian Refugees. Doctoral dissertation, University of Utah.
Gold, Steven J.
1992 Refugee Communities: A Comparative Field Study. Newbury Park, CA: Sage.
González, Norma, Luis C. Moll, Martha Floyd-Tenery, Anna Rivera, Patricia Rendón, Raquel Gonzales, and Cathy Amanti
1993 Teacher Research on Funds of Knowledge: Learning from Households. Educational Practice Report: 6. National Center for Research on Cultural Diversity and Second Language Learning. Santa Cruz, CA: University of California.
González, Norma, ed.
1995 Educational Innovation: Learning from Households. Practicing Anthropology 17(3).
Hackett, Beatrice Nied
1988 Family, Ethnicity, and Power: Chinese Cambodian Refugees in the Washington Metropolitan Area (District of Columbia). Ph.D dissertation. American University
Hagan, Jacqueline Maria
1994 Deciding to Be Legal: A Maya Community in Houston. Philadelphia: Temple University Press.
Haines, David W.
1982 Southeast Asian Refugees in the United States: The Interaction of Kinship and Public Policy. Anthropological Quarterly 55(3):170–181.
1993 Sentiment in Public Policy: The Southeast Asian Diaspora. Selected Papers on Refugee Issues: II. MaryCarol Hopkins and Nancy D. Donnelly, eds. Pp. 42–52. Arlington, VA: American Anthropological Association.
Haines, David W., ed.
1985 Refugees in the United States: A Reference Handbook. Westport, CT: Greenwood.
1989 Refugees as Immigrants: Cambodians, Laotians, and Vietnamese in America. Totowa, NJ: Rowman and Littlefield.
Hansen, Judith Friedman
1979 Sociocultural Perspectives on Human Learning: An Introduction to Educational Anthropology. Englewood Cliffs, NJ: Prentice Hall.
Heigel, J. P.
1982 Psychological Needs of Refugees. Western Psychiatric and Kru Khmers' Approach to the Problems. Caring Role of TMC's in the Khmer Holding Camp. Report to U.N. High Commission on Refugees' Workshop on Mental Health in Primary Health Care Settings. Bangkok, Thailand.
1983 Collaboration with Traditional Healers: Experience in Refugees' Mental Care. International Journal of Mental Health 12(3):30–43.

Holtzman, Wayne H., and Thomas H. Bornemann, eds.
   1990 Mental Health of Immigrants and Refugees: Proceedings of a Conference Sponsored by the Hogg Foundation for Mental Health and the World Federation for Mental Health. Austin: Hogg Foundation for Mental Health.
Hopkins, MaryCarol
   1992 Becoming Bicultural: Preserving Culture Through Adaptation. Selected Papers on Refugee Issues. Pamela A. DeVoe, ed. Pp. 71–80. Arlington, VA: American Anthropological Association.
Hopkins, MaryCarol, and Nancy D. Donnelly, eds.
   1993 Selected Papers on Refugee Issues: II. Arlington, VA: American Anthropological Association.
Huffman, Franklin E.
   1981 The Ethnolinguistic Background of the Khmer. Special publication of the Outreach Office of the Southeast Asian Program. Ithaca: Cornell University.
Huyck, Earl, and Rona Fields
   1981 Impact of Resettlement on Refugee Children. International Migration Review 15: 246–254.
Jackson, Karl D.
   1989 Cambodia 1975–1978: Rendezvous with Death. Princeton, NJ: Princeton University Press.
Jockenhovel-Schieke, Helga
   1986 Realities of Life and Future Prospects Within Two Cultures. International Migration 24:573–602.
Kalman, Bela, and Joan Lebold Cohen
   1975 Angkor: Monuments of the God-Kings. New York: Harry N. Abrams.
Katona-Apte, Judit, and Mahadev L. Apte
   1980 The Role of Food and Food Habits in the Acculturation of Indians in the United States. *In* The New Ethnics: Asian Indians in the United States. Parmatma Saran and Edwin Eames, eds. Pp. 342–362. New York: Praeger.
Keo, Chanbo
   1987 Southeast Asian Refugees and their Mental Health. St. Paul: Office of Refugee Mental Health, Minnesota Department of Human Services.
Kibria, Nazli
   1993 Family Tightrope: The Changing Lives of Vietnamese Americans. Princeton: Princeton University Press.
Kiernan, Ben
   1985 How Pol Pot Came to Power: A History of Communism in Kampuchea, 1930–1975. New York: Routledge, Chapman, and Hall.
   1993 Genocide and Democracy in Cambodia: The Khmer Rouge, the U.N., and the International Community. New Haven: Yale University Press.
Kimball, Solon T., and Jaquetta Hill Burnett, eds.
   1973 Learning and Culture. Proceedings of the 1972 Annual Spring Meeting of the American Ethnological Society. Seattle: University of Washington Press.
Kulig, Judith
   1988 Conception and Birth Control Use: Cambodian Refugee Women's Beliefs and Practices. Journal of Community Health Nursing 5:(4):235–246.
   1990a Childbearing Beliefs Among Cambodian Refugee Women. Western Journal of Nursing Research 12(1):108–118.
   1990b A Review of the Health Status of Southeast Asian Refugee Women. Health Care for Women International 11:49–63.

1991 Role, Status Changes and Family Planning Use Among Cambodian Refugee Women. Ph.D. dissertation, University of California, San Francisco.

1994 Sexuality Beliefs Among Cambodians: Implications for Health Care Professionals. Health Care for Women International 15(1):69.

Lamphere, Louise

1987 Feminism and Anthropology: The Struggle to Reshape Our Thinking About Gender. *In* The Impact of Feminist Research in the Academy. Christie Farnham, ed. Pp. 11–33. Bloomington: Indiana University Press.

Ledgerwood, Judy L.

1990 Changing Khmer Conceptions of Gender: Women, Stories, and the Social Order. Ph.D. dissertation, Cornell University.

Longmire, B. Jean

1992 Teaching Values: Interaction in a Cambodian Classroom. Papers from the First Annual Meeting of the Southeast Asian Linguistics Society. Martha Ratliff and Eric Schiller, eds. Pp. 251–256. Tempe: Arizona State University Program for Asian Studies.

MacDonald, Jeffery, and Amy Zaharlick, eds.

1994 Selected Papers in Refugee Issues 1994:III. Arlington, VA: American Anthropological Association.

Marcucci, John L.

1986 Khmer Refugees in Dallas: Medical Decisions in the Context of Pluralism. Ph.D. dissertation, Southern Methodist University.

Marston, John

1987 An Annotated Bibliography of Cambodia and Cambodian Refugees. Minneapolis: Southeast Asian Refugee Studies, University of Minnesota.

Martin, Marie A., and Mark W. McLeod

1994 Cambodia, a Shattered Society. Berkeley: University of California Press.

Martin, M. Kay, and Barbara Voorhies

1975 Female of the Species. New York: Columbia University Press.

Mason, Linda, and Roger Brown

1983 Rice, Rivalry, and Politics: Managing Cambodian Relief. Notre Dame, IN: University of Notre Dame Press.

Matthiasson, Carolyn J., ed.

1974 Many Sisters: Women in Cross-Cultural Perspective. New York: Free Press.

May Someth

1986 Cambodian Witness: The Autobiography of Someth May. New York: Random House.

Mitrsomwang, Suparvadee S.

1992 Family Values and Behaviors in the Academic Performance of Indochinese Refugee Students. Doctoral dissertation, Vanderbilt University.

Mollica, Richard

1990 Refugee Trauma: The Impact of Public Policy on Adaptation and Disability. *In* Mental Health of Immigrants and Refugees: Proceedings of a Conference Sponsored by Hogg Foundation for Mental Health and World Federation for Mental Health. Wayne H. Holtzman and Thomas H. Bornemann, eds. Austin: University of Texas Press.

Mortland, Carol

1987 Transforming Refugees in Refugee Camps. Urban Anthropology 16(3–4):375–404.

1993 Patron-Client Relations and the Evolution of Mutual Assistance Associations. *In* Refugee Empowerment and Organizational Change: A Systems Perspective. Peter W. Van Arsdale, ed. Pp. 15–36. Washington, DC: American Anthropological Association.

Mortland, Carol, and Judy Ledgerwood

1988 Refugee Resource Acquisition: the Invisible Communication System. *In* Cross-Cultural Adaptation: Current Approaches. Young Yun Kim and William B. Gudykunst, eds. Pp. 286–306. Newbury Park, CA: Sage Publications.

Moua, Jean

1994 Research on Cambodian and Hmong Education: The Role of the School. A Symposium Sponsored by The Center for Language Minority Education and Research, California State University at Long Beach, April 27–28. Comments.

Murdock, George Peter

1967 Social Structure. New York: Free Press.

Needham, Susan

1991 Khmer Literacy Learning and Instruction in the Cambodian Community of Long Beach, California. Paper presented to the American Anthropological Association Annual Meeting, subsequently published in Papers from the Second Annual Meeting of the Southeast Asian Linguistic Society, 1994.

New York Times

1994 55,000 Cambodians Flee Homes as Khmer Rouge Increase Raids. May 4, A5:3.

Ngor Haing

1987 A Cambodian Odyssey. New York: Macmillan.

North, David, and Nim Sok

1989 Profiles of Some Good Places for Cambodians to Live in the United States. Washington, DC: U.S. Department of Health and Human Services, Office of Refugee Resettlement.

Noup, Celia Vann

1988 House of Donuts. *In* New Americans: An Oral History. Al Santoli, ed. Pp. 207–233. New York: Ballantine.

Ogbu, John

1974 The Next Generation: An Ethnography of Education in an Urban Neighborhood. New York: Academic Press.

1981 Black Education: A Cultural-Ecological Perspective. *In* Black Families. H. P. McAdoo, ed. Beverly Hills: Sage.

Pack, Susan

1989 Cambodian Odyssey. Long Beach, California, Press-Telegram, April 30, J1–J5.

Pan, Renee

1986 Cambodian Funerals: Religious Traditions in the Homeland are Explained. Asian Business & Community News 5(6):15–16.

Pitman, Mary Anne, Rivka A. Eisikovits, and Marion Lundy Dobbert

1989 Culture Acquisition: A Holistic Approach to Human Learning. New York: Praeger.

Ponchaud, Rev. François

1977 Cambodia: Year Zero. New York: Holt, Rinehart and Winston.

1989 Social Change in the Vortex of Revolution. *In* Cambodia 1975–1978: Rendezvous with Death. Karl D. Jackson, ed. Pp. 151–177. Princeton: Princeton University Press.

Rasbridge, Lance A.

1991 Infant/Child Feeding among Resettled Cambodians in Dallas: Intracultural Variation in Reference to Iron Nutrition. Ph.D. dissertation, Southern Methodist University.

Rasbridge, Lance A., and Judith Kulig

1995 Infant Feeding among Cambodian Refugees. MCN, the American Journal of Maternal and Child Nursing 20(4):213.

Reiter, Rayna

1975 Toward an Anthropology of Women. New York: Monthly Review Press.

Rubin, Arnold
1989 Art as Technology: The Arts of Africa, Native America, Southern California. Beverly Hills: Hillcrest Press.

Rumbaut, Rubén
1989 Portraits, Patterns, and Predictors of the Refugee Adaptation Process: Results and Reflections from the IHARP Panel Study. *In* Refugees as Immigrants: Cambodians, Laotians, and Vietnamese in America. David W. Haines, ed. Pp. 138–182. Totowa, NJ: Rowman and Littlefield.

Rumbaut, Rubén G., and Kenji Ima
1987 Southeast Asian Refugee Youth Study: Final Report. Prepared for Office of Refugee Resettlement, U.S. Dept of Health and Human Services. Washington, DC: U.S. Government Printing Office.

Rutledge, Paul
1985 The Role of Religion in Ethnic Self-Identity: A Vietnamese Community. Lanham, MD: University Press of America.

Rynearson, Ann M., and James Phillips, eds.
1995 Selected Papers on Refugee Issues: IV. Arlington, VA: American Anthropological Association.

Sam-Ang Sam
1988 The Pin Peat Ensemble: Its History, Music, and Context. Ph.D. dissertation. Wesleyan University.
1994 Khmer Traditional Music Today. *In* Cambodian Culture since 1975: Homeland and Exile. May M. Ebihara, Carol A. Mortland, and Judy Ledgerwood, eds. Pp. 39–47. Ithaca: Cornell University Press.

Sargent, Carolyn, and John Marcucci
1988 Khmer Prenatal Health Practices and the American Clinical Experience. *In* Childbirth in America: Anthropological Perspectives. Karen Michaelson, ed. Pp. 79–89. Westport, CT: Bergin and Garvey.

Sargent, Carolyn, John Marcucci, and Ellen Elliston
1983 Tiger Bones, Fire and Wine: Maternity Care in a Kampuchean Refugee Community. Medical Anthropology: Cross Cultural Studies in Health and Illness 7(4):67–80.

Shawcross, William
1979 Sideshow: Kissinger, Nixon and the Destruction of Cambodia. London: André Deutsch.
1984 The Quality of Mercy: Cambodia, Holocaust and Modern Conscience. New York: Simon and Schuster.

Sheehy, Gail
1987 Spirit of Survival. Toronto: Bantam.

Sin, Bo Chum
1991 Socio-Cultural, Psychological and Linguistic Effects on Cambodian Students' Progress Through Formal Schooling in the United States. Ph.D dissertation, University of Oregon.

Smith-Hefner, Nancy
1993 Education, Gender, and Generational Conflict among Khmer Refugees. Anthropology and Education Quarterly 24(2):135–158.

Stein, Barry N.
1986 The Experience of Being a Refugee: Insights from the Research Literature. *In* Refugee Mental Health in Resettlement Countries. Carolyn L. Williams and Joseph Westermeyer, eds. Pp. 5–23. Washington, DC: Hemisphere Publishing.

Stein, Barry, and Sylvano Tomasi, eds.
1981 Forward. Refugees Today. International Migration Review 15: 5–7.

Steinberg, David

 1959 Cambodia: Its People, Its Society, Its Culture. Survey of World Cultures 5. New
 Haven: HRAF Press.

Strand, Paul J., and Woodrow Jones, Jr.

 1985 Indochinese Refugees in America: Problems of Adaptation and Assimilation. Durham,
 NC: Duke University Press.

Sue, Derald Wing

 1973 Ethnic Identity: The Impact of Two Cultures on the Psychological Development of
 Asians in America. *In* Asian-Americans: Psychological Perspectives. Stanley Sue and
 Nathaniel Wagner, eds. Pp. 140–149. Ben Lomond, CA: Science and Behavior Books.

 1981 Counseling the Culturally Different: Theory and Practice. New York: John Wiley.

Time Magazine, Inc.

 1985 Immigrants: The Changing Face of America. 126(1):24–101.

 1987 Those Asian-American Whiz Kids. 130(9):42–51.

Tollefson, James W.

 1989 Alien Winds: The Reeducation of America's Indochinese Refugees. New York:
 Praeger.

United Nations High Commissioner for Refugees (UNHCR)

 [1994] The State of the World's Refugees 1993: The Challenge of Protection. New York:
 Penguin.

United States Department of Health and Human Services (USDHHS)

 1982 Report to the Congress. Refugee Resettlement Program. Office of Refugee
 Resettlement. Washington, DC.

 1993 Report to the Congress. Refugee Resettlement Program. Office of Refugee
 Resettlement. Washington, DC.

 [1994] Report to the Congress. FY 1993. Refugee Resettlement Program. Office of
 Refugee Resettlement. Washington, DC.

United States Department of State (USDS)

 1990 World Refugee Report: A Report Submitted to the Congress as Part of the Con-
 sultations on FY 1991 Refugee Admissions to the United States. Department of State
 Publication 9802. Washington, DC: Bureau for Refugee Programs.

Van Arsdale, Peter

 1987 Accessing Human Services: Ethnographic Perspectives on Refugee Communities and
 Mutual Assistance Associations. Information and Referral 9:1–25.

 1993 The Role of Mutual Assistance Associations in Refugee Acculturation and Service
 Delivery. *In* Selected Papers in Refugee Issues:II. MaryCarol Hopkins and Nancy D.
 Donnelly, eds. Pp. 156–176. Arlington, VA: American Anthropological Association.

Vickery, Michael

 1984 Cambodia: 1975–1982. Boston: South End Press.

 1990 The Rule of Law in Cambodia. Cultural Survival Quarterly 14(3):82–83.

Volkman, Toby Alice

 1990 Imagining Cambodia. Cultural Survival Quarterly 14(3):3–5.

Washburn, Sherwood

 1971 On the Importance of the Study of Primate Behavior for Anthropologists. *In*
 Anthropological Perspectives on Education. Murray Wax, Stanley Diamond, and Fred
 Gearing, eds. Pp. 91–97. New York: Basic.

Weinstein-Shr, Gail

 1990 Literacy and Social Process: A Community in Transition. *In* Discourse, Context and
 Ideology: Essays in Anthropology and Literacy. B. Street, ed. Oxford: Cambridge
 University Press.

Welaratna, Usha

1993 Beyond the Killing Fields: Voices of Nine Cambodian Survivors in America. Stanford, CA: Stanford University Press.

Welty, Paul Thomas

1970 The Asians: Their Heritage and Their Destiny. Philadelphia: J.B. Lippincott.

White, Leslie

1949 The Science of Culture. New York: Grove Press.

1959 The Evolution of Culture. New York: McGraw-Hill.

Williams, Carolyn L., and Joseph Westermeyer, eds.

1986 Refugee Mental Health in Resettlement Countries. Washington, DC: Hemisphere Publishing Corporation.

Yathay Pin

1987 Stay Alive My Son. New York: Free Press.

Index

achaa, 91–92, 96

adolescence (teenagers), 26, 40, 45, 48, 56–57, 59–61, 65, 71–72, 77, 89, 103, 119, 121, 126–130, 134–136, 141–143, 145n. 4, 150

adult-child relationships, 120. *See also* parent-child relationships

aesthetics, 26, 31, 77, 96, 99–103, 107–108, 131, 150

affinal kin, 30, 45, 49, 52, 61–63, 79, 148

age, age relationships, 28–29, 44–45, 51–52, 59–61, 69, 72–81, 85, 98, 126, 129, 139, 142, 147–151

Agency, the, 25, 33, 83, 114–118, 123

Aid to Families with Dependent Children (AFDC), 91, 116

Americans, 25, 60, 86, 111–123, 153–155

ancestors, 26, 49, 61, 65, 95–96, 149

Angkor Wat, 9, 10

arrival, situation upon, 27

arts, 87, 99–108, 109n. 1, 120–121, 150

barriers, 25, 74, 79–80, 117, 122–123, 123–124n. 2, 132–137, 147, 151–156

birth control, 37, 39–40

birthdays, 48, 75, 90

Buddhism, 9–10, 39, 49, 70–72, 87–98, 100–102, 109n. 1, 130, 149

Cambodia
  geography, 8
  history, 9–12, 15n. 4
  present situation, 13, 64

Camino, Linda, 14

ceremonies, 72, 87, 89–98, 108, 151

Chandler, David, 15n. 4

childbirth, 38, 40–41, 46n. 3, 54

childcare, 57–60, 66, 71, 73–76, 115–116, 142

children, 37, 48, 57–59, 76–77, 79–80, 94–95, 97, 103–107, 120, 129–131, 138–139, 150

children's art, 106–108, 120–121

church, Christian, 24, 33, 92, 107–108, 112, 114, 118–123

clothing, 28–32, 97, 99

Committee on Refugees and Immigrants (CORI), 15nn. 1, 8

community celebrations, 22. *See also* ceremonies

community relations and organization, 69, 81–86, 94–98, 122, 149

Criddle, Joan D., and Theeda Butt Mam, 15n. 6, 73

culture change, 44–45, 55, 90–91, 97, 99, 104–106, 108, 111–124

culture conflict, 24–25, 27–28, 31, 33–35, 37–39, 41–42, 49, 55, 60–61, 66, 71, 74, 76, 78–79, 117, 119, 120, 126–137, 141, 155

dance, 88, 103–106
dating, 6, 40, 51, 57, 78, 121, 129
death, 12–13, 30–31, 35–36, 48, 66, 81, 84, 89, 92, 114, 132, 143
dental care, 38, 41
descent, 51–52
DeVoe, Pamela A., 15n. 8
Donnelly, Nancy, 4, 15nn. 8, 9

Ebihara, May M., 2, 10, 11, 13–14, 17, 29–30, 32, 40, 47, 49–53, 59, 61–62, 66, 67nn. 1, 2, 4, 69–70, 72, 77, 83, 85–89, 130, 148
economics, 20, 45, 48–49, 64, 72, 79, 83-84, 92–95, 121, 132
education, 125–146. See also schools, schooling
    primary, 133–135
    secondary, 133–136, 141–143
    higher, 135, 144–145
    for teachers, 144–145
    recommendations, 138–145
    traditional, 89
elders, 34, 36, 53-56, 65, 72–73, 88–89, 95, 109n. 7
electronics, 26, 42–45
employment, 32–33, 60, 71, 80, 89, 153
English, 37, 42, 79–80, 117, 120
ESL
    for adults, 117, 132
    for children, 126, 133–134

family, 47–48, 52, 63–64, 66, 73, 79, 128–131, 136, 151–152
fictive kin, 63
food, 17–25, 38, 48, 93–97
France, French influence, 10
Funds of Knowledge for Teaching Project, 144–145, 146n. 6
funerals, 89, 92, 109n. 4

gender, 14, 45, 52, 69, 70–72, 81, 85–86, 89, 98
gifts, gift-giving, 48–49, 88–95
González, Norma, 146n. 6

Haines, David, 15n. 9, 122
hair, 30, 91
health, 12, 13, 34–42
health care, 14, 34–42, 46nn. 1, 2, 3,

153. See also medicine
Hopkins, 4, 15 n.8, 151
housing, 25–27, 100, 113

illness, 12, 13, 34–35
infants, 23–24, 41, 57–58, 74–75, 116
in-laws, 62–63, 79
insurance, 34, 41

jewelry, gold, etc., 29–31, 48, 88, 93

Kathen, 49, 65, 89, 94–97
Khmer language, 98, 120, 133
Khmer Rouge, 11, 12, 48, 131–132. See also Pol Pot era
Kiernan, Ben, 15n. 4
kinship, 47–67
kmauit, 61
kru Khmer, 36
Krulfeld, Ruth, 14
Kulig, Judith, 14, 23, 46n. 3

Ledgerwood, Judy, 2, 13–14, 51, 149

Marcucci, John L., 14, 46nn. 1, 3
marriage, 49–50, 78, 91. See also weddings
May Someth, 15n. 6
medicine. See also health care
    traditional, 35, 36, 40–41, 46nn. 1, 3
    western, 14, 35–42, 46n. 1, 2, 3
mental health, 12, 13, 35, 36, 38–39, 46 n. 1, 131, 154
methods, research, 47, 33
monks, 36, 71, 88–92, 94–97, 109n. 3, 130
Mortland, Carol, 2, 13–14, 15n. 7, 86, 149
mother-child relationships, 22–24, 29, 36–40, 44, 47–48, 51–60, 63– 65, 69, 74, 76, 81, 103, 115–116, 119, 127. See also parent-child relationships
mother-daughter relationships, 38, 54–57, 65, 78–79, 121
mourning, 30
music, 43, 96–97, 106, 109 n.7
mutual assistance association (MAA), 81-83, 86, 111–112, 140
names, 8, 38, 52, 73, 117, 139

Needham, Susan, 128, 139
New Year, 22–23, 89, 94, 97
Ngor Haing, 15n. 6
Noup, Celia, 15n. 6

One Hundred Days, 48–49, 65, 89–90

parent-child relationships, 52–59, 64, 74,
    77, 84, 120, 129, 131, 136, 141
patron-client relationships, 83, 86, 112,
    118
Phchum, 61, 64, 89, 94
Phnom Penh, 126–127
play, 70, 76, 95, 104
Pol Pot era (Khmer Rouge), 15nn. 4, 6,
    48–49, 60, 64, 73, 84, 131–132
Ponchaud, Rev. François, 15n. 4, 48
poverty, 25, 27, 153
pregnancy and childbirth, 39–41
prewedding, 72, 93–94

Rasbridge, Lance 14, 23
refugee research, 14, 15nn. 1, 4, 7, 8, 9
religion, 87–90, 118–121. *See also*
    Buddhism
residence patterns, 33, 50–52, 54, 61,
    63, 65, 70, 119
respect, 49, 57, 61, 64, 66, 72–73, 77,
    109 n.7, 129
Rumbaut, Rubén, 7, 126

Sam-Ang Sam, 15n. 5, 109n. 7
Sargent, Carolyn, 46n. 3
schools, schooling
    in Middle City, 127, 132–137
    in U.S., 14, 74, 80, 125–146, 154
    in Cambodia, 128, 130, 132
    problems, 126–129, 133–137
sewing, 30
Shawcross, William, 15n. 4
Sheehy, Gail, 15n. 6
shoes, 30, 102
siblings, 51–52, 59–61, 65–66, 67n. 4,
    74, 103

Sin, Bo Chum, 14
social class, 56, 69, 83–84
sponsorship, 111–112, 143, 154–155

teenagers, 26, 40, 45, 48, 56–57, 59–61,
    65, 71–72, 77, 89, 103, 119, 121,
    126–130, 134–136, 141–143, 145n.
    4, 150
temple (wat), 10, 13–14, 22–23, 30, 34,
    43, 45, 50, 53–54, 60, 69, 71, 75–76,
    78, 80, 82, 84, 86, 88–89, 92,
    95–102, 107–108, 109 n.1, 116, 120,
    123, 128, 140, 149–151. *See also*
    wat
Thailand, refugee camps in, 12, 13,
    48–49, 64, 132, 152
toddlers, 57–58, 75–76, 116
transportation, 32–34, 71, 80

United Nations High Commissioner for
    Refugees (UNHCR), 1, 12
United States Department of Health and
    Human Services (USDHHS), 2, 118,
    123n. 2
U. S. law and policy, 49, 64, 92, 109n.
    3, 113, 122, 123–124n. 2, 152–153

values, 26, 40, 47, 57, 59–60, 65–66,
    73, 75–77, 82, 85–86, 87–90, 92,
    102, 108, 126–130, 136–137,
    149–151
Van Arsdale, Peter, 86
Vickery, Michael, 15n. 4

wat (temple), 54, 80, 88–90, 94, 97,
    110, 120, 140
weddings, 22, 30–31, 48–49, 72, 79,
    89–92
Welaratna, Usha, 15n. 6
wife-husband relationships, 30, 45, 49,
    52, 61–62, 148

Yathay Pin, 15n. 6

About the Author

MARYCAROL HOPKINS is Associate Professor of Anthroplogy at Northern Kentucky University.